Leadership in Committee

A Comparative Analysis of Leadership Behavior in the U.S. Senate

With a New Preface for the Paperback

C. Lawrence Evans

Ann Arbor

THE UNIVERSITY OF MICHIGAN PRESS

To Susan

First paperback edition 2001
Copyright © by the University of Michigan 1991
All rights reserved
Published in the United States of America by
The University of Michigan Press
Manufactured in the United States of America
⊗ Printed on acid-free paper

2004   2003   2002   2001   4   3   2   1

A CIP catalog record for this book is available from the British Library.

Library of Congress Cataloging-in-Publication Data

Evans, C. Lawrence, 1958–
    Leadership in committee : a comparative analysis of leadership
behavior in the U.S. Senate / C. Lawrence Evans.
       p.   cm.
    Includes bibliographical references and index.
    ISBN 0-472-10237-0 (alk. paper)
    1. United States. Congress. Senate—Committees.   2. United
States. Congress. Senate—Leadership.   I. Title.
JK1239.E93   1991
328.73'071—dc20   91-21272
                                                                                                  CIP

ISBN 0-472-08825-4 (pbk. : alk. paper)

Preface to the Paperback Edition

Early in 2001, following the closest national election in decades, the U.S. Senate confronted some daunting institutional challenges. Along with dimpled chads and a landmark Supreme Court case, the 2000 campaign had produced a Senate split right down the middle, with 50 Republicans and 50 Democrats. The first task for the 50-50 Senate was to organize itself internally. Would Republicans or Democrats chair the Senate's eighteen standing committees? Which party would determine the legislative agenda in committee and on the floor? How would committee assignments be divided between the two parties? How would committee staff and other legislative resources be allocated? And what would happen when the inevitable party-line votes occurred in committee—deadlock or something else?

Not surprisingly, Republicans and Democrats strongly disagreed about the proper response to these questions. From staffing allotments to control over the agenda, Tom Daschle, the Senate Democratic leader, demanded that the traditional powers of the majority party be equally divided. Initially, he suggested that Republican and Democratic committee leaders serve together as cochairs. Republican leader Trent Lott and other GOP lawmakers rejected the Democratic demands as unworkable. Remarked one, "It's very hard to drive a car when two people have their hands on the wheel."[1]

Lott believed that his party held the trump card in this dispute. After the January 20 inauguration of President George W. Bush, Vice President Cheney would be able to cast the tiebreaking vote in favor of the Republican position on party-line matters. As a result, Lott argued, his party should function as the Senate majority party (assuming, of course, that they did not lose a seat via party switching, resignation, or death). Republicans should chair the committees, and the party should operate with a numerical majority on each panel. The Democrats rejected Lott's argument and threatened to tie the chamber in knots unless a bipartisan compromise was achieved on organizing the Senate.

After weeks of public posturing and private bargaining, the two sides struck such an accord. Republicans would chair all of the committees, but panel memberships would be equally divided between the parties, as would control over committee staff resources. If a tie vote occurred in committee during the 50-50 Senate, either party leader could move to bring the issue before the full body.[2]

The vexing organizational issues that the Senate confronted in January 2001 are reflected in most of the major topics in this book, including the vital importance of agenda control in Congress; the relationship between staff expertise and legislative effectiveness; the interconnections between committee and chamber decision making; the consequences of the partisan and ideological makeup of a committee for leadership and coalition building; and most important, *the central roles played by committees and committee leaders in the modern Senate.*

Although *Leadership in Committee* was first published in 1991, and much of the descriptive data is from the 99th Congress (1985–86), the analytical framework advanced here has enduring value for explaining what Senate committee leaders do and how their behavior varies. More concretely, I portray committee chairs and ranking minority members (the committee leader for the minority party) as rational actors who make choices in a manner that promotes the achievement of their policy and political objectives. Individual characteristics of the relevant leader, especially the nature of the leader's policy preferences, prior leadership experience, and proximate career plans (e.g., a possible presidential run), condition committee leadership behavior. However, in explaining how leaders behave, I primarily rely on contextual factors, especially the distribution of policy preferences within the relevant panel, and structural characteristics of the committee, such as staff allotments and the role of subcommittees.

The noteworthy changes that have occurred in the Senate over the past decade have not fundamentally altered the important causal relations that exist between these individual and contextual characteristics, on the one hand, and the behavior and impact of Senate committee leaders, on the other. Moreover, because of the diversity of their operating styles, committee leaders in the Senate continue to provide us with valuable perspective on the broader subjects of leadership and lawmaking on Capitol Hill.

Consider, for instance, the ongoing scholarly debate about the foundations of congressional organization. Over the past decade, three competing theoretical perspectives have shaped how scholars think about the nature of the lawmaking process. According to the distributive theory, committees and the other structural features of Congress are primarily designed to promote logrolling and bargaining between important clientele groups and constituencies.[3] Committee and floor leaders use their prerogatives and resources to build and maintain these distributive coalitions. The informational theory, in contrast, asserts that the internal structures of Congress are designed to encourage members to specialize and develop expertise in important issue areas, thereby enhancing the informational efficiency of the chamber as a whole.[4] The third perspective, the partisan theory, holds that congressional operations are intended to promote the policy and electoral objectives of the majority party.[5] Majority party members grant their leaders important procedural powers so that the leadership can advance the party's agenda and maintain party unity.

Congressional scholars disagree about which theoretical perspective is most useful for explaining the internal operations of the institution. One implication of this book, however, is that we should focus less on which theory is best and more on the specific conditions under which each one is most useful for understanding Congress and the lawmaking process. The nature of the impact exerted by legislative leaders varies by committee and by issue. Not surprisingly, then, the explanatory value of our leading theories of congressional organization differs significantly across the four Senate panels under focus in this study—Commerce, Environment and Public Works, Judiciary, and Labor. The relevance of the distributive, informational, and partisan theories also varies across the eight individuals who led these committees during the period under focus—Lloyd Bentsen, Joseph Biden, John Danforth, Orrin Hatch, Ernest Hollings, Edward Kennedy, Robert Stafford, and Strom Thurmond.

Take the Commerce Committee, for example, which has jurisdiction over issues that evoke the (relatively) parochial interests of particular industries and groups—broadcast spectrum, airport construction, and the like. Also consider the Environment and Public Works Committee (EPW), which deals with a number of important distributive policy areas, including surface transportation, public buildings, and water resources development. On these issues, I argue, the primary contribution of leaders in committee is to help balance the interests of competing constituencies à la distributive theory. The other half of the EPW jurisdiction relates to environmental policy, by all accounts one of the most technically complex issue areas in U.S. politics. On these matters, because of seniority and access to expert committee staff, committee leaders tend to develop important informational advantages relative to other lawmakers. Consistent with informational theory, a key contribution of formal leaders in the environmental area is to provide policy expertise to the full chamber.

The Judiciary and Labor Committees, in contrast, largely consider issues that are prominent on the programs of one or both political parties. According to partisan theory, the central leadership prerogative in Congress is control over the decision-making agenda. Indeed, my description of leadership behavior within the two panels emphasizes procedural tactics and agenda strategies, as the two parties compete to advance their respective policy initiatives through committee and to derail the policy priorities of the opposing party. Thus, by focusing our attention on how and why leadership influence varies by committee and by issue, the analytical framework in this book sheds useful light on the central conceptual debate in congressional scholarship—the conditions under which competing theories of Congress can best explain legislative procedure, strategy, and leadership.

As mentioned, however, the Senate did change somewhat as an institution over the past decade. How do these changes relate to the Senate committee system and the main arguments presented in *Leadership in Committee*?

First, partisan control of the Senate has changed hands several times since the mid-1980s, and, over time, substantial turnover has occurred at the committee leadership level. An important strength of this book is the rich portrait it provides of eight committee leaders in action. Certain of the names and faces are different now. In early 2001, Ernest Hollings and Edward Kennedy still served as the Democratic leaders on the Commerce and Labor Committees, respectively, just as they had during the mid-1980s. Joseph Biden, Orrin Hatch, and Strom Thurmond also remained prominent members of the Senate, but they had moved on to other leadership posts within the chamber.[6] The other committee leaders featured in this book—Lloyd Bentsen, John Danforth, and Robert Stafford—had all retired from the Senate.

Still, the analytical framework and descriptive details in this study transcend specific committees and specific committee leaders. Indeed, my conceptual approach is useful for exploring how turnover at the leadership level alters committee decision making. Recall that I single out three individual characteristics for understanding committee leadership behavior— a leader's personal policy preferences, leadership experience, and proximate career plans. During the 99th Congress, Commerce chair John Danforth was new to committee leadership, had no apparent national ambitions, and mostly shared the policy preferences of the Republican contingent on his panel. As described in this book, for reasons of inexperience and his instinctive moderation, Danforth was not a commanding figure within the Senate on Commerce Committee issues.

In early 2001, John McCain wielded the gavel on the Commerce panel. Unlike Danforth, the Arizona Republican had ample committee leadership experience; a national constituency from his remarkable 2000 presidential run; and strong, if not strident, views about many issues within the Commerce jurisdiction. On certain committee matters, such as tobacco policy and teenage smoking, McCain's views diverged sharply from the position of the Republican leadership. The Commerce Committee had not changed much in structure, jurisdiction, or ideological makeup, but McCain was far more aggressive and active as chairman than had been the case with Danforth.[7] The striking differences in their operating styles can be analyzed and understood via the conceptual framework presented in this book.

Second, during the 1990s the Senate adopted some incremental procedural and structural changes that touch on committee leadership behavior. In 1995, for example, the majority Republicans adopted a rule requiring their members to vote on a GOP party agenda prior to the selection of committee chairs. Some moderates feared the vote would become a litmus test for chairmanship selection, but it appears to have had limited impact. That year, the Senate Republican Conference also adopted six-year term limits for GOP committee chairs and ranking minority members. These limits will not become binding until 2003 or later, and the consequences for leadership behavior remain unclear.

A number of modifications also occurred in the structure of individual committees, including the four panels under focus here. On the Labor Committee, for example, the number of subcommittees was reduced, and jurisdiction over health policy was transferred from full committee to the new Subcommittee on Public Health. Such alterations in committee structure matter because they affect the resources and prerogatives available to chairs and ranking minority members and thus their ability to shape committee bills.

Recently, Vincent Moscardelli has extended the arguments in this book to identify the conditions under which changes occur in Senate committee structure, and his findings have broader implications for our understanding of leadership in Congress.[8] Moscardelli demonstrates that new committee leaders often push through adjustments in the structure of their panels to promote their policy and political goals. This strategic restructuring is particularly prevalent when the policy preferences of a new chair diverge substantially from the views of his or her predecessor. So committee leaders can influence as well as respond to the context within which they operate. In the short run, however, contextual factors, such as committee structure and a panel's ideological makeup, can be treated as fixed constraints that influence leadership behavior.

Third, and most important, decision making within the Senate became more partisan during the 1990s, with implications for leadership and lawmaking in committee. The incidence of party-line voting grew, both in committee and on the floor. Increasingly, party leaders have used the filibuster, cloture motions, and other procedural tactics to advance their party's agenda and stymie the opposition. Whereas party voting on cloture motions (the procedure for cutting off a filibuster) was relatively rare in the 1980s, it became the norm during the 1990s. In the contemporary Senate, filibuster threats often take the form of a "hold," in which a senator communicates to party leaders the intent to engage in obstructionist tactics. Although the leadership repeatedly attempted to clamp down on anonymous holds during the 1990s, their efforts were mostly unsuccessful. The combination of increased partisanship and obstructionism has created what Barbara Sinclair calls "a sixty-vote Senate," in which the passage of major legislation often requires that the majority party secure the supermajority necessary to shut down a filibuster.[9]

Much of the heightened partisan conflict concerns the message agendas that the congressional parties now devise at the beginning of a new Congress. These messages are comprised of "issues, themes, and policy symbols that legislators believe will generate a positive response toward their party among voters."[10] In early 2001, for example, the Bush administration and the Senate and House Republican leadership agreed to advance a message agenda structured around four key themes—tax reduction, defense readiness, protecting Social Security, and education reform. Congressional Democrats countered with their own message of tax fairness, debt reduction, protecting Social Security and Medicare, and education investment. The two parties attempted to focus the congressional agenda on their own priorities and proposals, and they used elaborate communications strategies (town hall meetings, public statements, television advertisements, interest group outreach) to publicize and mobilize public sentiment behind their respective messages. On message issues, the process of legislating is inseparable from the process of party campaigning.

The rise of message politics influences all aspects of the lawmaking process, including committee leadership behavior. For instance, the drafting and initial consideration of message proposals often occur in party task forces, rather than in the committees of jurisdiction, to promote party unity and avoid obstructionism by the opposition. On message issues, committee leaders serve as agents for their party caucuses, rather than for the narrower constituencies associated with their jurisdictions. And on message items, committee chairs and ranking minority members are integrally involved in the party communications and public relations efforts that have become so important on Capitol Hill.

Education policy, for example, is central to the message agendas of Senate Republicans and Democrats. These issues fall within the jurisdiction of the Labor Committee, which was renamed the Committee on Health, Education, Labor, and Pensions (HELP) in early 1999. In fall 1999, the panel attempted to mark up a measure to reauthorize the Elementary and Secondary Education Act. Both parties sought to use the legislation as a vehicle for advancing their respective education messages.[11] Consistent with the conceptual framework in this book, the partisan battle that ensued was shaped by the distribution of preferences within the HELP Committee, along with the policy views and other individual characteristics of the chairman.

The chairman was James Jeffords of Vermont. A moderate Republican with strong interests in education, Jeffords eventually would leave the GOP in June 2001, switching party control of the Senate to the Democrats. Along with Jeffords, in 1999 the HELP Committee also included nine Republican conservatives, as well as eight liberal Democrats under the leadership of Edward Kennedy.[12] Jeffords was running for reelection in a moderate state and believed that he could not publicly endorse legislation that reflected the conservative GOP message on education. If he voted with the Democrats in committee, however, Republicans would lack the votes necessary to report their measure to the floor. As a result, the committee process on education issues essentially imploded in fall 1999. Conservative Republicans on the panel met privately with GOP leaders to craft an education package for their party. Jeffords did not attend many of these sessions. When the markup finally occurred in March 2000, the chairman agreed to vote "present" on a number of issues to avoid undermining the Republican message. Trent Lott attempted to bring up the bill on the floor in May, but Kennedy threatened to offer amendments dealing with the volatile issue of gun control, and the majority leader pulled the measure from the agenda.

Readers of this book will recognize that the 1999–2000 fight over education legislation was an inversion of the agenda game played within this same committee during the mid-1980s by Kennedy and Orrin Hatch, who then served as chair. Indeed, as I document in the pages that follow, most of the key ingredients of contemporary message politics were apparent in the Labor and Judiciary Committees of the 1980s, as Hatch, Kennedy, Thurmond, Biden, and their fellow partisans competed for influence over the legislative agenda.

More generally, I believe that the arguments put forth in *Leadership in Committee* are as relevant to the current Congress as they were when the book was originally researched and published. The U.S. Senate may not be, as it often is described, "the greatest deliberative body in the world." But it continues to be a fascinating and important chamber, nonetheless, and its members and committees have much to teach us about the nature of legislative leadership in U.S. government.

NOTES

1. Helen Dewar, "Senate GOP Reelects Leaders: Party Seems Cool to Democratic Demands for Power-Sharing," *Washington Post,* December 6, 2000, A33.

2. A decision about the partisan composition of conference committees was left for later in the session.

3. Kenneth A. Shepsle and Barry R. Weingast, eds., *Positive Theories of Congressional Institutions* (Ann Arbor: University of Michigan Press, 1995).

4. Keith Krehbiel, *Information and Legislative Organization* (Ann Arbor: University of Michigan Press, 1991).

5. Gary Cox and Mathew McCubbins, *Legislative Leviathan: Party Government in the House* (Berkeley: University of California Press, 1993); David W. Rohde, *Parties and Leaders in the Postreform House* (Chicago: University of Chicago Press, 1991); and Barbara Sinclair, *Legislators, Leaders, and Lawmaking: The U.S. House of Representatives in the Postreform Era* (Baltimore: Johns Hopkins University Press, 1995).

6. Biden moved from ranking Democrat on Judiciary to an analogous position on the Foreign Relations Committee; Hatch shifted from Labor to Judiciary chair; and Thurmond continued to serve as Senate president pro tempore in 2001 but no longer chaired committees because of his advanced age.

7. Consult, for example, Carroll J. Doherty, "All in a Day's Battle: McCain, the Eager Warrior," *Congressional Quarterly Weekly Report,* May 23, 1998, 1356–59.

8. Vincent G. Moscardelli, "Transforming Leadership in Senate Committees: An Analysis of the Effects of Leadership Behavior on the Senate Committee Environment" (Ph.D. diss., Emory University, 2000).

9. Barbara Sinclair, "The New World of U.S. Senators," in *Congress Reconsidered,* 7th ed., ed. Lawrence C. Dodd and Bruce I. Oppenheimer (Washington, D.C.: Congressional Quarterly Press, 2001).

10. C. Lawrence Evans, "Committees, Leaders, and Message Politics," in *Congress Reconsidered,* 7th ed., ed. Lawrence C. Dodd and Bruce I. Oppenheimer (Washington, D.C.: Congressional Quarterly Press, 2001), 219.

11. My summary of Senate action on education issues derives from interviews that I conducted with a sample of Senate chiefs of staff.

12. One of the other nine Republicans on the HELP Committee was Susan Collins of Maine, a moderate like Jeffords. On education issues, however, Collins was more likely to support the party position.

Preface

This book is about the behavior of legislative leaders in Congress: what they do, how their tactics vary, and why. As yet, we have not accumulated a large body of knowledge about legislative leadership. Certainly we know a lot about individual leaders: Uncle Joe Cannon, Sam Rayburn, Lyndon Johnson, Wilbur Mills, and Tip O'Neill are just a few of the names that come to mind. But because scholars usually focus their research on just one or two leaders, an analytical framework has not been developed that allows us to explain the behavior of different leaders across different leadership contexts. In the following pages, my purpose is to begin filling this gap in our knowledge by analyzing the leadership styles of eight U.S. senators who served as committee leaders during the 99th Congress (1985–86). My goal is to develop a framework for explaining leadership behavior that can be usefully applied to a variety of legislative leaders and leadership contexts.

My theoretical perspective is derived primarily from rational choice theory, although the exposition is informal and no mathematical symbols are employed. Theory plays two roles in this study. First, it is used to develop hypotheses about leadership and power in Senate committees, hypotheses that are evaluated with data gleaned from extensive fieldwork on Capitol Hill. But my field research also involved a lot of what Richard Fenno calls "soaking and poking—or just hanging around," generating new hypotheses and leading me to reformulate many of the questions guiding this project. In my case, the process of question reformulation was shaped significantly by the literature on rational choice theory. Thus, in addition to generating preliminary hypotheses, theory also functions in this study as a screening device for organizing the overabundance of new information that emerged during the process of empirical investigation.

All authors owe a large debt to those who spur them on, and I owe more than most. Richard Fenno has been an invaluable source of advice and encouragement since my first exposure to congressional politics in his graduate seminar at the University of Rochester. I have yet to meet an individual who can match his ability to spark enthusiasm for the study of Congress. Larry Bartels also provided extensive and thoughtful comments on earlier versions of this project, and my work is much improved because of his input and example. And Richard Hall has been an important and much appreciated source of constructive criticism throughout the five years of research and writing that resulted in this book.

David Rohde and Steven S. Smith read the entire manuscript and provided detailed suggestions. David Canon, Roger Davidson, Keith Krehbiel, Barbara Sinclair, and Darrell West commented on portions of previous drafts. I also have benefited from the assistance of Larry and Barbara Evans, John and Judy Talbert, and Bernard Rapoport. Financial support was provided by the University of Rochester, the Brookings Institution, and the summer research grant program of the College of William and Mary. And Colin Day, Christina Milton, and others at the University of Michigan Press have gone out of their way to facilitate the publication process.

A large portion of what I know about the Senate was taught to me by the senators and Senate staff persons who agreed to be interviewed for this project. Unless otherwise attributed, all quotations in this book are from these interviews, conducted by the author in Washington, D.C. As an academic observer of congressional politics, I often have been amazed and gratified by the willingness of participants in the legislative process to open their doors and share their knowledge. I have tried to repay their kindness with a book that captures the rhythms of the Senate in an accurate and compelling fashion. But, in truth, I owe them a debt that cannot be repaid.

Most important, I thank Susan, Jack, and Becky Evans for motivation, perspective, refuge, and humor. My efforts, as always, are dedicated to them.

Contents

Introduction

Leadership in Congress is much discussed, but little understood. Candidates for office promise to provide leadership. Studies of electoral behavior reveal that perceptions of leadership ability influence the voting decision. Journalists cover Congress by focusing on the actions of party and committee leaders. And there exists a large scholarly literature on leadership selection, as well as a number of highly valuable studies of individual leaders. But in spite of our tendency to view Congress through the lens of leadership, our understanding of the tactics and strategies employed by congressional leaders to build coalitions remains at best underdeveloped.

Our lack of understanding of legislative leadership reflects more fundamental uncertainties about the nature of leadership in American politics. It is often repeated that leadership is followership, that American political leaders lack the formal powers necessary to command collective responsibility, and that the real source of most important change lies in the constellation of constituencies and groups that structures the electoral arena. Richard Neustadt, for example, tells us that presidential power is the "power to persuade" and likens the office to "chief clerk."[1] Roger Davidson reflects a scholarly consensus when he labels leaders in the Senate "janitors for an untidy chamber" and observes that the Senate "stubbornly resists being led."[2] And John Manley summarizes his portrait of Wilbur Mills, one of the most powerful committee chairmen in recent years, when he asserts that Mills's notion of going on the offensive was "to lean forward in his foxhole."[3]

Politicians certainly emphasize their constraints, but they also emphasize the potential for creative leadership. Consider Alan Simpson's comments about his successful efforts at shepherding a major immigration reform bill through the Senate, by all accounts one of the most significant legislative achievements of the 1980s.

> Why did I do it? Perversity! Sometimes you just have to press on. Persistence. There were times when I decided to junk it. . . . One thing about the Senate, if you look obsessed, you get defeated. They smile and ram it to you. . . . I was in a restaurant a while ago and the waiter invited

me back into the kitchen for a toast [in honor of the bill]. They all yelled "Viva Simpson." I loved it.[4]

Most observers of the U.S. Congress would agree with Simpson that leadership is more than followership, that certain procedural prerogatives of leadership can matter a great deal, and that legislators are more than simple articulators of constituency preferences. But if legislative leaders can make a difference, when do they make a difference, and why? What tactics and strategies are available to legislative leaders for building coalitions? How does leadership behavior vary? What do leaders contribute to legislative work on Capitol Hill? And, most important, what can we reasonably expect from legislative leaders in an institution as fragmented and individualistic as the modern Congress?

The purpose of this book is to begin answering these questions through an exploration of committee leadership behavior in the U.S. Senate. My primary focus is on the legislative styles of eight senators who served as full committee chairs or ranking minority members during the 99th Congress (1985–86): Lloyd Bentsen of Texas, Joseph Biden of Delaware, John Danforth of Missouri, Orrin Hatch of Utah, Ernest Hollings of South Carolina, Edward Kennedy of Massachusetts, Robert Stafford of Vermont, and Strom Thurmond of South Carolina. Because it is impossible to understand leadership outside of the context of incentives and constraints that shapes leadership behavior, I also focus on the four panels these individuals led: the Senate Committees on Commerce, Science and Transportation; Environment and Public Works; Judiciary; and Labor and Human Resources.

Leadership in Committee

The main premise of this study is that it is useful to examine the tactics and strategies of legislative leadership from the perspective of leadership behavior in Senate committees. This assumption has analytical value for three reasons: the policy-making importance of Senate committees, the scope of the job of committee leader, and the possibility of comparing a large number of Senate committee leaders across a wide variety of leadership contexts.

The modern Senate is characterized by rampant individualism and a broad dispersion of legislative power. And in recent years, the tide of individualism has risen markedly.[5] However, this has not erased the primary feature of legislative life in the Senate: Most legislative work occurs in committee. Policy alternatives tend to be formulated in the committee of jurisdiction. The coalition-building process begins (and often ends) in committee. And committee recommendations usually emerge relatively unscathed from consideration by the full Senate. As Richard Fenno recently observed, "If there is any uncontested generalization about the operation of the United States Senate, it is that the policy-making work of the body is done in its committees."[6] Thus, the comparative analysis of leadership behavior in Senate committees is important because Senate committees themselves are important.

In addition, committee leadership in the Senate encompasses a wide range of procedural prerogatives, formal responsibilities, and informal expectations. A committee chair is responsible for his or her panel's agenda and determines which bills are considered and which bills sink from view. Both the chair and the ranking minority member—the committee leader for the minority party—confront the often diverse demands of rank-and-file committee members from both sides of the aisle. And committee leaders operate within the larger context of American national government. As a result, their behavior is often conditioned by expectations about what will happen in succeeding stages of the legislative process: in the full Senate, in the House, in the executive branch. In short, the job of committee leadership is complex enough to provide useful information about legislative leadership in general.

There also are tactical reasons for focusing on leadership in committee. Party leaders are more visible than committee leaders, but at any point in time, there is just one Senate majority leader and one Senate minority leader, just one Speaker of the House and one House minority leader. As a result, studies of party leadership in Congress usually focus on only one or two leaders, and generalization is problematic. In his pathbreaking study of Wilbur Mills, John Manley explains why:

> First, the extreme variability of personalities . . . stands as a barrier to generalization; and, second, . . . it is hard to say how much of the legislative process is due to individuals and how much is due to the situational factors that confront them.[7]

Thus, to develop general propositions about legislative leadership, it is crucial that we move beyond case studies of individual leaders. We need to examine a variety of leaders to explore how characteristics of leaders as individuals shape their behavior. And we need to examine leadership behavior in a variety of leadership contexts to explore how situational factors influence a leader's choice of tactics and strategies. Only by systematically comparing the behavior of different leaders across different leadership contexts can we avoid the analytical difficulties to which Manley refers.

This is precisely the advantage of conducting a study of legislative leadership at the committee level. There are currently sixteen standing committees in the U.S. Senate, led by sixteen chairs and sixteen ranking minority members. As a result, focusing on leadership in committee allows us to examine many leaders and leadership styles across a wide range of political contexts and environments. Congressional committees often are described as "little legislatures."[8] As such, they are highly useful laboratories for analyzing the tactics and strategies of legislative leadership.

The Concept of Legislative Leadership

The subject of political leadership is rich and complex. It has been analyzed by political scientists as a personal quality, as a relationship between two or more individuals, and as a characteristic of formal institutional positions.[9] Politicians themselves speak readily of leadership, and their remarks reflect these ambiguities.

Asked to describe Strom Thurmond's chairmanship of the Senate Judiciary Committee, his onetime colleague, former Senator Paul Laxalt of Nevada, recalled that the position seemed to energize Thurmond: "When the Republicans won the Senate, it took twenty years off him. . . . As chairman, he was tough but acted with eminent fairness." A staff assistant who handled Judiciary Committee issues for Orrin Hatch described Thurmond's leadership in the following terms:

> He's a grand senator who uses his seniority with great aplomb. Nobody can tell Thurmond no very gracefully because, although he never says it, it's kind of implicit there that "hey sonny, I was here in the Senate when you were in diapers." So they defer to him a great deal. If he ever really wants something, from our perspective, he's probably going to get it. That respect is probably not equally reflected on the other side of the aisle. They see him in a different context. But with them he is a little more short and curt at times, and driving and dynamic and impatient.

According to a senior aide to committee Democrat Edward Kennedy of Massachusetts:

> Thurmond has, like any wise chairman, tried to be open and fair. He has his constituents and we on the Democratic side have ours. . . . He tries to get his agenda through and sometimes we try to stop it. The most recent breakdown was over the habeas corpus thing. In the middle of the committee's markup, he pulled it off the agenda and reintroduced it on the floor.

Thus, participants in the process also perceive legislative leadership to be multifaceted; to be at once a personal trait (e.g., fairness, energy, impatience), a characteristic of a social interaction (e.g., respect, deference), and a procedural prerogative (e.g., agenda control).

In this book, my focus is on leadership behavior. For purposes of analysis, the leadership style of a committee chair or ranking minority member is conceptualized as the culmination and aggregation of a series of discrete decisions made over time. As such, I am not defining leadership as a personal trait, a type of interaction, or a prerogative of office, although these characteristics of the general phenomenon of political leadership are certainly relevant. Rather, references to leadership or leadership style (I use these terms interchangeably) are references to *patterns of behavior* revealed during the course of committee work.

The issue here is not so much a question of exclusion as it is one of emphasis. Traits, interactions, and institutional position all play a role in the analysis that follows. But in conceptualizing political leadership, our focus should be driven by the larger questions of interest. And in this study, the overriding concern is the policy-making capacity of the Senate. The proximate leadership variables for understanding coalition building in the Senate are the legislative inputs Senate leaders often provide: the setting of priorities, the formulation of alternatives, and the mobilization of support.[10] These leadership inputs are best conceptualized as forms of behavior, as a set of discrete actions. Personal traits are important to the extent that they shape behavior. Interactions between leaders and the led also play a central role, but the emphasis is on the patterns of behavior that characterize these interactions. And institutional position identifies the actors of interest.

Aspects of Leadership Behavior

If our focus is to be on behavior, what aspects of leadership behavior should we explore? Committee leadership encompasses a wide array of actions and interactions, ranging from scheduling decisions to supervising preparation of committee reports. But even casual observation of Senate committees at work reveals that certain aspects of leadership behavior are crucial to the process of coalition building. In particular, four sets of questions need to be addressed if we are to understand leadership behavior in Senate committees:

—A chair's most significant procedural prerogative is control over the full committee agenda. What factors shape a chair's scheduling decisions? How do a chair's agenda tactics vary by issue area? And how do scheduling decisions vary across different committee chairs?

—Within Senate committees, legislation often is assigned to a subcommittee of the full panel for preliminary action. On some bills, subcommittee chairs and subcommittee ranking minority members play very significant legislative roles. On others, they are relatively inactive. Why do full committee chairs and ranking minority members delegate significant legislative responsibility to subcommittee leaders or other committee members in certain instances but not in others? How and why does the role played by subcommittee leaders vary across different panels?

—The strategic interaction between the two full committee leaders is also an important variable in committee leadership. On some panels, for instance, the chair and ranking minority member often work together, while on others, relations between the two full committee leaders are rife with conflict. What factors shape how the chair and ranking minority member interact? How and why does the pattern of interactions between two full committee leaders vary across different pieces of legislation? How and why does it vary across different committees?

—Committee leaders often are concerned about potential floor problems with their legislation, and their strategies and tactics in committee may be influenced by a desire to maximize the probability of success in the full Senate. On other pieces of legislation, though, committee leaders do not legislate in committee with an eye to the floor. Why not? Why do some chairs and ranking minority members moderate their legislative efforts in committee to facilitate passage on the floor, while others ignore the mood of the full chamber?

These questions structure my approach to the analysis of legislative leadership. Committee leadership is conceptualized in terms of four variables that capture different forms of committee leadership behavior: (1) the use of agenda prerogatives; (2) interactions with subcommittee leaders; (3) interactions between the two full committee leaders; and (4) the extent to which committee leaders take into account the mood of the full Senate during committee deliberations. These four aspects of leadership behavior function as dependent variables in the analysis that follows.

Although the variables represent different aspects of leadership behavior, they are interdependent. For example, decisions made at the agenda level determine the type of issues that are actively considered in committee, and thus shape relationships between the two full committee leaders and other panel members, as well as strategic behavior vis-à-vis the Senate floor. Similarly, conflict between the chair and ranking minority member may influence the type of issues the panel opts to focus on, affecting decisions made at the agenda level of the process. The four aspects of leadership behavior are addressed in separate chapters, but their interdependence is recognized and explored throughout.

Additionally, these four aspects of leadership behavior vary from issue to issue for individual leaders. Perhaps the most often recognized, but least explored, aspect of congressional leadership behavior is the simple fact that it varies across different issues considered by the same leader, as well as across different leaders. That is, the behavior of a committee leader depends in part on the portion of the committee's jurisdiction that is under consideration. The typical congressional committee considers a wide range of legislation, and when we examine committee leadership behavior on different issues, the mix of tactics and strategies can change significantly.

Of course, often there are important patterns in leadership behavior across the legislation considered by a single panel, and isolating and explaining these patterns is a primary goal of this book. Issue areas are not distributed to committees randomly. Judiciary Committee issues, for example, are particularly likely to be salient and steeped in conflict. And because Judiciary Committee leaders regularly confront controversial legislation of broad national interest, certain patterns develop in their leadership behavior. But we cannot let the existence of interesting patterns blind us to the considerable variation in behavior that we observe for each leader. Such variation is an important aspect of leadership behavior, and it also provides further insight into the reasons that committee leaders do what they do.[11]

Explanatory Variables

The four dependent variables just discussed are useful tools for organizing and describing committee leadership behavior, but my goal is to explain, as well as to organize and describe. Thus, in addition to analyzing how each aspect of leadership behavior varies across individual leaders and different issue areas, I attempt to provide an explanatory framework that can be usefully applied to a broad range of legislative leaders and leadership contexts. Two categories of explanation are employed: *contextual characteristics* of the environments in which these eight leaders function and *individual characteristics* of each leader. These contextual and individual characteristics are discussed at length in the next chapter, and they serve as explanatory variables in the chapters that follow.

The central argument of this study is that most of the variation we observe in the behavior of political leaders can be understood from the perspective of contextual factors alone. Individual characteristics of particular leaders do matter, and they are incorporated in the discussion that follows. But from agenda tactics to preparation of the final report, it is apparent that the environment of leadership shapes the contours of leadership behavior in committee. Two aspects of the leadership environment are emphasized in this book: the *preference context* and the *structural context*. The preference context refers to the distribution and intensity of preferences on a committee's issues in committee and in the full Senate. The structural context refers to the distribution of agenda prerogatives and staff resources.

Individual characteristics of legislative leaders also influence their behavior. But by "individual characteristics," I am not referring to aspects of a leader's personality. Psychological factors are important, but they also are beset by conceptual ambiguities and measurement problems. There are, however, certain individual characteristics of the eight committee leaders—and political leaders in general—that are important for understanding leadership behavior, as well as sufficiently objective to allow analysis. In this study, I focus on three: a committee leader's *policy preferences, leadership experience,* and *proximate career plans.*

The contextual and individual characteristics emphasized here are significant because they affect the political viability and efficiency of the various alternatives from which committee chairs and ranking minority members select their strategies and tactics. Throughout this book, committee leaders are portrayed as rational and goal-oriented. They choose forms of behavior that best allow them to achieve their aims, subject to opportunities and constraints that are shaped by their personal characteristics and characteristics of the political contexts within which they lead. I am not arguing that committee leaders (or any political actors, for that matter) are omniscient. Indeed, chairs and ranking minority members often operate under conditions of significant uncertainty, and, as we shall see, they make decisions that in retrospect appear to be mistakes. But given the constraints within which they lead, they allocate their time and resources in such a way as to maximize the probability of achieving their goals.[12]

Data

An in-depth description of the methodology employed in this study can be found in appendix A, but at this point it is useful to briefly describe the data. As mentioned, my focus is on the chairs and ranking minority members of four authorizing committees of the Senate, primarily during the 99th Congress, the last two years of Republican control of the chamber. The four panels are the Senate Committees on Commerce, Environment and Public Works, Judiciary, and Labor. Such an emphasis may raise questions about the generality of my arguments. But it will be apparent that these committees and this period are a valuable window into the larger phenomenon of committee leadership in the Senate. They provide the opportunity to examine a wide variety of leadership contexts and tactics. And together, these panels have considered some of the most salient and controversial legislation on the national agenda. The jurisdiction of the Commerce Committee consists of consumer and regulatory issues. Environment and Public Works is responsible for infrastructure development and the nation's environmental laws. The Judiciary Committee has been the scene of heated debate over criminal law matters and the social agenda of the "New Right," and the programs of the Great Society largely fall within the jurisdiction of the Senate Labor Committee.

Eight Committee Leaders

In addition to having jurisdiction over a wide range of issue areas, the Commerce, Environment and Public Works, Judiciary, and Labor Committees were led during the 99th Congress by senators with strikingly different ideologies, backgrounds, career ambitions, and operating styles.

During this period, the Senate Commerce Committee was chaired by John C. Danforth of Missouri, first elected to the Senate in 1976. An heir to the Ralston-Purina fortune, an ordained Episcopal priest, and a Yale-educated lawyer, Danforth first entered politics as a reform-minded candidate for attorney general of Missouri in 1968. After eight years as attorney general, he ran successfully for the U.S. Senate. Danforth has been very much in the mainstream of the national Republican party. Indeed, during the period of Republican control of the Senate from 1981 to 1987, he was considered one of a group of moderately conservative midwesterners who often held the balance of power in the institution as a whole. As a new chairman in 1985, Danforth was responsible for leading a panel with one of the largest and most diverse jurisdictions in Congress. As he recalled, "I haven't had any experience before or since that was like chairing that committee."

The ranking minority member of the Commerce Committee during the 99th Congress was Democrat Ernest F. Hollings of South Carolina, a member of the Senate since 1967. Even when in the minority, Hollings was an important presence. Asked to characterize Hollings, Commerce Committee Democrat Wendell Ford of Kentucky described him as "forceful," while a Republican on the panel claimed that a more appropriate description would be "forcefully erratic." But there is a consensus among observers of the Senate that, when interested, Hollings tends to have a major impact on the work of the chamber. For a few months in 1980, he was chairman of the Senate Budget Committee, and from 1981 to 1983 he served as that panel's ranking minority member. But at the beginning of the 98th Congress, Hollings chose to assume the ranking position on the Commerce Committee (where he was also the senior Democrat), largely out of frustration with the Senate's failure to confront the federal budget deficit. In 1984, Hollings was a candidate for the

Democratic presidential nomination, but after a poor performance in the New Hampshire primary, he withdrew from the race and refocused his attention on the U.S. Senate.

Republican Robert T. Stafford of Vermont was chairman of the Environment and Public Works Committee during the 99th Congress. Stafford began his long political career as Rutland County state's attorney in 1947 and went on to serve as Vermont's deputy attorney general, attorney general, lieutenant governor, and governor, as well as a member of the House, before his appointment to the Senate in 1971. A self-described "pragmatic environmentalist," Stafford was generally supportive of the environmental programs within his committee's jurisdiction.[13] When he became chairman in 1981, however, the panel faced a Senate body that had moved solidly to the right, as well as an administration aiming to relax regulations on industry. As a result, much of Stafford's attention as chairman was directed at efforts to protect and reauthorize Superfund, the Clean Air Act, the Clean Water Act, and other major environmental programs—programs that tended to generate significant controversy on the Senate floor, as well as in the executive branch. Stafford retired from the Senate in 1989.

Stafford's Democratic counterpart on Environment and Public Works during the 99th Congress was Lloyd Bentsen of Texas. Bentsen first achieved national prominence as Michael Dukakis's vice-presidential running mate in 1988, but he has been in and out of congressional politics since his election to the House of Representatives in 1948 at the age of twenty-seven. Bentsen left the House after just three terms and then reentered electoral politics in 1970 by defeating incumbent Senator Ralph Yarborough in the Democratic primary. In the general election, Bentsen out-polled then Congressman George Bush of Houston, and he has been reelected three times. Bentsen briefly ran for the Democratic presidential nomination in 1976, but he was unable to erode Jimmy Carter's base of support in the South, and withdrew from the race. Since 1976, his attention has focused primarily on the Senate, where he is now regarded as one of the institution's most influential members. Bentsen's performance in the 1988 campaign was impressive—at least in comparison to the other participants in the race—and he was widely mentioned as a future prospect for the Democratic presidential nomination.

Strom Thurmond of South Carolina chaired the Senate Judiciary Committee during the 99th Congress. Both in duration and diversity, Thurmond's political career is unique among contemporary senators. He was elected to the South Carolina state senate in 1932, served as governor of South Carolina from 1947 to 1951, and achieved national prominence in 1948 as the States' Rights Party nominee for president of the United States. He was first elected to the U.S. Senate in 1954 as a Democrat (and a write-in candidate). In the early years of his Senate career, Thurmond was best known for his maverick style and firm opposition to federal efforts aimed at desegregating the South. Indeed, in 1957, he set the record for the longest individual filibuster in Senate history—over 24 hours—and, in 1964, he made the front pages of the *New York Times* and *Washington Post* after wrestling then Senator Ralph Yarborough of Texas to the floor in an attempt to block an important civil rights initiative. Later in 1964, Thurmond switched to the Republican party, and when the Republicans took control of the Senate in 1981, he became chairman of the Judiciary Committee, as well as president pro tempore of the full chamber. After the Voting Rights Act of 1965 effectively enfranchised black voters in South Carolina, Thurmond's position on civil rights moderated significantly, but he remains one of the most conservative members of the Senate.

The ranking Democrat on the Judiciary Committee during the 99th Congress was Joseph R. Biden, Jr., of Delaware. Elected to the Senate in 1972 at the age of twenty-nine, Biden was at the time the second youngest individual ever to serve in the institution. When the Republicans assumed control of the Senate in 1981, Biden had less seniority on the Judiciary Committee than his Democratic colleague Edward Kennedy of Massachusetts. But Kennedy, the senior Democrat on both the Judiciary and Labor Committees, opted to be ranking minority member on Labor, opening up a committee leadership position for Biden on the Judiciary Committee. As ranking minority member on the panel, Biden often took a backseat to other committee Democrats, including Kennedy, Howard Metzenbaum of Ohio, and Dennis DeConcini of Arizona. Although his legislative output has been modest, Biden is widely recognized as one of the most articulate Democrats in the Senate and, early in the campaign, was considered a serious contender for the 1988 Democratic presidential nomination.

During the 99th Congress, the chairman of the Senate Labor Committee was Orrin G. Hatch of Utah. First elected to the Senate in 1976, Hatch quickly earned a reputation as a staunch opponent of organized labor. His first major impact as a member of the chamber occurred during the late 1970s, when he successfully filibustered two initiatives favored by the labor movement, leading some critics to nickname him "Borin' Orrin." According to Hatch, after the defeat of a labor law bill in 1978, then AFL-CIO President George Meany told him, "No hard feelings, but if it costs us $4 million, we'll get rid of you in 1982."[14] In 1981, after just four years in the Senate, Hatch became chairman of the Labor Committee. As chairman, he led a coalition of seven conservative Republicans, but committee liberals had an important strategic advantage. Hatch faced a solid coalition of seven liberal Democrats, and, as a result, the balance of power centered on the panel's two swing voters, moderate Republican Robert Stafford of Vermont and liberal Republican Lowell Weicker of Connecticut. Indeed, the Labor Committee during this period illustrates well how the ideological complexion of the rank and file can constrain legislative leadership. As Hatch put it, "The chairman can't just snap his fingers and expect things to happen."[15]

Hatch's Democratic counterpart was Edward M. Kennedy of Massachusetts. Kennedy was first elected to the Senate in 1962, and by the 99th Congress, he was one of the most senior members of the chamber. The moderate to liberal majority on the Labor Committee provided Kennedy with strategic advantages that were not available to the other ranking minority members examined in this book. Indeed, Kennedy was often referred to as "the only Democratic chairman in the Senate" during the years of Republican control. Such a characterization is misleading: Hatch held the formal prerogatives of leadership, and the balance of power on close votes clearly lay with Robert Stafford and Lowell Weicker. Still, little progress was made in committee on controversial matters without the cooperation of the ranking minority member. Further buttressing Kennedy's role on the Labor Committee was his national prominence in American politics. Few Senate Democrats can match his ability to generate media coverage. And since 1968, much of the prenomination jockeying and calculation among Democrats has turned on whether or not Edward Kennedy would be a candidate for the Democratic presidential nomination. Indeed, during the first session of the 99th Congress, he was considered a potential front-runner for the Democratic nomination in 1988.

Data pertaining to these eight senators and the panels they led constitute the raw material of this study. As a group, they are not in any sense a scientifically designed random sample of the Senate or of Senate leaders. But they do vary significantly in their ideologies, backgrounds, and career plans. And, as we shall see, they led committees that were significantly different in ideological composition and formal structure. In short, these eight committee leaders are sufficiently different from one another and sufficiently representative of committee leaders in the Senate to allow exploration of some fundamental questions about legislative leadership.

Evidence

The evidence in this book was gathered from three main sources: a statistical analysis of certain aspects of committee behavior on a sample of sixty-two bills considered by the four panels, interviews with Senate staff who participated in or closely observed the legislative work of the four committees, and interviews with members of the Senate.

First, a sample of legislation considered by the four committees in 1985 was analyzed to promote systematic generalization about the behavior of committee leaders. A listing of the bills is provided in table A.1 of appendix A. For each bill, data was gathered about voting and amending behavior during the committee stage of the process. These data are used in a statistical analysis of participation in committee which is described in appendix B and discussed in chapters 3 and 4.

Interviews with Senate staff—the second major source of data— provided additional information about the sample of committee bills and also unearthed more general information about legislative leadership in the four panels. Approximately 100 semistructured interviews were conducted with current and former Senate staff persons who had significant responsibility for one or more of the bills in the sample. These discussions were conducted on a "not-for-attribution" basis. Thus, none of these individuals are quoted directly. And because of the length and complexity of my discussions with them, these interviews were tape-recorded and transcribed. A list of current and former Senate staff persons who were interviewed as part of this study is provided in appendix A.

The third major source of data is derived from interviews conducted with twenty-one individuals who were members of the Senate during the 99th Congress, including seven of the eight full committee leaders under focus (I was unable to interview Joseph Biden). Most of the senators interviewed were members of the four committees being considered, and the sample is skewed toward the leadership level. Indeed, thirteen of the twenty-one had experience as full committee chairs, ranking minority members, or both. All have served as subcommittee chairs or subcommittee ranking minority members. And included in the sample are the current majority leader of the Senate, George Mitchell of Maine, and the assistant floor leader for Senate Republicans, Alan Simpson of Wyoming. In contrast to the staff interviews, my discussions with senators were "on the record." And, to promote rapport, I chose not to tape-record the member interviews. Instead, verbatim notes were taken during the course of each interview, and the discussion was reproduced as completely as possible immediately following the meeting. A list of the senators interviewed is also provided in appendix A.

Outline of the Book

Since our subject is leadership behavior in Senate committees, rather than the tactics and strategies of particular leaders, the chapters that follow are explicitly comparative, drawing on evidence pertaining to all eight leaders (except chapter 2, which focuses on the four committee chairs). Chapter 1 discusses the contextual and individual characteristics that shape leadership behavior. Chapter 2 examines the most significant form of procedural power employed by committee chairs in the Senate: control over the agenda. The interaction between full committee leaders and subcommittee leaders is the subject of chapter 3, and chapter 4 explores the relationship between the two full committee leaders themselves. Chapter 5 presents an analysis of the impact of succeeding stages of the legislative process on leadership in committee. Chapter 6 examines the legislative influence exerted by chairs and ranking minority members in Senate committees, and it offers some concluding observations about leadership and power in Congress.

Notes

1. Neustadt 1980, particularly chapters 1 through 3.
2. Davidson 1985, 250.
3. Manley 1970, 151.
4. Unless a citation is provided, the quotations in this book are from interviews conducted by the author. See appendix A.
5. See Ehrenhalt 1982; Rohde, Ornstein, and Peabody 1985; and Sinclair 1989.
6. Fenno 1989, 1.
7. Manley 1970, 99.
8. Goodwin 1970.
9. Useful overviews of the literature on legislative leadership are provided in Peabody 1985 and Sinclair 1990. Additionally, the various chapters in Mackaman 1981 and Kornacki 1990 are a sampling of the state of the art in congressional leadership research. For a discussion of rational choice theories of political leadership, see Fiorina and Shepsle 1989. A comprehensive discussion of the sociological literature on leadership can be found in Bass 1981.
10. A study of the various inputs into coalition building in Senate committees is provided by David Price (1972).
11. Richard Hall first directed my attention to the variance in the styles of individual committee chairs and ranking minority members across different components of their jurisdictions. Such variation is implicit in Hall and Evans 1990.
12. Thus, this study is squarely in the tradition of "purposive behavior" that has dominated legislative studies for two decades. For an overview, see Sinclair 1983b.
13. Koch 1981, 343.
14. Cohodas 1981, 1954.
15. Cohodas 1981, 1954.

CHAPTER 1

Understanding Leadership Behavior

Given the observation that different committee leaders behave differently, what characteristics of the context within which they lead, and what characteristics of the leaders as individuals, can help us understand the differences in behavior that we observe?

I asked a senior staff assistant to Ernest Hollings to explain Hollings's leadership style. The response was visceral and immediate: "You're not going to dissect Senator Hollings with some political science model." This chapter is not an attempt at dissection, and no full-fledged analytical model is provided. Rather, I present and discuss five factors that are important for understanding leadership behavior in committee, are relevant to a wide range of leaders and leadership contexts, and are sufficiently concrete to function as explanatory variables in the chapters that follow.

The two most powerful explanatory variables pertain to the context of committee leadership: the preference context and the structural context. The other three are individual characteristics of the eight senators under study: their policy preferences, leadership experience, and proximate career plans.

As will become apparent, the order in which these explanatory variables are presented reflects their relative importance for understanding leadership behavior. Throughout its history, the Senate has been home to some of the most colorful and idiosyncratic individuals in American politics; we thus cannot avoid considering individual characteristics of the eight committee leaders being studied. But members of the Senate are also professional politicians, and as professional politicians, they are highly responsive to the opportunities and constraints arising out of the electoral and legislative environments. Individual characteristics do matter, but the influence of contextual factors tends to dominate.[1]

Contextual Characteristics

The Preference Context

The policy preferences of a committee leader's rank and file are the single most important factor for understanding leadership behavior. Senators generally perceive a political issue in terms of one or more alternatives, or potential outcomes. Each of these potential outcomes is associated with a certain value, or level of satisfaction. The alternative a senator values most highly becomes his or her preferred outcome, or *preference*, for the issue under consideration.

If all committee members prefer the same outcome, then the distribution of preferences in committee on the issue is perfectly homogeneous, and decision making is consensual. When the policy preferences of committee members diverge, conflict arises. And when legislators have markedly different views, the distribution of preferences becomes heterogeneous, and decision making becomes rife with controversy. As we shall see, the distribution of preferences in committee influences a committee leader's choice of tactics and strategies. For example, when preferences are heterogeneous, building coalitions becomes more difficult, and committee leaders are less able to achieve their policy goals.[2]

In addition to the distribution of preferences on an issue, we need to consider the intensity with which these preferences are held. If a senator values achieving his or her preferred outcome on one issue more highly than achieving his or her preferred outcome on another, then the senator's preferences on the first issue are more *intense* than are his or her preferences on the second. The level of preference intensity on an issue will usually vary from member to member, but on some items, the preferences of most committee members will be relatively intense. The reauthorization of a major environmental program, for example, typically generates wide interest, and senators' preferences tend to be more intense on such legislation than they are on more routine matters. Levels of preference intensity on an issue also have consequences for leadership behavior. For instance, when preferences among the rank and file are intensely held, more members participate, and committee leaders tend to be more constrained in their choice of tactics and strategies.

At this point, two caveats deserve mention. The first is conceptual. Both the distribution and intensity of member preferences on committee issues are determined in large part by characteristics of a panel's jurisdiction, as well as by the constellation of interest groups activated by the jurisdiction. Aspects of a committee's jurisdiction certainly influence leadership behavior, and jurisdiction is discussed throughout this study, but it is not formally included as an explanatory variable. The reason is straightforward: The nature of a panel's jurisdiction, the outside interests activated by committee issues, and the distribution and intensity of member preferences are all closely associated, and gauging the independent impact of each on leadership behavior is problematic, to say the least. As a result, I have chosen to focus on preferences in committee and to explore the effects of jurisdiction and the interest group environment primarily through their impact on the intensity and distribution of member preferences.

The second caveat is about measurement. I have chosen to depend, in part, on interest group ratings of congressional voting records for information about the underlying policy preferences of committee members. For instance, I use ratings by the Chamber of Commerce of the United States (CCUS) as indicators of the preferences of Commerce Committee members on issues within their jurisdiction. Each year the CCUS—an interest group representing the views of American industry—examines congressional voting on business-related questions and rates all members of Congress on a scale ranging from 0 (antibusiness) to 100 (strongly probusiness). Interest group ratings designed for the jurisdictions of the other three panels are also employed in the pages that follow.

These voting scores provide valuable information about legislators' preferences, but they must be interpreted with care. Issues decided by roll call tend to be more controversial than the typical policy decision made on Capitol Hill, where most questions are settled through quiet negotiation, rather than a formal vote. As a result, relying on interest group ratings alone may lead us to exaggerate the extent to which preferences in a committee are polarized. In this book, however, these ratings are used only in conjunction with the more informal perceptions of senators and staff assistants. And, for the most part, their observations are relatively consistent with the voting scores. Additionally, reliance on small distinctions in the interest group ratings can be lowered by collapsing each rating (all of which range from 0 to 100) into just three categories: low (0 to 33), medium (34 to 66), and high (67 to 100).[3]

Danforth, Hollings, and the Commerce Committee

CCUS ratings of the voting records of Commerce Committee members in 1985 are provided in table 1.1. As mentioned, senators are divided into three groups, depending on how they were rated by the Chamber; low (CCUS score from 0 to 33), medium (CCUS score from 34 to 66), and high (CCUS score from 67 to 100).

During the 99th Congress, the ideological breakdown along business-related issues on the panel was eight to seven to two; that is, eight senators received a high rating, seven fell in the middle category, and two received a low rating. Committee chairman John Danforth was solidly in the upper (generally more conservative) category, while ranking Democrat Ernest Hollings was in the middle (relatively moderate) grouping. Thus, the distribution of preferences in the Commerce Committee was consensual, with a preponderance of moderates and moderate conservatives.

The Republican side of the committee was particularly cohesive. Eight of the nine Republican committee members earned a high ranking, and the remaining Republican, Bob Packwood of Oregon, was just one point short of the highest category. In addition, Danforth was very close to the median for his party. The minority side of the committee was also relatively homogeneous, with six of the eight Democrats falling in the moderate category. In contrast to Danforth, however, Ernest Hollings's CCUS rating for 1985 was the highest among committee Democrats. Indeed, throughout his long career in the Senate, Hollings has been characterized as a moderate to conservative Democrat, and he usually agreed with Danforth about issues before the panel.

Systematic data about the intensity of preferences on the typical Commerce Committee bill are unavailable, but some tentative generalizations can be offered. The audience for most Commerce Committee issues is a group of one or more industries, as well as the administrative agencies charged with regulating them. Senators join the committee to aid industries located in their states. Asked why he joined the panel, Wendell Ford of Kentucky voiced the modal response: "The state—tobacco, aviation. It all comes through the Commerce Committee. . . . Louisville is building two runways [and] I'm concerned about service to rural areas."

As a result, the intensity of a senator's preferences on Commerce Committee legislation is generally a function of the relevance of the affected industry to the folks back home. On product liability and other consumer issues, the audience of interested outsiders is relatively broad, and a majority of committee members have intense preferences. But on the typical Com-

TABLE 1.1. Preference Distribution for the Senate Commerce Committee, 1985

	Republicans	Democrats
Low		Daniel K. Inouye (24)
		Donald W. Riegle, Jr. (24)
Medium	Bob Packwood (66)	J. James Exon (46)
		Wendell H. Ford (48)
		Albert Gore, Jr. (41)
		Ernest Hollings (55)
		Russell Long (39)
		John D. Rockefeller, IV (36)
High	John C. Danforth (75)	
	Barry Goldwater (88)	
	Slade Gorton (69)	
	Nancy Landon Kassebaum (69)	
	Larry Pressler (71)	
	Bob Kasten (72)	
	Ted Stevens (78)	
	Paul S. Trible, Jr. (90)	

Source: Data from Sharp 1988.

Note: Voting evaluations by the Chamber of Commerce of the United States for 1985 are provided in parentheses. The highest possible rating is 100; the lowest is 0. The low range is from 0 to 33; medium, from 34 to 66; high, from 67 to 100.

merce Committee bill, interest is low, and usually just three or four senators are intense in their views, while remaining committee members tend toward indifference. The consensual distribution of preferences combines with relatively low levels of preference intensity to make the Commerce Committee one of the most bipartisan panels in the Senate.[4]

Stafford, Bentsen, and the Environment
and Public Works Committee

The jurisdiction of the Environment and Public Works Committee is bifurcated: The panel considers important environmental programs, but it also has jurisdiction over traditional public works items such as highway construction, public buildings, and water projects.

The public works side of the jurisdiction is relatively bipartisan and consensual. Subject to budget constraints, individual projects are aggregated into huge omnibus packages that disburse federal largess widely across states. Particularly among members less sympathetic to the position of environmental groups, public works issues tend to be an important reason for joining the panel. For example, asked why he selected Environment and Public Works, conservative Republican Steve Symms of Idaho responded:

> Trucking, transportation; they're important to my state. . . . I could never give Environment and Public Works up now. It's too important to the state of Idaho. There's so much work to do. We're behind the eight ball on highways. It's a young state. . . . I sometimes joke that when I become chairman, I'm going to change the name of the committee to Public Works and Environment.

It is difficult to generalize about the distribution of preferences on public works legislation, except to note the obvious: Senators tend to prefer the alternative that targets the greatest quantity of federal assistance to their own states. As a result, decision making on these issues is bipartisan and consensual, characterized by norms of reciprocity and universalism.[5]

Environmental policy is more controversial. The League of Conservation Voters (LCV) provides ratings of senators' voting records on environmental issues, and LCV scores for each member of the Environment and Public Works Committee can be found in table 1.2. As was the case with the Commerce Committee, the distribution of preferences on Environment and Public Works was relatively homogeneous, with a coalitional structure of eight to three to four (eight senators received a high rating from the League, three fell in the middle third, and four ranked low). Thus, the panel was clearly dominated by environmentalists.[6]

Republican members were heterogeneous in their preferences, ranging from Gordon Humphrey of New Hampshire, whose rating was very high, to a coalition of less environmentally oriented westerners, including James Abdnor of South Dakota, Pete Domenici of New Mexico, Alan Simpson of Wyoming, and Steve Symms of Idaho. Committee chairman Robert Stafford's LCV rating was the committee median, however, and he was solidly in the environmentalist camp. The Democratic side was more homogeneous, with five of the seven minority members earning a high rating, although ranking Democrat Lloyd Bentsen of Texas fell in the middle category. Consequentially, the distribution of preferences in committee generated patterns of bipartisan decision making on environmental issues, as well as on public works legislation.

When we consider the intensity of preferences on Environment and Public Works Committee issues, however, important differences from the Commerce Committee become apparent. Most important, preferences in Environment and Public Works tend to be more intense. Once again, the key factor for understanding preference intensity is the nature of the committee's audience. The audience of interested outsiders tends to be larger for environmental issues and public works programs than for the typical Commerce Committee bill. On the environmental side, the panel activates affected producer interests and environmental organizations such as the National Wildlife Federation and the Sierra Club. And because of the complexity of most environmental legislation, the committee relies on the expertise of various executive agencies, most prominently the Environmental Protection Agency.

TABLE 1.2. Preference Distribution of the Senate Environment and Public Works Committee, 1985

	Republicans	Democrats
Low	James Abdnor (11) Pete V. Domenici (23) Alan Simpson (22) Steve Symms (0)	
Medium	David Durenberger (64)	Lloyd Bentsen (60) Quentin Burdick (44)
High	John H. Chafee (75) Gordon J. Humphrey (94) Robert Stafford (70)	Max Baucus (72) Gary Hart (75) Frank Lautenberg (100) George Mitchell (89) Daniel P. Moynihan (89)

Source: Data from Sharp 1988.

Note: Voting evaluations by the League of Conservation Voters for 1983–84 are provided in parentheses. The highest possible rating is 100; the lowest is 0. The low range is from 0 to 33; medium, from 34 to 66; high, from 67 to 100.

On the public works side of the committee's jurisdiction, individual water and highway projects have narrow appeal, but aggregated into large packages, these measures are of major interest to a wide array of constituency groups and legislators.

The intensity of member preferences on Environment and Public Works Committee issues complicated decision making on the panel. Coalitions in the Commerce Committee were built on sand, and they shifted from issue to issue. The coalitional structure on Environment and Public Works was more regularized and more constraining, and a degree of conflict was more likely. Although the panel was oriented toward consensus, there were pockets of dissension, often led by Republican Alan Simpson of Wyoming. And the intensity of member preferences reduced the range of strategies and tactics available to the leadership. As a result, Stafford and Bentsen were far more constrained than Danforth and Hollings, the full committee leaders on the Commerce Committee.

Unlike the Commerce, Judiciary, and Labor panels, a proper understanding of the preference context on Environment and Public Works requires that we consider the distribution of preferences in the full Senate, as well as in committee. In contrast to the other three panels, Environment and Public Works was unrepresentative of the institution as a whole: Committee members were significantly more pro-environmentalist than the full Senate.[7] In committee, decision making was dominated by moderate environmentalists, but conflict often broke out on the floor between environmentalists and pro-industry forces, who were better represented in the parent chamber. And, as we shall see, the unrepresentativeness of the panel influenced leadership behavior in committee, as well as on the floor.

Thurmond, Biden, and the Judiciary Committee
The distribution of preferences in the Judiciary Committee is summarized in table 1.3. Since Judiciary Committee issues tap into traditional liberal-conservative cleavages, a rating of ideological liberalism, compiled by the Americans for Democratic Action (ADA), is provided for each committee member, with 100 the most liberal rating, and 0 the most conservative. The Judiciary Committee was clearly more polarized than the previous two panels, with a coalitional structure of nine to three to six: nine conservatives, three moderates, and six liberals.

Both the chair and ranking Democrat were representative of their fellow partisans on the committee. Chairman Strom Thurmond was one of the most conservative members of the panel, but his position did not diverge sharply from the preferences of the median Republican. Ranking minority member Joseph Biden, a liberal, was also close to the median position for committee Democrats.

Thurmond and Biden faced strikingly different strategic contexts, however. Most important, the chairman had a solid working majority. In contrast, committee Democrats had to pick up all three of the moderate swing votes to block Republican initiatives, and passing their own legislation required the support of all six committee liberals, all three of the moderates, and the vote of at least one conservative. Thus, Biden and the other liberal Democrats were severely constrained by the configuration of preferences.

It is also important to examine the homogeneity, or cohesion, of the various voting blocs. Thurmond could count on the support of a very cohesive coalition of seven conservative Republicans. This preference homogeneity among committee Republicans was no accident. For the purposes of analysis, it is useful to interpret the distribution of preferences in committee as exogenous to leadership behavior—as a cause and not a consequence of the tactics and strategies of the committee chair and ranking minority member. But, in reality, committee leaders influence the committee assignment process and thus affect the preference distribution in their own panels. Indeed, Strom Thurmond systematically sought out conservative Republicans for the Judiciary Committee. Asked why he joined the committee, Paul Laxalt of Nevada replied: "My background as a lawyer. I was a prosecutor. Also Thurmond. Thurmond was very persuasive. He needed more conservative votes."

TABLE 1.3.   Preference Distribution for the Senate Judiciary Committee, 1985

	Republicans	Democrats
Conservative	Jeremiah Denton (5) John East (0) Charles E. Grassley (10) Orrin G. Hatch (10) Paul Laxalt (0) Mitch McConnell (5) Alan K. Simpson (10) Strom Thurmond (0)	Howell Heflin (25)
Moderate	Arlen Specter (55)	Robert C. Byrd (65) Dennis DeConcini (45)
Liberal	Charles McC. Mathias (70)	Joseph R. Biden, Jr. (75) Edward M. Kennedy (85) Patrick J. Leahy (70) Howard M. Metzenbaum (100) Paul Simon (85)

Source: Data from Sharp 1988.

Note: Voting evaluations by the Americans for Democratic Action for 1985 are provided in parentheses. The highest possible rating is 100; the lowest is 0. The conservative range is from 0 to 33; moderate, from 34 to 66; liberal, from 67 to 100.

Steve Symms described the process through which he secured his committee assignments in similar terms. After selecting the Finance Committee on the first round of the committee assignment process, Symms had to choose between Judiciary, Labor, and Environment and Public Works in round two.

> Strom Thurmond really wanted me on Judiciary. He offered to set up a subcommittee and let me chair it. I'm not a lawyer. Thurmond said: "You don't have to be a lawyer—you've got common sense. I'll hire you a lawyer. If you don't like him, I'll hire you another one." . . . I have enormous respect for Strom Thurmond. He's a statesman. But I ended up choosing Environment and Public Works.

An aide to Jeremiah Denton of Alabama described how his boss—another nonlawyer—ended up on the Judiciary Committee in 1981.

> Senator Denton and Senator Thurmond have a very close personal relationship. In 1980, when the freshmen came up, Senator Denton wanted Armed Services and Labor and Human Resources. Thurmond sought him out and said, "Admiral, because of what you've been through [seven and a half years in a North Vietnamese POW camp], no one can speak with more expertise on the subject of terrorism." He told Senator Denton that he was creating a new subcommittee on terrorism, and he wanted Denton to chair it. Senator Denton was reluctant because he wasn't an attorney, but Thurmond was insistent, and Denton accepted.

Thurmond's penchant for attracting to the committee nonlawyers with firm conservative credentials is instructive. He could count on their votes, and without backgrounds in the law, it was unlikely that they would become highly involved in committee issues.

In contrast to committee Republicans, Democratic members of the panel were relatively heterogeneous in their preferences, ranging from liberals such as Edward Kennedy and Howard Metzenbaum to conservative Howell Heflin of Alabama. To some extent, this heterogeneity was dampened by Democratic attempts to draw liberals to the panel and thus counter Thurmond's recruitment efforts. But from table 1.3, we can see that committee Democrats remained a diverse lot. Biden was constrained by the spread of Democratic preferences on the committee, as well as by the voting split.

Unlike the distribution of member preferences, the intensity of preferences on Judiciary Committee issues significantly limited the discretion of both leaders. The Judiciary Committee deals with some of the most salient and divisive issues in American politics—gun control, abortion, busing, the death penalty, and school prayer. According to Paul Laxalt: "The Judiciary

Committee is the garbage dump of the Senate. We get all the garbage. If it's controversial, it goes there." A former aide to Edward Kennedy explained why Kennedy chose ranking status on the Labor Committee in 1981 over a similar leadership position on Judiciary:

> Senator Kennedy went to the Labor Committee in 1981 after he lost the presidential election. His national constituencies had more at stake in the Labor Committee than they did on Judiciary. In Judiciary, you just get your brains beat in: abortion amendments and all this other stuff. There's no payoff for a Democrat; you can't get any press. Those are no-win issues.

The Judiciary Committee's audience tends to be national, and interest in the Senate on committee issues is broad-based and intense. As a result, both Thurmond and Biden often confronted a rank and file that had its mind made up.

Hatch, Kennedy, and the Labor Committee
The underlying preferences of senators on Labor Committee issues also can be effectively captured by ADA ratings of member liberalism. And, as indicated in table 1.4, the Labor Committee was the most polarized of the four panels, with a coalitional structure of seven to one to eight: seven conserva-

TABLE 1.4.   Preference Distribution for the Senate Labor Committee, 1985

	Republicans	Democrats
Conservative	Charles E. Grassley (10) Orrin G. Hatch (10) Paula Hawkins (15) Don Nickles (0) Dan Quayle (0) Strom Thurmond (0) Malcolm Wallop (0)	
Moderate	Robert T. Stafford (45)	
Liberal	Lowell P. Weicker (70)	Christopher J. Dodd (85) Edward M. Kennedy (85) John F. Kerry (85) Spark M. Matsunaga (95) Howard M. Metzenbaum (100) Claiborne Pell (95) Paul Simon (85)

Source: Data from Sharp 1988.

Note: Voting evaluations by the Americans for Democratic Action for 1985 are provided in parentheses. The highest possible rating is 100; the lowest is 0. The conservative range is from 0 to 33; moderate, from 34 to 66; liberal, from 67 to 100.

tives, one moderate, and eight liberals. On the Republican side, there was a very cohesive core group of seven conservatives, whereas the Democratic side was a wall of liberalism. Thus, decision-making parameters in the Labor Committee were set by two divergent, extremely partisan, and highly cohesive coalitions, each with seven members. The balance of power belonged to liberal Republican Lowell Weicker of Connecticut and moderate Republican Robert Stafford of Vermont (who also chaired the Environment and Public Works Committee).

As was the case on the Judiciary Committee, the polarization of preferences on Labor resulted in part from systematic efforts by committee leaders to bring like-minded senators to the panel. Kennedy influenced which Democrats were given assignments on the committee, and he was partially responsible for the remarkable cohesiveness on the Democratic side. And, as was the case with Thurmond on the Judiciary Committee, Orrin Hatch actively recruited conservative legislators to the Labor Committee.[8] Interestingly, one conservative who joined the panel at Hatch's request was Strom Thurmond. As Thurmond recalled: "Hatch asked me to join. I said I couldn't, I had my hands full. He said 'I need the conservative vote—give me your proxy when you can.'"

The data in table 1.4 demonstrate the central feature of Labor Committee politics during the Hatch chairmanship: Hatch lacked the votes necessary to control his own committee. To pass legislation, the chairman had to hold all seven conservatives, pick up moderate Robert Stafford, and then gain the support of Lowell Weicker or at least one of the liberal Democrats. Asked about his leadership, Hatch immediately mentioned the distribution of preferences in committee.

> It was difficult. We had a majority of nine to seven . . . , but when you added two liberal Republicans—Lowell Weicker and Bob Stafford—to the Democrats, it was nine to seven in favor of them. So we had some votes that were nine to seven, and some that were eight to eight.

Particular attention should be paid to the political relationship between Hatch and Weicker. During his years in the Senate, Weicker was generally characterized as a maverick: a liberal Republican in a party that was rapidly turning to the right. One of Weicker's aides discussed her boss's relationship with Orrin Hatch.

> His [Hatch's] situation is very difficult. Senator Hatch is a very nice man who really wants to try and accommodate and compromise, particularly on these issues [assistance to the handicapped], even though they beat the hell out of each other on virtually everything else. School prayer and abortion—Weicker and Hatch are the two major opponents on these issues in the Senate.

In addition, Weicker's strategic position on the Labor Committee was reinforced by his chairmanship of the Appropriations subcommittee with jurisdiction over Labor Committee issues. Hatch chaired the authorizing committee, but Weicker led the panel that controlled the purse strings. Thus, to win in his own committee, Orrin Hatch had to pick up the support of a moderate senior Republican (Robert Stafford), as well as the vote of a liberal adversary with a legitimate claim to formal leadership in the jurisdiction (Lowell Weicker).

The intensity of preferences on committee issues further complicated coalition building. Like the Commerce Committee, the Labor Committee has an audience that is primarily composed of interest groups. But, in contrast to Commerce, groups in the Labor Committee's audience have memberships that are geographically dispersed.[9] Labor unions, the National Education Association, the American Medical Association, and organizations promoting the interests of the disabled and the aged—all are part of the committee's audience, but none are concentrated in one state or region. Executive agencies play a role in drafting legislation, but most initiatives originate in advocacy organizations, with the agencies providing technical expertise. The broadbased memberships of the groups in the Labor Committee's audience translate into a relatively broad-based interest among senators on most issues in the jurisdiction. As a result, preferences on committee issues tend to be intense.

The preference contexts described in this section represent modal tendencies. However, intense conflict occasionally broke out during committee deliberations in Commerce and Environment and Public Works. And on some Labor and Judiciary Committee issues, the distribution of preferences was consensual. Orrin Hatch did not lack a working majority across all components of his panel's jurisdiction, and Strom Thurmond was occasionally in the minority on the Judiciary Committee. Thus, the tables in this section reflect general patterns, but there is variation in the configuration of preferences across different issues considered by each panel. Understanding why the behavior of individual leaders varies from bill to bill—and it does—will require consideration of how preferences vary from bill to bill, as well as the modal tendencies. As a result, additional information about preferences on particular issues is incorporated in the chapters that follow.

The Structural Context

The internal structure of a committee is the second contextual factor that shapes leadership behavior. By *structure,* I am referring to the role of subcommittees and the allocation of committee staff resources. Structure matters because it influences the distribution of information and agenda prerogatives in committee. When a panel is centralized, the two committee leaders tend to have a relatively large informational advantage and near-monopoly control over the schedule. These asymmetries lessen in degree, however, as committee structure becomes more decentralized.

In the Senate, the legislative importance of subcommittees varies from panel to panel. Committee (and subcommittee) meetings are generally hearings or markups. During a hearing, legislators receive testimony from other members, agency officials, interest group representatives, and other witnesses. Markups, in contrast, are bill-writing sessions, where amendments can be offered and votes may be cast. On some committees, subcommittees regularly mark up legislation, while on others, markups only occur in full committee, and subcommittees are primarily vehicles for holding hearings.[10] When subcommittee markups are not held, control over the agenda is concentrated in the hands of the full committee chair and, to a lesser extent, the ranking minority member.

In contrast, the occurrence of a subcommittee markup limits a full committee leader's legislative veto power. Committee leaders can still refuse to schedule legislation for full committee consideration, but the potential political costs are higher if a bill has already been marked up in subcommittee. Other members have allocated time and resources to the effort. And marking up a bill, even at the subcommittee level, raises its profile and contributes to the legislation's momentum. Sponsors of the bill might respond to the delaying tactics of a full committee chair by going directly to the floor, or by offering the legislation as a rider to some other measure.[11]

Agenda prerogatives are also an instrument for rewarding supporters and punishing opponents. Panel members who systematically oppose the chair often find it difficult to move their own legislation through committee. An aide to Ernest Hollings on the Commerce Committee explained.

> In the Senate, it's usually not possible to please everybody, but one thing you really try to avoid is getting into a pissing contest with the chairman. If a senator has introduced a bill and he wants to see it move, you can pretty much count on the fact that if he really goes after the chairman on some other issue, he's not going to get what he wants on his own bill. His own bill may never see the light of day.

Thus, decentralizing agenda control attenuates the bargaining leverage of the two full committee leaders, particularly the chair.

Although the distribution of agenda prerogatives matters, control over the committee staff is the more consequential structural feature, and it also varies widely across committees. Personal and committee staff aides are the primary resource for processing the information necessary to participate effectively in legislative work in the modern Senate. Committee aides are particularly valuable because of their substantive expertise. They are more likely to be specialists in the policy area and usually have longer tenure on Capitol Hill than the average personal staff member. Indeed, a typical career path for staffers desiring to stay on the Hill is to move from a personal staff position to a position on one of the committee staffs.[12]

Senators speak readily about the expertise of committee staffers. Asked about their role, Nancy Landon Kassebaum of Kansas replied:

> Occasionally I think committee staff run the Senate. It depends on the degree to which members are engaged by an issue. They [aides] generate a lot of the amendments—some seem to drop out of the sky around here. They also have institutional memory. . . . We all know of cases of staff members having enormous influence.

Two committee aides emphasized the links between staff resources, information, and power:

> The chairman is usually the most informed about the issues. . . . The committee staff works for him, and we're able to alert him to potential pitfalls so he can steer around a lot of them and outmaneuver other senators.

> Because they control the staff, the chairman and ranking minority member are obviously going to have more information. . . . If knowledge is power, they're going to be in the best position to win.

In general, the greater the percentage of committee staff resources controlled by the chair and ranking minority member, the greater the informational asymmetry between the two leaders and the committee rank and file. On the other hand, allowing subcommittee leaders to hire and fire a portion of the committee staff results in a more equal distribution of information, and committee leaders will be more constrained by effective participation from other members of the panel.

If the four committees examined in this study are characterized by the relative decentralization of their internal structures, then Commerce is the most centralized, while Judiciary and Labor are clearly decentralized. Environment and Public Works exhibits a mixed pattern.[13]

Danforth, Hollings, and the Commerce Committee

The most striking aspect of the Commerce Committee is its centralization. Almost all committee issues are assigned to a subcommittee for the purpose of holding hearings, but subcommittees on the Commerce Committee do not mark up legislation. All markups are held at the full committee level. As one aide generalized:

In the Commerce Committee, subcommittee chairmen are basically people who chair hearings that the chairman [of the full committee] is too
busy to chair. . . . We don't even call them the full committee chairman
and the subcommittee chairmen. It's the chairman and everybody else.
The bottom line is that they don't hold markups.

The full committee orientation of the Commerce Committee is reflected
in the structure of the staff. Because of the panel's wide-ranging jurisdiction,
the Commerce Committee staff is one of the largest in the Senate. Committee
staffers are specialists. They are assigned subcommittee duties, and most of
the majority staff works out of the various offices of the subcommittees. The
minority staff is less specialized because of its smaller size (a trend on all four
panels), but minority staff aides on the Commerce Committee also tend to
focus on the work of one or two subcommittees. On both the majority and
minority sides, however, the power to hire and fire staff rests in the hands of
the relevant full committee leader.

John Danforth maintained these centralized staffing arrangements when
he became chairman of the Commerce Committee in 1985, although his
control was not complete. As Danforth recalled:

I made accommodations with some senators: "We're going to have a
vacancy in your area, and I'd be interested in any suggestions you might
have." [But] I retained the ability to hire and fire.

Committee Democrat Wendell Ford of Kentucky described staffing practices
on his side of the aisle in similar terms: "Fritz [Hollings] will usually ask, 'Do
you have any objections?' There might be a list of two or three people, and
he'll ask, 'Do you have a preference?'"

Although hired by full committee leaders, committee staffers work most
closely with the leaders of the subcommittees to which they are assigned.
Still, the loyalty lines of the staff become apparent when the views of the full
committee chair and the relevant subcommittee chair diverge. One Republican aide who experienced the predicament described his response.

Yeah, that's a tough situation. You just have to try and wear two hats.
Sometimes it works and sometimes it doesn't. You wear a Danforth hat
and a Kasten hat. You have to be very careful about what you say to one
senator about what the other senator is doing because you're likely to be
privy to information the other senator shouldn't have. If you can, you try
to have different staffers staff each member. But if a conflict of interest is
unavoidable, I go with the chairman. He hired me.

Because of the smaller size of the minority staff, minority aides are particularly likely to follow the lead of the ranking minority member. As one of Hollings's staffers put it:

> Hollings comes first and foremost, but we do work with other senators when they have an interest in individual issues that they need help on. But if Senator Hollings has an interest and wants to see an issue come out a certain way, he will say, "You're my staff, do it." If someone else comes in and asks for help, I would have to say "no, I'm working with Hollings and he is against you." My loyalty is to the senator that hired me.

Thus, in both staff structure and the legislative role of its subcommittees, the Commerce Committee is one of the most centralized panels in the Senate.

Stafford, Bentsen, and the Environment and Public Works Committee

The Environment and Public Works Committee is also relatively centralized, but less so than the Commerce Committee. Indeed, in the legislative role of its subcommittees and in the structure of its staff, the committee reveals a mixed pattern. In contrast to Commerce, subcommittees on Environment and Public Works regularly hold formal markup sessions. However, senators and staff stress that the real action often occurs in full committee. According to a Republican staffer:

> The rules of this committee are structured so that, technically, doing things at the subcommittee level is quaint, but not necessary. You can have full committee hearings. In fact, whether you mark a bill up in subcommittee is almost completely irrelevant on this committee. The only thing that matters is how a bill is marked up in full committee. The only purpose of marking bills up in subcommittee is for PR value and to get something printed. The full committee markup is the real thing. Everything else is showtime.

The committee staff is also relatively centralized but, again, less so than is the case on Commerce. The Environment and Public Works Committee staff is small, cohesive, bipartisan, and very experienced. Indeed, during the 99th Congress, a number of committee aides had worked for the panel for almost two decades. During the years of the Stafford chairmanship, the staff revolved around a core group of four or five senior aides, some working for the majority and some for the minority. This core group embodied much of the committee's institutional memory and was active on almost all committee issues. As will become apparent, the loyalties and policy-making role of the staff are crucial for understanding leadership behavior on the Environment and Public Works Committee.

On Environment and Public Works, it is particularly important to examine staffing arrangements from the perspective of loyalty lines, rather than simply relying on organizational charts. Technically, all staffers work for the full committee, but, in practice, the more senior committee members have considerable influence over a number of slots. Two aides to the committee described their terms of employment.

> Who do I work for? Abdnor or Stafford? Well, kind of split the difference. The way it works is I am employed by the committee and by Stafford, but my assignment is to work with Abdnor [a subcommittee chair]. Stafford hired me, but I wouldn't have been hired if I hadn't passed muster with Abdnor. It's a little difficult.

> I was hired by Stafford and interviewed only by Stafford. After I got here it became obvious that I had expertise in _____. Durenberger was interested in doing some work there, so I worked with him, and that has led to my doing other work for him. . . . The only place that could be a problem is if Stafford and Durenberger got out of sorts on some issue, and in that case my primary loyalty would be to the chairman.

Thus, although the formal structure of the committee's staff is fairly centralized, senior committee members often have control over some staffing slots, and loyalty lines in general are relatively fluid.

In summary, the structure of the Environment and Public Works Committee is mixed. Unlike the Commerce Committee, certain portions of the jurisdiction are relatively decentralized, while others are held at full committee. Under Stafford's chairmanship, Superfund and the Clean Air Act were not referred to subcommittee, primarily because of his interest and commitment in these areas. In other issue areas—for example, the Clean Water Act, nuclear power, and water resources development—subcommittees played a significant role. Thus, the structural context on Environment and Public Works reveals a degree of issue-specific variation—variation that is important for understanding the leadership of both Robert Stafford and Lloyd Bentsen.

Thurmond, Biden, and the Judiciary Committee
The internal structure of the Judiciary Committee is highly decentralized. Subcommittees regularly hold markups, and most committee staff resources are controlled by subcommittee leaders.

The importance of formal subcommittee markups varies from issue to issue, but almost the entire jurisdiction of the Judiciary Committee is parceled out to one or more subcommittees. As a result, there is little issue-specific variation in the structural context on the Judiciary Committee. During the years of Republican control, however, an important exception was antitrust policy, which was held at full committee. When Strom Thurmond became chairman in 1981, he chose not to recreate the Subcommittee on Antitrust, in part because of his own interest in the issue area. But it also was widely reported at the time that another reason for holding antitrust at full committee was that an antitrust subcommittee would have been chaired by liberal Republican Charles McC. Mathias, and Thurmond wanted to keep the jurisdiction out of Mathias's hands. Holding antitrust at full committee added a degree of centralization to a very decentralized panel.

The staff of the Judiciary Committee is one of the most decentralized in the Senate, and subcommittees on Judiciary have much larger staffs than the subcommittees of the other three panels under consideration. Subcommittee staffers are hired and fired by the subcommittee chairs and subcommittee ranking minority members alone, and there is no control exercised by full committee leaders. Thurmond retained a small full committee staff to cover antitrust legislation and to monitor the activities of certain of the subcommittees. A former full committee counsel outlined his job description.

> There were seven attorneys on the full committee staff, which is very small: Each subcommittee had almost as many staffers as we did. The full committee counsels were each assigned one to three subcommittees to oversee, depending on activity levels. It was basically an oversight role for those subcommittees Thurmond was not a member on. Thurmond was on three subcommittees, but not on immigration, this time. My job was to do that bill for him.

Ranking Democrat Joseph Biden lacked the staff resources to employ a similar strategy. Indeed, one committee aide described Biden as "strapped": "He doesn't have the resources to keep a hold on every issue. They don't have much staff."

Hatch, Kennedy, and the Labor Committee
The structure of the Labor Committee is also decentralized, and subcommittee markups are often the scene of significant legislative work. The decentralization embodied in the subcommittee system is often diluted, however, by decisions to hold important areas of the Labor Committee jurisdiction at the full committee level. In the late 1970s, for example, labor issues were kept at full committee because of their importance to the policy goals of then chairman Harrison Williams of New Jersey. Similarly, both Orrin Hatch and Ed-

ward Kennedy have a strong interest in health policy, and in 1981, Hatch chose not to create a subcommittee on health.[14] Holding health policy at full committee added an important component of centralization to the internal structure of the Labor Committee. Because of a general lack of funds for social service programs, the panel has been devoting more attention to health issues in recent years. Thus, we need to distinguish between health policy and other areas of the jurisdiction in evaluating the impact of structural arrangements on leadership behavior.

As was the case with the other three panels, control over the Labor Committee staff mirrors the legislative role of the subcommittees. A senior aide to Hatch described the staff structure on Labor.

> Each subcommittee has its own staff, which is accountable to the subcommittee chairman or ranking minority member. Senator Hatch doesn't hire them. He gives each subcommittee chairman a sum of money with which to run the subcommittee in terms of staff. There is absolutely no veto power or clearance at the full committee level on personnel decisions. They can hire whomever they want. Because of that, our committee may be less efficient than a committee like Commerce, where the staff is kept at the full committee level, increasing the chairman's control.

The loyalty lines of subcommittee staff were apparent when the positions of Hatch and a subcommittee chair diverged.

> My boss and Hatch disagree on a lot of issues, but that's no problem for the subcommittee staff. Senator Weicker does the hiring and never checks with Hatch. He has complete autonomy in hiring decisions. When they disagree, I go with Weicker absolutely. It's clear-cut.

The Democratic staff under Kennedy was less decentralized, primarily because of its smaller size, but also because Kennedy was able to keep a much tighter grasp on the role of the minority than Hatch was able to keep on Republican members.

Although control of much of the Labor Committee staff was decentralized through the subcommittee system, there coexisted a large and active full committee staff. Both the majority and minority had health policy offices, with staffers hired and fired by the relevant full committee leader. In addition, as was also the case on Judiciary, a group of full committee staffers was assigned monitoring duties over the subcommittees to protect the full committee chair's interests.

Individual Characteristics

Contextual factors shape leadership behavior, but individual characteristics of particular chairs and ranking minority members can also influence their choice of tactics and strategies. As a result, a proper understanding of leadership behavior in the Senate requires that we consider important differences in the eight individuals who are the focus of this study.

But which individual characteristics should be considered? Beyond their Republican identification, Robert Stafford and Strom Thurmond have little in common. Along what personal dimensions can we usefully compare Edward Kennedy and Orrin Hatch? At a certain level, all politicians are simply different. They have distinct temperaments, metabolisms, and life histories. I asked an aide to Howard Metzenbaum why his boss employs obstructionist tactics. The response was typical: "Why? You're asking [about] something that's deep within the psyche of Howard Metzenbaum. I'm afraid it's not something that lends itself to analysis very well." The staffer was correct, of course. Psychological characteristics are important, but they also tend to be ambiguous and extremely difficult to measure.[15] Thus, although it is important to consider individual characteristics of the eight senators in our attempt to understand their behavior, these characteristics need to be concrete enough for analysis. I focus on three: a committee leader's policy preferences, leadership experience, and proximate career plans.

Policy Preferences

A committee leader's policy preferences influence his or her leadership behavior. This is not to say that liberalism or conservatism alone is associated with a particular style of leadership. But certain aspects of a leader's policy preferences do have an independent impact on his or her choice of tactics and strategies.

Most important, we need to consider the location of a committee leader's preferences relative to the distribution of opinion in the committee as a whole. I have already discussed how well the policy preferences of each leader meshed with the preference contexts on their panels. Full committee leaders on Commerce and Environment and Public Works tended toward the middle of the preference distributions in their committees. On Judiciary and Labor, however, the preference contexts were more heterogeneous, and full committee leaders diverged from the median viewpoint.

Additionally, the ideological distance between the two full committee leaders is also an important variable for understanding how they interact. On Commerce and Environment and Public Works, the policy preferences of the chair and ranking minority member were proximate, promoting cooperation at the leadership level. In contrast, on Judiciary and Labor, full committee leaders confronted each other from opposite ends of the ideological spectrum, and maintaining cooperation at the leadership level on these two panels often was problematic.

We also need to consider the *intensity* of a leader's policy preferences because preference intensity influences a leader's willingness to delegate decision-making responsibility to other committee members. Leadership resources are scarce, and committee chairs and ranking minority members have to choose when to be active and when to let other senators take the lead. The more intense a leader's preferences are on an issue, the greater the value the leader will place on achieving a policy outcome close to those preferences, and the more willing the leader will be to allocate leadership resources to the issue. John Danforth, for example, is particularly interested in consumer policy and traffic safety, and on those items, he is less likely to defer to other senators. Similarly, Edward Kennedy has a long-standing interest in health policy and clearly takes the lead among Labor Committee Democrats in this issue area. Indeed, all eight of the committee leaders under study cared more about certain portions of their jurisdictions than they did about others, and leadership styles varied significantly from issue to issue, depending on the intensity of a leader's policy preferences.

Leadership Experience

A second individual characteristic that is useful for understanding the behavior of these eight leaders is experience: experience in the particular leadership position each held in 1985, experience with committee leadership in general, and experience as a member of the Senate.

Committee leadership involves a complex array of tasks, ranging from scheduling to anticipating the mood of the parent chamber. The key input into a leader's output is information, both about substantive policy alternatives and about the preferences of committee members (and senators in general) between these alternatives. Indeed, policy alternatives are best conceptualized as bundles of information. On most issues, a committee leader has access to an overabundance of information from staff aides, other offices, and outside actors such as interest group representatives and agency officials. As an aide to a senior Democrat told me: "There's no shortage of facts, there's a surplus. But the information isn't knowledge if it isn't useful to us, if it isn't in the right form."

The leader's task is thus one of information management: interpreting information and translating it into usable form, subject to the extreme time pressures that characterize the modern Senate. There generally will be little uncertainty about the underlying ideological preferences of the rank and file, but there often is significant uncertainty about the relationship between concrete policy alternatives and those underlying preferences. Thus, effective coalition building requires that a committee leader's office collect politically useful information about viable alternatives, and then interpret those alternatives in terms of the underlying preferences of committee members.[16]

The committee staff is essential for fulfilling these tasks, but the expertise of committee leaders themselves is also crucial. This is particularly the case for chairs, who ultimately are responsible for running their panels. Committee leaders tend to be more effective at managing information the longer they have held the position, the broader their experience as a committee leader, and the longer they have been in the Senate. Of course, the link between experience and expertise is not perfect, but participants in the process stress that there is a learning period for new committee leaders, particularly chairs.

Thus, it is useful to consider the backgrounds of the eight senators in evaluating their behavior as committee leaders. Some summary data is provided in table 1.5. If we examine experience in the leadership position each held during the 99th Congress, two of the committee chairs stand out—Strom Thurmond and John Danforth.

By the beginning of the 99th Congress, Strom Thurmond had been a senator for three decades, a full committee leader since 1971, and chairman of the Judiciary Committee for four years. Procedural ingenuity has long been a hallmark of the Thurmond style, and he is extremely adept at using Senate rules to achieve his goals. In 1957, for example, after drying himself out in a steamroom for two days, Thurmond held the floor of the Senate for 24 hours

TABLE 1.5. Leadership Experience by Committee

Committee	Years in Current Leadership Position	Years as a Committee Leader	Years in Senate
Commerce			
Danforth	0	0	8
Hollings	2	5	18
Environment and Public Works			
Stafford	4	8	14
Bentsen	0	2	14
Judiciary			
Thurmond	4	14	30
Biden	4	4	12
Labor			
Hatch	4	4	8
Kennedy	4	6	22

Source: Congressional Staff Directory, various editions.
Note: Years of experience at the beginning of 1985

and 18 minutes in a futile attempt to block an important civil rights matter—an effort that is still the longest sustained filibuster by an individual in Senate history.[17] In 1964, Thurmond, in one of the more innovative quorum strategies ever employed, wrestled then Senator Ralph Yarborough of Texas to the floor outside the Commerce Committee meeting room in order to keep the panel from reporting out a nomination he opposed. A journalist described the exchange on the front page of the *New York Times* the following morning.

> Within minutes of their encounter, the 200 pound Texan and the 170 pound South Carolinian, both with their coats off, were rolling and thrashing across the marble floor to the startled dismay of an audience of secretaries and clerks. At one point in the 10-minute encounter Senator Thurmond, who had Senator Yarborough pinned to the floor, offered to quit if the Texan would give up. They did struggle to their feet once, but immediately fell again without any pretense of playful good humor.[18]

The discussion ended after Frank Lausche of Ohio walked by and warned his colleagues that they were both courting heart attacks, and committee chairman Warren Magnuson of Washington emerged from the meeting room and asked them to desist.

As ranking minority member of the Judiciary Committee in the late 1970s, Thurmond was more subtle in his use of quorum strategies to delay the flow of liberal legislation backed by then chairman Edward Kennedy. An aide to Patrick Leahy of Vermont, a committee Democrat, described Thurmond's approach.

> During the 96th Congress, it used to be that Thurmond would walk in and sit there by himself until the Democrats made quorum. Then, on cue, the other guys, who had been sitting in an anteroom, would come on in. If there weren't enough Democrats, no meeting.

In short, Thurmond has a well-honed ability for using the rules of the institution to his advantage, an ability developed during a Senate career that has spanned over three decades. Committee structure and the distribution of preferences are important for understanding his leadership of the Judiciary Committee from 1981 to 1987, but it is also instructive to examine his leadership style from the perspective of the length and breadth of his experience as a senator and a committee leader. As one Democratic staffer on the panel quipped, "Thurmond can run a meeting in his sleep—I've watched him do it."

In contrast, upon assuming the chairmanship of the Commerce Committee in 1985, John Danforth had no experience at all as a full committee chair or ranking minority member. Danforth described the transition period that is inherent when a senator assumes leadership on a panel with a jurisdiction, staff, and work load as large as the Commerce Committee's.

> I thought there was a transition. I haven't had any experience before or since that was like chairing that committee. It really is hard. Just being a senator is a time-consuming job. Before becoming chairman, I was just a senator with a personal staff following the Senate for me, following my personal interests.

> The demands on a chairman are different. Fisheries is not exactly a cutting-edge issue in Missouri, but I had to deal with the issue as chairman, had to be briefed on the bills. Aviation is not my beat. But the work always needs to be done. . . . I felt more comfortable with it the second year. Also, when I first became chairman, there was a sense that I had to prove my mettle to other senators.

In general, most observers agreed that Danforth was more adept at leading the committee during his second year, and that there was clearly a period of learning and transition during the months after he assumed the chairmanship in January, 1985. As a result, a key factor in understanding Danforth's leadership style over the period was simply that he was new to the job.

Proximate Career Plans

The third individual characteristic contributing to an understanding of committee leadership behavior is a leader's proximate career plans. The concern is not so much with each senator's long-term ambitions, but with those career plans that had a significant and direct impact on their leadership styles during the period of interest. Thus, my focus is on what the eight leaders believed they would be doing in the years immediately following the 99th Congress. Four career paths are of interest: (1) no change: a leader planned to stay in his or her current position for the foreseeable future; (2) leadership on another panel: a leader planned to move to a leadership position on another committee; (3) the presidency: a leader was considered a serious presidential prospect for 1988; and (4) retirement.

A committee leader's proximate career plans influence his or her commitment to the panel. When a leader intends to stay in a position, that committee's jurisdiction will tend to dominate the leader's policy agenda. As indicated in table 1.6, both Commerce Committee leaders—John Danforth and Ernest Hollings—intended to be in leadership positions on the committee for the foreseeable future. Danforth would have preferred to chair the Finance

Committee, but he had to wait in line behind Bob Packwood and William Roth, Jr., who had greater seniority. Ernest Hollings probably would have preferred the ranking position on the Appropriations Committee, his other assignment, but was well down the line in seniority. As a result, the Commerce Committee jurisdiction was central to the issue agendas of both Danforth and Hollings.

As table 1.6 indicates, at different points in 1985 and 1986, three of the committee leaders planned to assume a leadership post on another panel at the beginning of the 100th Congress. In February, 1985, Russell Long of Louisiana, ranking minority member on the Finance Committee, announced that he would not be running for reelection. The Finance Committee Democrat immediately behind Long in seniority was Lloyd Bentsen, then ranking minority member on Environment and Public Works. Because Finance was more central to Bentsen's policy interests, he planned to give up his position on Environment and Public Works to become Democratic leader on the Finance Committee as soon as Long retired. One effect of Bentsen's expected shift was to pull his attention away from the Environment and Public Works Committee during the two years he was ranking Democrat on the panel. Bentsen spoke to the point.

> Yes, it [the prospect of a leadership post on Finance] did have an effect on how I allocated my time. The Finance Committee has the broadest jurisdiction of any congressional committee. . . . If I had not become chairman of the Finance Committee, I would have retired from the Senate.

TABLE 1.6. Proximate Career Plans by Committee

Committee	Plans
Commerce	
Danforth	No change
Hollings	No change
Environment and Public Works	
Stafford	Retirement
Bentsen	Leadership position on Finance Committee[a]
Judiciary	
Thurmond	Leadership position on Armed Services Committee[b]
Biden	Presidential campaign
Labor	
Hatch	Leadership position on Judiciary Committee[b]
Kennedy	Presidential campaign[c]

[a] After February, 1985
[b] 99th Congress, second session
[c] Kennedy announced he would not be a candidate on December 19, 1985.

Indeed, when Bentsen became chairman of Finance at the beginning of the 100th Congress, he gave up his assignment on the Environment and Public Works Committee.

Similar dynamics were at work on the Judiciary and Labor Committees, although the magnitude of the effect was less pronounced. During the early 1970s, Strom Thurmond was ranking minority member on the Senate Armed Services Committee. In 1977, however, Thurmond gave up that position to become ranking minority member on Judiciary (on which he was also the senior Republican), in order to block the Judiciary Committee Republican next in line—liberal Charles McC. Mathias of Maryland.[19] Consequentially, when Republicans organized the Senate in the 1980s, Thurmond chaired the Judiciary Committee. By 1986, however, it was apparent that both Mathias and Barry M. Goldwater of Arizona (then chairman of Armed Services) would not be running for reelection. As a result, during most of his last year as chairman of the Judiciary Committee, Thurmond intended to shift to a leadership position on the Armed Services Committee at the beginning of the next congress.

The prospect of a Thurmond move had implications for Orrin Hatch as well. In 1985, Hatch was fourth in line on Judiciary, behind Thurmond, Mathias, and Paul Laxalt of Nevada. Laxalt announced his retirement from the Senate in August, 1985. Thus, when Mathias announced that he would not be running for reelection and it became apparent that Thurmond would soon move to Armed Services, Orrin Hatch expected to be the next chairman of the Judiciary Committee, a panel he preferred to the Labor Committee. As a result, Hatch also spent most of 1986 believing he soon would be assuming leadership on a different committee.

In fact, when the Democrats won back the chamber in November, 1986, Thurmond opted to retain his leadership post on the Judiciary Committee, and Hatch retained his position on Labor.[20] For our purposes, however, *expectations* are what matter, and during most of the second session of the 99th Congress both senators *believed* that they would soon be moving to leadership positions on other panels. These expectations led to a shift in attention in the expected direction, particularly for Orrin Hatch. Close observers of Labor Committee politics from both parties noted that Hatch's commitment to the panel seemed low in 1986, at the same time that he was often described by staffers as Thurmond's "vice-chairman" on the Judiciary Committee.

By most accounts, two of the committee leaders—Joseph Biden and Edward Kennedy—were actively considering campaigns for the 1988 Democratic presidential nomination at some point during the 99th Congress. Biden eventually ran, while Kennedy announced his noncandidacy in December, 1985. The prospects of a presidential campaign typically influence a senator's legislative agenda in the years immediately preceding the official announcement of candidacy. Successfully running for president requires that a candidate appeal to a national audience. As a result, laying the groundwork for a presidential campaign tends to broaden a committee leader's issue agenda, and it influences how a committee leader allocates his or her time among the different issues in the panel's jurisdiction. For instance, according to some observers, one reason Biden deferred so extensively on Judiciary Committee issues was that taking the lead on legislation relating to busing, school prayer, and abortion was not viewed as a useful strategy for winning the Democratic presidential nomination.[21]

Finally, according to knowledgeable staff, one of the eight committee leaders planned to retire from public life at the end of his term: Robert Stafford, chairman of the Environment and Public Works Committee.[22] The decision to retire from politics effectively severs the electoral connection, and a senator is free to pursue his or her own policy interests relatively unencumbered by constituency pressures and the need to generate publicity for the purposes of reelection.[23]

Summary

Five factors are employed in this book to explain the behavior of committee leaders in the U.S. Senate. The two most powerful explanatory variables are contextual: the preference and structural contexts. But individual characteristics of the eight leaders also matter, and we will focus on three: a leader's policy preferences, leadership experience, and proximate career plans.

On the Commerce Committee, the preference context was consensual, and the structural context was (and remains) centralized. Thus, committee chair John Danforth and ranking Democrat Ernest Hollings had the political support, agenda control, and staff resources necessary to exert strong leadership. In addition, the policy preferences of the two full committee leaders seldom clashed on committee issues, facilitating cooperation at the leadership level. Danforth was new to the chairmanship in 1985, however, and faced a period of learning and transition. Both senators planned to remain as leaders on the Commerce Committee for the foreseeable future.

The preference context on Environment and Public Works was also oriented toward consensus, but there were pockets of dissension among conservative westerners on the panel. And because the committee was unrepresentative of the prevailing opinion in the full Senate on environmental issues, the prospect of floor problems loomed large. The personal policy preferences of chairman Robert Stafford and ranking minority member Lloyd Bentsen usually did not diverge significantly. Like the Commerce Committee, Environment and Public Works is also relatively centralized in structure, but subcommittee leaders hold markups and have greater control over the committee staff.

The proximate career plans of both Stafford and Bentsen affected their behavior on Environment and Public Works. Stafford was about to retire from the Senate, and Bentsen planned to move to a leadership position on the Finance Committee at the beginning of the next congress.

Preferences on the Judiciary Committee were polarized, with committee chairman Strom Thurmond and ranking minority member Joseph Biden often disagreeing on the issues. The panel is also decentralized, further complicating the jobs of the two leaders. Both senators had committee leadership experience at the beginning of the 99th Congress, but few members could match the length and breadth of Strom Thurmond's career in the institution. And the proximate career plans of Thurmond and Biden had consequences for their leadership. For most of 1986, Thurmond expected to move to a leadership position on the Armed Services Committee at the beginning of the next congress, and Biden was considered a leading prospect for the 1988 Democratic presidential nomination.

The Labor Committee was the most polarized of the four panels, and committee chairman Orrin Hatch often lacked a working majority. As was the case on the Judiciary Committee, the structure of the Labor Committee is highly decentralized (except for health issues). The ideological distance between Hatch and ranking Democrat Edward Kennedy was significant, hindering cooperation between the two full committee leaders. And the proximate career plans of Hatch and Kennedy were also relevant if we are to understand their leadership. During the second session of the 99th Congress, Hatch believed he would soon replace Thurmond as the Republican leader on Judiciary, while for most of the first session, Kennedy was considered a potential candidate for the Democratic presidential nomination in 1988.

Notes

1. Recent scholarly research has emphasized the contextual foundations of leadership behavior in Congress, and my discussion of committee leadership is in this tradition. In particular, see Cooper and Brady 1981 and Jones 1968.

2. The discussion in this paragraph is primarily adopted from Cooper and Brady 1981, as well as from Rohde and Shepsle 1987. Both studies emphasize the importance of the distribution of preferences among the rank and file for understanding party leadership behavior, and both focus on preference homogeneity as a condition for strong party leadership in Congress. Also see Ornstein, Peabody, and Rohde 1986. Unekis and Rieselbach 1984 describe how the preferences of House committee leaders relate to the factional structures of their panels. Also see Parker and Parker 1985 for a systematic analysis of voting factions in House committees.

3. Of course, care is necessary in interpreting scores falling near the boundary of a category. On the limitations of interest group ratings as indicators of legislators' preferences, see Fowler 1982, Hall and Grofman 1990, and VanDoren 1990. As an additional check, I converted the interest group ratings used in this book into ordinal

measures, but no significant substantive changes resulted. The Commerce Committee did appear somewhat more consensual, but since the unconverted CCUS ratings also generated a consensual distribution of preferences, and were easier to interpret, I used them in table 1.1.

4. In table 1.1, Republicans on the Commerce Committee cluster in the high category, while most committee Democrats are in the middle category. However, low levels of preference intensity countervailed any tendencies toward partisanship on the panel (see also note 3). While the issues considered by the Commerce Committee during the 1960s and 1970s—consumer safety, truth in advertising, deregulation— were highly salient, mobilizing a broad audience, the committee's agenda in recent years has been dominated by a plethora of relatively routine reauthorizations. For a discussion of the Commerce Committee in the 1960s, see the work of David Price (1972, 1975).

5. For discussions of congressional decision making on public works issues, see Ferejohn 1974 and Murphy 1974.

6. Because environmental issues do not translate directly into liberal-conservative distinctions, there are some surprises. One of the most ardent environmentalists on the panel, for example, was Gordon Humphrey of New Hampshire, an extremely conservative Republican. Similarly, Quentin Burdick of North Dakota, generally considered a liberal Democrat, received an LCV rating of just 44, the lowest among committee Democrats.

7. Krehbiel 1990.

8. It has long been difficult to draw conservative Republicans to the labor committees in both the House and Senate because the assignment regularly places them in a position to vote against the side of organized labor. See Price 1972, Fenno 1973, and Hall 1987.

9. For a discussion of the political environment in which the House and Senate labor committees operated in the 1960s, see Fenno 1973. The group-oriented character of that environment has not changed significantly.

10. A discussion of subcommittee activity levels in the House and Senate can be found in Smith and Deering 1984, chapter 5.

11. The chamber's standing rules allow a senator to bypass the committee of jurisdiction and bring a matter directly to the Senate floor. Placing a bill on the calendar does not imply that it will be scheduled for floor consideration, however. Party leaders control the schedule of the full Senate, and they tend to defer to the wishes of committee leaders. Bills that bypass committee against the wishes of the chair usually die a quiet death.

12. Fox and Hammond 1977.

13. It should be noted that committee structure is not necessarily exogenous to committee decision making. Richard Fenno, for example, has argued that both structural arrangements and leadership behavior are shaped by a common set of factors (1973, chap. 4). That is, there may be a pattern between various degrees of structural decentralization and leadership behavior, but the correlation may arise because they are determined by the same variable, rather than through a causal link from structure to leadership tactics. Indeed, to a certain extent the internal structures of Senate committees are endogenous to committee decision making. Subcommittees are created, abol-

ished, and reconstituted depending on member interest, and staffing practices also change over time. And, as will be apparent in the paragraphs to follow, the staff structures of the four panels under study reflected their preference distributions to a certain extent. In particular, structural decentralization and preference heterogeneity appear to be closely associated. But altering structure changes the distribution of power within committee. Those who stand to lose agenda prerogatives or staff resources will tend to oppose the change. If attempts to alter structure are unsuccessful, those senators benefiting from the status quo may retaliate. Thus, altering structural arrangements is not without cost. As a result, a committee's internal organization is at least partially exogenous to member preferences, and structural factors can be usefully conceptualized as having an independent impact on leadership behavior. Senate committee leaders and their aides certainly believe that the role of subcommittees and the distribution of committee staffers influence how they do their work. On the partial exogeneity of institutional arrangements, see Shepsle 1986.

14. Kennedy also chose not to create a health subcommittee when he became chairman in 1987.

15. For a different and highly influential view, see the various studies of James David Barber (1965, 1966a, 1966b, 1972).

16. The intuition behind this paragraph is drawn from John Kingdon's analysis of decision making on the House floor (1989). A more abstract formulation can be found in Austen-Smith and Riker 1987. See also Gilligan and Krehbiel 1987, 1989, 1990. A discussion of the role of "interpretation" in legislative decision making is provided by Richard A. Smith (1984).

17. Calmes 1987b, 2115.

18. Phillips 1964, L1, 10.

19. Ehrenhalt, 1987, 1366.

20. Thurmond opted for the ranking minority membership on Judiciary to be in the forefront of Republican efforts to protect Reagan's judicial nominees. In addition, his choice allowed John Warner of Virginia to fill the ranking position on Armed Services. At the time, Warner anticipated a tough reelection fight and believed that a leadership position on Armed Services would enhance his prospects at the polls.

21. For a discussion of the Senate as a "presidential incubator," see Peabody, Ornstein, and Rohde 1976.

22. Stafford formally announced his retirement from the Senate in April, 1987.

23. On the importance of the electoral connection to legislative behavior, see Mayhew 1974.

CHAPTER 2

Agenda Control

In comparing the legislative styles of committee leaders in Congress, our attention turns first to the most significant formal prerogative of leadership: control over the full committee agenda. Agenda control is primarily exercised by chairs. Ranking minority members also have a degree of influence over the agenda, but that influence is exerted through their working relationships with their majority counterparts. As a result, in this chapter we explore the agenda styles of the four chairmen: John Danforth, Robert Stafford, Strom Thurmond, and Orrin Hatch.

Agenda prerogatives play a crucial role in congressional policy-making. If a bill survives the chair's scrutiny, legislative action usually begins with a hearing. Formal committee hearings fulfill a variety of functions, ranging from information gathering to mobilization.[1] But because of the large number of bills introduced each year and the scarcity of time and money for committee hearings, most legislation dies a quiet death very early in the process when the relevant full or subcommittee chair decides not to schedule hearings. Thus, the agenda-setting stage in committee is the major bottleneck in the legislative process.

Committee leaders can accelerate or delay legislation throughout committee deliberations, but there are a few key junctures. For legislation considered at both the subcommittee and full committee levels, agenda prerogatives are shared. The subcommittee chair can close the gates on an initiative by not funding hearings or by refusing to hold a subcommittee markup, while the full committee chair controls the schedule once the legislation emerges from subcommittee. If there is no subcommittee layer to the process, as often happens in Senate committees, agenda control belongs to the full committee chair, and he or she decides which bills are considered and which bills disappear.

Agenda Control and Legislative Strategy

The policy-making importance of a chair's control over the full committee agenda, the strategic nature of agenda politics, and the general role of procedural tactics in committee deliberations were all particularly apparent dur-

ing one political fight between Orrin Hatch and Lowell Weicker in the Labor
Committee in 1985. In April, 1985, Weicker introduced S.974, a bill authorizing $10 million to support legal advocacy programs for residents of mental
institutions. Hatch, who chaired the Labor Committee, was suspicious of the
initial Weicker draft and favored greater reliance on state programs already in
place. Because Weicker chaired the subcommittee of jurisdiction and had
agenda control at the subcommittee level, scheduling hearings was not a
problem. But given Hatch's prerogatives at the full committee level, a collision of some form was inevitable, and it occurred when Weicker marked up
the bill in his Subcommittee on the Handicapped.

Hatch was not a member of the subcommittee, but subcommittee members Strom Thurmond of South Carolina and Don Nickles of Oklahoma acted
for him. A Kennedy staffer who was in attendance described the meeting.

> The subcommittee markup was unbelievable. Nickles and Thurmond
> tried to kill the bill by offering about twenty amendments. There's a rule
> in the Senate that you can't let a markup go on more than two hours after
> the Senate goes into session [usually noon], and Thurmond and Nickles
> were trying to use up the time.

The Hatch staff was primarily responsible for drafting the amendments, which
were offered by Strom Thurmond during the course of subcommittee deliberations. Indeed, the Thurmond amendments first arrived at Lowell Weicker's
office in Hatch envelopes.

Hatch and Thurmond were unsuccessful in their attempts to derail S.974
in subcommittee, however. Procedures exist for circumventing the two-hour
limit. A senator can ask for a waiver of the two-hour rule on the Senate floor,
and permission to continue the meeting is granted if there are no objections.
Weicker's office anticipated the Hatch-Thurmond strategy and secured the
necessary waiver in advance. An aide who was staffing the meeting for
Weicker recalled the outcome.

> We wanted to continue. . . . You need to put a unanimous consent re-
> quest in on the floor that your committee be [allowed] to meet past the
> noon hour. It has to be actually said. Our backup staff work at the
> markup [made clear] the logistics of it, and [we] were smart enough to
> make the phone calls and get the chair of the Senate to request unan-
> imous consent, and it was granted. They were not banking on that at
> all. . . .

> At one point, Thurmond tried to end the markup and Weicker said, "We
> have permission to continue." You should have seen the look on Thur-
> mond's face and the faces of the Hatch staffers. Their ploy was "we'll

have so many amendments that time will run out." . . . It would be a real pain in the ass to schedule another subcommittee markup. Weicker just wanted to keep things moving.

The amendments were defeated by a margin of five to two, and the bill was eventually reported out of subcommittee unanimously, but getting it on the agenda of the full committee was another matter. Outmaneuvered once, Hatch was not going to be outmaneuvered again. Like all Senate chairmen, Hatch controlled his committee's agenda, and he refused to schedule S.974 for full committee markup until his views had been accommodated. Weicker could have taken the bill directly to the floor through a variety of parliamentary procedures, but as one of his staffers noted, "In the current administrative climate, you just never know what is going to happen when you circumvent committee." So after much prodding from Weicker and Hatch, staff aides for the two senators found middle ground, and Weicker and Hatch united behind a compromise bill. The legislation was then placed on the full committee agenda, marked up, reported to the floor, and quickly passed by the full Senate.

The procedural duet between Hatch and Weicker on S.974 has implications for how we should approach agenda control as an aspect of leadership behavior.

Time and Timing

As the Weicker bill makes very clear, decisions about a committee's agenda are decisions about priorities, and decisions about priorities are inherently political. Agenda politics is about power. It is well known that procedural maneuvering in Congress is almost always wrapped up in substantive differences over policy, and this is particularly the case with scheduling decisions. In the modern Senate, members and their staff work subject to unprecedented time constraints.[2] Claiborne Pell of Rhode Island, first elected in 1960, commented on how time pressures have changed since he became a senator.

> The Senate was much more agreeable when I came here, more fun. Pastore [former Senator John Pastore of Rhode Island] used to spend two hours on the floor in the afternoon. I'd love to do that . . . but I don't have the time, with meetings and appointments. Mike Mansfield [a former majority leader] and I once took a five-week trip around the world. I could never do that now.

Lloyd Bentsen, first elected to the House in 1948, a business executive during the 1950s and 1960s, and a senator since 1971, also emphasized changing time constraints in Congress.

I never put in hours like this when I was in the private sector. We were on the floor until 2:30 last night. I came home and set the alarm for 7:00. I can't remember the weekend when I didn't bring a briefcase home. There's so much to read. I brought in a management consultant who had worked for me in the private sector to look at the organization of the staff. He was amazed at how hard we work. . . .

I came to Washington in 1948 at age twenty-seven, the youngest member for two terms. We used to go out in July. It was more casual. I used to have a poker game at my house on Friday nights. LBJ would come, Stuart Symington, Fred Vinson. That would never happen now. Go to the house of a freshman?

. . . There's been incredible change. LBJ used to call and say, "Let's go play nine holes at Burning Tree," on a Wednesday. On a Wednesday! Now we have beepers and phones in our cars. I got the beeper three years ago, the car phone a year and a half ago. Warren Rudman saw my car and asked why I had two antennas. I told him one was for the phone and one was for the FAX machine. I was joking, but there's been incredible change.

As political scientist Bruce I. Oppenheimer has demonstrated, time pressures pervade the modern Senate, and the implications for decision making are profound.[3] One consequence has been to raise the stakes involved in agenda politics. It is well known that committee chairs in Congress can derail legislation by refusing to place it on the agenda. What is perhaps less well known, however, is how damaging even minor delays in a bill's progress can be for the probability of final passage.

By all accounts, the burgeoning Senate work load has led to an increased level of demand for time on the floor. Sessions of Congress are longer than they were twenty years ago, and the amount of floor time available for considering legislation in the full Senate has increased significantly. But growth in the amount of business has more than countervailed the increase in available floor time, and, as a result, securing the floor time necessary to consider complex or controversial legislation has become much more difficult.

The probability that a bill will be passed by the full Senate is in part a function of time. The more quickly an item moves through committee, the greater the time available for floor consideration, increasing the prospects for final passage. Conversely, bottling up legislation in committee—even for just a few months—is often sufficient to kill it. Particularly toward the end of a session of Congress, the institution simply lacks the time to deal with controversial legislation that is not of the utmost importance. As a result, senators and staff aides place great emphasis on getting legislation to the floor as quickly as possible.

The process of agenda setting influences the timing of committee deliberations. By placing a bill near the top of the full committee agenda, the chair facilitates timely action in committee and thus increases the time available for floor consideration. Placing an item at the bottom of the agenda delays committee action and decreases the probability that the bill will become law. And, of course, refusing to place an item on the full committee agenda usually kills the legislation outright. Thus, given the pressing time constraints that characterize the modern Senate, the agenda-setting stage is crucial. Weicker was certainly concerned about timing in his handling of S.974. He moved it to the top of his subcommittee's agenda and devised a strategy for countering dilatory tactics by conservatives during the subcommittee markup. Similarly, time constraints increased the effectiveness of Hatch's threat not to schedule the bill for full committee consideration.

Strategy

In addition to the general importance of time and timing in the modern Senate, it should also be emphasized that the process of agenda setting is fundamentally strategic in character. Although control over the full committee agenda is a formal procedural prerogative, agenda politics consists of a sequence of strategic interactions between the chair and other members of the committee. On S.974, both Hatch and Weicker had a range of feasible tactics from which to choose their strategies, and the utility of each alternative depended in part on the actions of the other senator.

For Weicker, one alternative was to challenge Hatch directly and attempt to have the full Labor Committee vote S.974 onto the agenda. A second alternative was to cut a deal with the chairman and trade substantive concessions on the legislation for a place on the schedule. Still another option was to circumvent committee and attempt to add the bill as an amendment to some other measure on the floor. Finally, Weicker could have done nothing: He could have moved on and blamed the bill's demise on Hatch.

As chairman of the full committee, Orrin Hatch was faced with his own array of alternatives. One was to refuse to schedule any Weicker initiative in this area without dramatic revision. Another was to initiate active negotiations and reach a compromise solution. A third alternative was to obstruct the bill during the subcommittee stage of the process. Or, finally, Hatch simply could have scheduled the Weicker bill in its original form and then attempted to modify the legislation in committee or on the floor.[4]

The choice of tactics by Hatch and Weicker depended on how they perceived the benefits and costs of each option, which in turn depended on their expectations about the other senator's behavior. We need to think about agenda control as more than a formal prerogative of leadership. Rather, it is useful to conceptualize agenda setting as the interdependent decision making of two or more political actors: as a set of strategic interactions between the chair and other committee members, conditioned by the chair's formal powers.[5]

Understanding Agenda Politics

Before exploring the agenda strategies of the four chairs, it is useful to make some preliminary arguments based on the contextual and individual factors discussed in the previous chapter. Both sets of characteristics shape decision making at the agenda stage of the process.

Contextual Characteristics

The structural context sets the boundaries of a chair's discretion over scheduling decisions: It determines the distribution of agenda resources. On centralized panels such as the Commerce Committee, in which subcommittees do not mark up legislation, formal agenda prerogatives are concentrated in the hands of the chair. In contrast, on relatively decentralized committees such as Judiciary, agenda control is shared with subcommittee chairs. Thus, the structural context sets the parameters of formal power and informal responsibility within which agenda politics takes place.

Within these structural boundaries, the preference context is the central characteristic for understanding a chair's scheduling decisions. For instance, Commerce and Environment and Public Works are both relatively centralized, but decision making at the agenda stage was strikingly different on the two panels. Similarly, both Judiciary and Labor tend to be more decentralized, but Strom Thurmond and Orrin Hatch behaved differently in setting their panels' agendas. For all four chairs, the key factors influencing scheduling practices were the distribution and intensity of preferences on committee issues.

Most pieces of legislation considered in the Senate are relatively noncontroversial. If the distribution of preferences on a bill is consensual, the importance of agenda politics declines. Consider the routine reauthorizations that constitute so much of the institution's work load. As mentioned, processing reauthorizations is considered part of the job of a committee. Most action occurs at the staff level, and scheduling decisions are handled so as to promote efficient decision making. Moving noncontroversial items to the top of the agenda can be a tactic for delaying other pieces of legislation that are waiting in line, but on committees with primary jurisdiction over consensual legislation, a chair's agenda prerogatives are less crucial determinants of his or her leadership behavior. Given its jurisdiction over a wide range of relatively routine reauthorizations, the Commerce Committee tends to fall in this category.

On other issues, the intensity and location of member preferences generate significant conflict, complicating the process of coalition building. And, in addition to the level of conflict, *where* controversy occurs in the legislative process also has implications for a committee chair's agenda strategies.

Agenda Control to Counter Dilatory Tactics
When significant conflict exists in committee, there are incentives for opposing senators to engage in obstructionism. We know quite a bit about the procedural tactics available to senators for obstructing legislation on the floor—the filibuster is an integral part of Senate lore.[6] What is less well known is the potential importance of dilatory tactics during the committee stage of the process. Committee members who lack the votes to win on substance have access to a wide range of tactics for delaying or blocking committee action. For example, Senate committees cannot meet in the absence of a quorum, usually a simple majority of committee members. In 1984, Democrats on the Labor Committee were able to block committee consideration of a bill relating to the *Grove City v. Bell* Supreme Court decision simply by boycotting scheduled meetings.

In addition, under the Senate's standing rules, subcommittees and committees cannot meet beyond two hours after the Senate has gone into session unless a waiver from the floor is obtained. This effectively places a time constraint on committee deliberations and provides incentives for opponents of a bill to filibuster in committee by extending debate or by simply showering legislation with amendments (the Hatch approach on S.974). According to Claiborne Pell of Rhode Island, current chair of the Senate Foreign Relations Committee:

> You can do an 80 percent filibuster in committee—not a full one, but 80 percent. [Still] it's very difficult to stop. Six to eight weeks before the end of a session, the leadership will not countenance that, [but] if you want to be an SOB, you can block something.

The dilatory potential of extended debate in committee was particularly apparent in an exchange between Strom Thurmond and liberal Democrat Patrick Leahy, which occurred during a Judiciary Committee markup held in 1984. Thurmond wanted to move a piece of legislation to the floor, and Leahy wanted to slow it down.[7]

> *Thurmond.* Will you object to voting on it today, this bill?
> *Leahy.* Well, I do not think we have time enough for me to cover some of my concerns about the bill.

Thurmond. Senator, you know what you are doing, you are filibustering if you take that position.

Leahy. Mr. Chairman, I have spoken for seven minutes—

Thurmond. Just be frank. You are within your rights. I just ask you the question. I do not want to keep all of the members here. . . .

Leahy. Mr. Chairman, I define a filibuster by the all-time standard set by our chairman. That is a filibuster. Eight and a half minutes of discussion of an amendment is not a filibuster. . . . I do have a number of issues to cover that probably would not be covered by noon.

Thurmond. In other words, you are going to filibuster?

Leahy. No, that is not so.

One strategy for countering dilatory tactics in committee is for the chair to use his or her control over the agenda to accelerate deliberations. Indeed, much of Strom Thurmond's leadership as chairman of the Judiciary Committee can be understood as an attempt to use his formal prerogatives in response to dilatory tactics by liberal Democrats such as Leahy.

Maximizing Floor Time

If the distribution and intensity of preferences in committee promote conflict on an issue, conflict will almost certainly exist on the floor of the Senate as well. If anything, the procedural prerogatives of individual senators are greater on the floor than they are in committee, and those who lose in the first stage of the sequence are likely to carry on their fight in the full Senate. Conflict in committee implies conflict on the floor.

The reverse does not hold true, however. Senators select their committee assignments, and, as a result, the membership of a committee is not necessarily representative of the chamber as a whole. If a panel is unrepresentative of the full Senate on an issue, it is possible that consensus may be achieved during committee deliberations, even in the face of significant opposition from senators not on the committee.

If preferences in committee are consensual but conflict is expected on the floor, incentives exist for the chair to use agenda prerogatives to accelerate the pace of a bill, even in the absence of delaying tactics during committee deliberations. Placing an item at the top of the full committee agenda speeds up committee action and maximizes the time available for floor consideration. As we shall see, scheduling was an important component of Robert Stafford's leadership on Environment and Public Works, even though there was a broad pro-environmentalist consensus in committee, because significant controversy was generally expected on the floor. Thus, the agenda was important on Environment and Public Works, as well as on the Judiciary Committee, but the underlying political dynamics were different because the locus of conflict was different.

Individual Characteristics

The structural and preference contexts are the key factors for understanding agenda politics, but individual characteristics of committee chairs also have an impact. Most important, we must consider the location of the chair's policy preferences relative to the preferences of other committee members. The further a chair's policy preferences from the median viewpoint in committee on an issue, the more likely that he or she will lack a working majority.[8] As a result, there will be incentives for the chair to lean heavily on agenda control as a substitute for political support by blocking consideration of issues on which the chair lacks the votes to win. Of the four chairmen, John Danforth and Robert Stafford seldom diverged significantly from the median positions on their panels, and Strom Thurmond had a solid base of conservative support during his six years as chair of the Judiciary Committee. On the Labor Committee, however, Orrin Hatch's preferences tended to diverge sharply from the median position, generating incentives for Hatch to systematically use his scheduling prerogatives to block legislation supported by a majority of committee members.

Additionally, a chair's proximate career plans influence scheduling decisions because they shape the level and nature of the commitment a leader has to the jurisdiction. And committee leadership experience also matters to a certain extent, as exemplified by the agenda practices of John Danforth on the Commerce Committee.

John Danforth and the Commerce Committee

Agenda politics was less important for understanding leadership on the Commerce Committee than was the case for the other three panels. Structural centralization plays a role. The absence of subcommittee markups rests full control of the agenda in the hands of the full committee chairman. Thus, John Danforth did not have to systematically use his agenda prerogatives to block legislation being pushed by subcommittee chairs with independent forums.

The nature of the preference context also reduced the importance of agenda setting as a source of political power. Recall that the distribution of preferences in the Commerce Committee was conducive to bargaining, accommodation, and compromise. The panel's coalitional structure was highly consensual, and preferences on the typical Commerce Committee bill were not intense. As a result, there was not a cohesive minority coalition of significant size on the committee capable of systematically pushing issues opposed by the chairman. Danforth's position close to the center of the distribution of preferences on the Commerce Committee further reduced the likelihood that opening the gates and allowing legislation to flow freely would result in personal defeat.

There were also few incentives for Danforth to use his scheduling prerogatives to systematically accelerate the pace of committee deliberations.
The bulk of the panel's jurisdiction is composed of relatively routine reauthorizations, items that seldom evoke much controversy. In the absence of significant conflict, there are few incentives for the chair to use his or her control
over the agenda to put committee bills on a fast track. Indeed, in the Senate,
consensual legislation is usually considered quickly on the floor by unanimous
consent. In short, the Commerce Committee's jurisdiction is bipartisan and
consensus-oriented, and the agenda-setting stage is not highly politicized.[9]

As is the case with all senators, though, certain portions of the jurisdiction were more relevant to Danforth's interests and goals than were others,
and the chairman's own policy preferences tended to be more intense on these
items. In Danforth's case, those issues were traffic safety, consumer policy,
and legislation of particular importance to his constituents in Missouri. As
Danforth said:

> The chairman's control of the agenda matters. Certain issues—product
> liability, traffic safety—that I wanted to do: They went on the agenda.
> They clearly became items. I was the chairman.

Danforth also used his control over committee priorities to accelerate
legislation that was important to his constituents. During 1985, two events in
Missouri generated particularly swift legislative responses by the chairman.
First, rumors emerged that the owner of the St. Louis Cardinals might move
the team out of state. Second, famed corporate raider Carl Icahn began to take
over TWA, one of the largest employers in Missouri. Both events generated
significant concern among Danforth's constituents, for obvious reasons.

Protecting communities from the prospect of losing professional sports
franchises was not a new legislative concern in 1985. During the 98th Congress, Commerce Committee member Slade Gorton of Washington introduced
a bill aimed at limiting relocations by professional football teams. Danforth
opposed Gorton's efforts, arguing that they constituted an undue interference
in the marketplace. The Gorton measure died on the floor in 1984, and he
reintroduced the legislation the following year. By this point, however, the
Cardinals had threatened to leave St. Louis, and Danforth—now chairman of
the Commerce Committee—switched his position on the question of legislation aimed at restricting team relocations. Working off of a draft provided by
the National Football League, committee staffers produced the "Professional
Sports Community Protection Act of 1985," which Danforth introduced and
placed near the top of the agenda. As a committee staffer recalled: "Because
Danforth was committee chairman, people looked away from Gorton to Danforth. Danforth's [bill] was the vehicle."

Carl Icahn's business activities produced a similar response, a response again made feasible by Danforth's control over the Commerce Committee agenda. There was significant concern that after purchasing TWA, Icahn would sell off its assets and put large numbers of Danforth's constituents out of work. Given the magnitude of the constituency interest, it was crucial that the chairman quickly devise a legislative response. Two committee staffers described the political dynamics.

> The hearings were real quick. We had coincidentally been holding a hearing with TWA. Then the Icahn thing broke and the hearing changed focus. The bill was drafted the next day. It was real fast. . . . TWA is the largest employer in the state of Missouri, and the bill is designed to help out Danforth, [to show that] he's responsible to constituents' concerns.

> Out of deference to the chairman and his need to act on behalf of his constituents, other members rolled over and silenced some of their very legitimate concerns about intruding in the marketplace, because it was so important to the chairman.

What is striking about this piece of legislation is the speed with which it was drafted and considered in committee. As chairman of the committee, Danforth was able to use his procedural prerogatives to quickly send a message to Icahn, as well as the folks back home. Thus, for legislation of special importance to the state of Missouri, the chairman's control of the agenda mattered a great deal.

The size of the Commerce Committee's work load complicates scheduling decisions. As Danforth recalled:

> The agenda is a little different on the Commerce Committee [relative to Judiciary and Labor]. The number of bills is so huge. It's a real firehose. You just want to get out of the way. It's unbelievable the number of things we had to do.

During his first year as chairman, observers of the committee perceived that scheduling decisions were not made as efficiently as they were during the tenure of Bob Packwood, Danforth's predecessor as chair. An aide to committee Democrats contrasted Danforth with Packwood in commenting on Danforth's first year in the position.

> They are definitely different. Danforth hasn't been chairman that long and his staff is new. It's a process of learning how to avoid problems, always talking with people, checking with them, and they have yet to get that all down just right. They hit snags.

For example, the first major legislation considered under Danforth's chairmanship was a bill to sell Conrail to the Norfolk Southern Railroad, marked up by the Commerce Committee in April, 1985. There was significant concern among committee members about the effect of the sale on midwestern carriers, however. One of the carriers was Kansas City Southern, located in Danforth's home state, and committee members believed that the chairman was going to offer an amendment aimed at protecting small railroads from anticompetitive consequences arising from the sale. Prior to the markup, however, a private agreement was struck between Kansas City Southern and Norfolk Southern, and Danforth did not offer the amendment. Although the chairman denied responsibility for the agreement, a number of senators voiced concern during markup about his decision not to offer the amendment and requested that the legislation be carried over until other railroads could be accommodated. Larry Pressler of South Dakota said that "if the Chairman's railroad is going to be accommodated and nobody else's is, I have a lot of trouble with that."[10] Paul Trible of Virginia noted that he had considered offering an amendment, but did not because he believed Danforth was going to act.

Danforth, in contrast, spoke against the motion to delay committee action and, instead, suggested that they proceed with other amendments to the legislation. But Pressler, Trible, J. James Exon of Nebraska, and Ernest Hollings all urged delay and consideration was postponed. This was not a major loss for Danforth. However, it is exactly the kind of dispute that a chair does not want to break out in open markup, and knowledgeable staffers pointed to his lack of experience in the position as an explanation.

In addition to matters of timing, there was some concern—again, particularly during 1985—that Danforth was not aggressive enough in protecting or expanding the Commerce Committee's agenda and jurisdiction. It is difficult to overestimate the importance placed on jurisdiction and turf in the U.S. Senate, as one veteran Senate staffer has expressed very well.

> People don't go for each others necks around here over issues. Policy is for gentlemen's debate. What draws blood around here is jurisdiction, who owns what issues. Possession of issues means television time, newspaper space, staffs; and to a great extent all those, especially staffs, add up to power within the Senate.[11]

The Commerce Committee has an extremely broad jurisdiction, and committee members expect the chair and ranking minority member to protect their panel's prerogatives. Turf fights are common in the Senate, but of the four chairmen, only Danforth was mentioned as not doing enough to protect his committee. For example, in characterizing Danforth's leadership style, committee member Wendell Ford of Kentucky, a senior Democrat, compared him to Ernest Hollings.

> Fritz [Hollings] is old school on jurisdiction. Danforth was not as forceful. Let me put it this way. They are both lawyers but if one was defending me, I'd want Hollings. Danforth would argue the law and the facts, Hollings would argue the case. Facts, law, case—Hollings would argue all three. . . . He wants to win.

An issue considered by the committee in September, 1985, is illustrative. Ted Stevens of Alaska pointed out that the Senate Agriculture Committee had just reported out a bill that dealt with the cargo preference issue, over which the Agriculture and Commerce Committees share jurisdiction. Danforth liked the provisions in the Agriculture Committee's bill, however, and preferred that the measure not be referred to his own panel, where he was in the minority on the issue. As a result, other committee members pushed for a sequential referral to establish the Commerce Committee's jurisdictional rights. A former aide to committee Republicans recalled the issue.

> Danforth liked what the Agriculture committee did. He doesn't like cargo preference, [so he] thought he was just going to let things be. Stevens, Long, Inouye, and others said, "There's a bill on the floor with Commerce Committee jurisdiction." . . . They instructed the chairman to protect the committee's jurisdiction, which he didn't want to do.

By all accounts, John Danforth is a thoughtful and hardworking legislator. However, as a new chairman in 1985, he was still in a period of adjustment and search, gathering information about the boundaries of his discretion. As with all complex tasks, there is a learning curve for committee leadership in the Senate.[12]

Robert Stafford and the Environment and Public Works Committee

Agenda control was a more important aspect of Robert Stafford's leadership style on the Environment and Public Works Committee. Like the Commerce Committee, the structural context on Environment and Public Works is relatively centralized. Thus, to understand differences between the way Danforth and Stafford handled their agendas, we need to look beyond committee structure and examine the preference context, as well as individual characteristics of the two chairmen.

On Environment and Public Works, there is a strong consensus among committee members about legislative priorities. The panel's jurisdiction is dominated by reauthorizations, but the reauthorizations considered by Environment and Public Works are relatively small in number, highly complex, and nationally salient. At the beginning of 1985, for example, there was substantial agreement among committee members that the agenda should focus on reauthorizing Superfund, the Safe Drinking Water Act, and the Clean Water Act, and on passing an omnibus water resources development bill.

Legislative priorities for the year were set in a meeting held in January. Stafford's office clearly set the agenda, but participants emphasized the bipartisan nature of agenda setting on the panel. A Republican staffer recalled:

> The majority side sets the agenda. If there is something of particular importance to Senator Bentsen, Senator Stafford would probably accommodate that. There was a meeting to set the agenda at the end of January this year. Stafford's people drew up a list of the chairman's priorities, and [they were] Superfund, Safe Drinking Water, Clean Water. Then he made Safe Drinking Water first because he thought it would have a good chance. It was done by the majority, but the minority had no problems. It was just so clear what was up. You have to look at what you have a shot at getting, but also things that will generate member interest. . . . The same things keep coming up.

An aide to committee Democrats also stressed consensus at the agenda level.

> Superfund was number one. Stafford directs that and just said, "We're doing it," and everybody agrees because it is a major bill. There isn't much disagreement about the order of things. Stafford sets the agenda. For instance, acid rain is coming up. Stafford decided it needed to come up after Superfund because we just needed to get it done, and there isn't much disagreement about that. Simpson may come in and say, "Why do we have to bother with this now?" But he's not going to object.

Bipartisanship at the agenda-setting stage was a result of the distribution and intensity of preferences in committee, as well as the location of the chairman's policy preferences. Since Stafford had a clear majority on issues of major importance, there was no need to systematically block initiatives being pushed by other committee members. As was the case with John Danforth, there was little probability that Stafford would lose control of his panel during the course of committee deliberations. Indeed, none of the committee members and staff aides I spoke with mentioned blocking power as a component of Stafford's leadership.

Additionally, Stafford did not have to use his control over the agenda to *accelerate* deliberations in response to conflict *within* the committee. The minority coalition of conservative westerners was intense in its opposition to the pro-environmentalist slant on the panel, but dilatory tactics in committee were extremely rare. I asked Stafford if he could recall any significant examples of obstructionism in the committee during his chairmanship.

> Not really. I think Symms was tempted to when he first joined the committee. And we always got a long speech from Al Simpson. I joked with him on Clean Air that we couldn't officially close the markup unless we had an Al Simpson speech.

Other committee members also noted the absence of dilatory tactics on Environment and Public Works.[13] As a result, there was little need to use the schedule to counter obstructionism in committee.

But agenda control was important on the Environment and Public Works Committee—important because of the distribution of preferences on the floor. Committee members realized that they were more pro-environmentalist than the chamber as a whole, and they knew the Senate floor potentially was an arena for conflict on these issues. And, as mentioned, environmental issues are among the most technically complex considered on Capitol Hill, often requiring a week or more of floor time to complete deliberations. As a result, there were powerful incentives for the Environment and Public Works Committee to bring its legislation to the floor as quickly as feasible. Indeed, Stafford placed particular emphasis on moving early in the session. During the organizational meeting in 1985, for example, the chairman announced that he would attempt to get the subcommittees working on legislation even before they were officially organized, primarily to provide the majority leader with as much leeway as possible in scheduling.

Stafford's leadership was crucial to the successful reauthorization of Superfund during the 99th Congress. The program is extremely technical, and in addition to consideration by the Environment and Public Works Committee, sequential referral to both the Finance and Judiciary Committees was necessary. To maximize the time available for floor consideration, as well as conference committee deliberations with the House, Stafford introduced the bill on January 3, 1985, held markup sessions the following month, and reported the legislation out of committee on the first of March. As a result, the Senate was able to pass the legislation in September, and the entire second session was available for conference committee action. Subsequent events confirmed that the time was necessary.

Stafford's use of the agenda to accelerate legislation was also apparent on less salient measures. In 1985, the committee considered legislation to amend the Safe Drinking Water Act. The substance of the bill was based on a House draft, with input from the Environmental Protection Agency, committee members Daniel Patrick Moynihan and Alan Simpson, and subcommittee chairman David Durenberger of Minnesota. Stafford was not significantly involved in shaping the content of the legislation, but he played a crucial role on timing. A staffer who worked on the bill recalled that

> Moynihan, Simpson, and Durenberger were the big three. Stafford made sure that we were kept on a fast agenda once he saw that it had a chance of passage. He was influential in that respect, pushing things forward. He didn't want to modify certain things. . . . Most of the staff was surprised we got it as far as we did. After subcommittee, Stafford jumped on it and said he thought it was a good bill and scheduled a full committee markup as soon as possible.

Stafford's actions on these bills reflect his general approach to leadership on the committee, an approach that was partially responsible for the panel's success in reauthorizing major environmental programs that were not strongly supported by the Reagan administration. According to Pete Domenici, "Stafford's stick-to-it-ness tended to get things going."

Strom Thurmond and the Judiciary Committee

It is when we turn to the Judiciary and Labor Committees that the importance of the chair's agenda prerogatives for committee politics becomes particularly apparent. In contrast to Commerce and Environment and Public Works, preferences in the Judiciary and Labor Committees were polarized and entrenched. Whereas Commerce and Environment and Public Works were bipartisan and oriented toward consensus, decision making in the Judiciary and Labor Committees was often highly partisan and rife with conflict. As a result, there was a different texture to agenda politics in the latter two panels. Keeping in mind the bipartisanship we found in Commerce and Environment and Public Works, consider the following conversation about the agenda, which occurred during a meeting of the Senate Judiciary Committee in 1985:[14]

> *Thurmond.* Now the first—well, suppose we ask first, is there any matter on here this morning that you feel is not controversial and that we can act on right away and get out? Is S.239 controversial?
> *Metzenbaum.* Oh, yes.
> *Thurmond.* Well . . . , we will come back to that. Is S.238 controversial?
> *Metzenbaum.* Yes.
> *Thurmond.* How is that?

Metzenbaum. I think it is, yes.

Biden. Yes, the habeas corpus [bill] is. Senator Leahy and myself, but particularly Senator Leahy, have been trying to work out some compromise on that legislation.

Thurmond. All right. Is S.237 controversial?

Metzenbaum. Yes.

Biden. Yes.

Thurmond. Is 1300 [an antitrust bill] controversial?

Metzenbaum. Yes.

Thurmond. Are you opposed to everything?

Metzenbaum. Yes.

Thurmond. Honest confession is good for the soul.

Of the four panels, agenda prerogatives are most decentralized on the Judiciary Committee. During the 99th Congress, the only major component of the jurisdiction not assigned to a subcommittee was antitrust policy. Subcommittee chairs controlled their own agendas, and thus had the power to begin deliberations on any issue they chose. The subcommittee chairs generally shared Thurmond's preferences, however, and he was not systematically confronted by subcommittee leaders pushing initiatives he opposed. And on antitrust, Thurmond had complete control over the agenda. Unlike Orrin Hatch on the Labor Committee, Strom Thurmond had a solid working majority of conservative Republicans and conservative to moderate Democrats during his six years as chairman. On some issues the panel split, with the balance of power residing in the hands of swing voters Arlen Specter, Dennis DeConcini, and Howell Heflin. But, for the most part, Thurmond had the votes to win. As a result, the strategic response of liberal Democrats on the committee was to use procedural tactics to obstruct legislation backed by Thurmond and other committee conservatives. An aide to Patrick Leahy of Vermont described the role of procedural tactics in Judiciary Committee deliberations.

> The Judiciary Committee is a better reflection of the Senate floor than any other. Everybody uses their procedural rights. People divide up earlier, and it feels like the floor. There are fights; there's screaming and yelling; . . . people filibuster in committee; [and] they exercise the right to break the committee meeting after two hours after the Senate goes in, a very effective tool for keeping things bottled up.

Liberal Democrats on the Judiciary Committee employed a variety of dilatory tactics, ranging from quorum strategies to simply asking a lot of questions. During the 98th Congress, for example, Edward Kennedy was able to delay consideration of the McClure-Volkmer gun bill by repeatedly raising technical questions about the legislation. A veteran aide to Kennedy described the strategy in the following terms:

> On McClure-Volkmer, Kennedy filibustered. It didn't look like one, but it had the effect of one. All he was doing was asking questions. It created what's called the disappearing quorum act. Get a quorum there. Kennedy insists on a quorum: "I have some serious amendments, but I want ten here not nine." Then he starts asking questions and talking and takes out this big book of materials, and you can just see the eyes glaze over, and one by one on the Republican side they disappear. Kennedy looks up, surprised, and says, "Mr. Chairman, I don't think there's a quorum here." Thurmond says, "Well sure there's not, they've heard these questions before." "Well Mr. Chairman, I'm here. I'm ready to act on it." That went on for six months.

Thurmond's responses ranged from extensive sermons about the importance of allowing the committee to vote, all the way to yanking legislation off of the committee agenda and taking it directly to the floor.

The centrality of procedural tactics to Judiciary Committee politics raises the stakes of the agenda-setting stage. Indeed, scheduling was a major part of the legislative game on the panel during much of the Thurmond chairmanship. As a result, it is useful to carefully examine how items were placed on the agenda, particularly the informal practices that were evident during his tenure. If we examine the formal rules of the committee, the chair controls the agenda, subject to the constraint that a majority of committee members can always vote a measure onto the schedule. Given Thurmond's solid working majority on the panel, such an occurrence was extremely unlikely. But liberal Democrats had access to a range of dilatory tactics for blocking consideration of legislation, tactics of the sort employed by Edward Kennedy on McClure-Volkmer. Thus, when we look at formal rules in isolation, the distribution of prerogatives is clearly a recipe for procedural warfare.

Within these parameters, however, there were incentives for a degree of cooperation over the agenda: a degree of cooperation that generated certain informal practices for determining the schedule. Simply put, there were incentives for all parties not to push their procedural privileges to the limit. Thurmond was concerned that the Democrats not engage in extreme forms of obstructionism such as regularly boycotting meetings or filibustering all conservative legislation. Of course, given the jurisdiction and the distribution of preferences, some use of dilatory tactics by liberal Democrats was inevitable, but there are varying degrees of obstructionism. It was in Thurmond's interest that Democrats not bring the panel to a grinding halt.

Because of the preferences and procedural prerogatives of other members of the panel, Thurmond was constrained in the degree to which he could use his own procedural prerogatives as chairman of the Judiciary Committee. An aide to Democrat Dennis DeConcini, occasionally a swing vote on the committee, explained.

> When he [Thurmond] is either pressured into it or feels a bill is ready to go on the calendar, it goes on the calendar. If we had a bill we thought was dynamite and had lots of support for, and he wouldn't put it on the calendar, at the next meeting we'd stand up and filibuster on the commemoratives or start voting no on the nominations or start voting no when it's nine to eight and he needs [our] vote. The bill would get on the agenda.

According to a staff assistant to Edward Kennedy:

> The majority sets the agenda and has a little of the element of surprise. But the minority has the element of surprise too. We can use dilatory tactics, not have a quorum, or filibuster. So it is not in the interest of the majority to always surprise [us] because that gets everybody's back against the wall, and we can do things like not show up.

Committee Democrats also had much at stake in scheduling decisions, generating incentives for them to curb dilatory action. Although conservatives had a clear majority, committee deliberations provided liberal Democrats with the opportunity to mobilize opposition, offer amendments, and slow the pace of legislation they adamantly opposed. Under the institution's standing rules, however, the chair can take legislation directly to the floor and bypass slow-down tactics in committee, a tactic Thurmond occasionally used during his tenure. As a result, there were incentives for Democrats on the Judiciary Committee to use their procedural prerogatives, but not to the extent that Thurmond was induced to pull legislation off the committee agenda and go directly to the full Senate.

In short, there were potential gains to cooperation on the agenda. Indeed, by the 99th Congress, an informal understanding had been reached that set guidelines for the agenda stage. Items new to the full Judiciary Committee agenda were to be placed at the bottom and would have to work their way through the queue to be marked up unless unanimous consent was obtained to bring them up out of order. An aide to Paul Laxalt explained the process for one bill.

> It was at the bottom of the agenda, and unanimous consent was required to bring it up out of order. Thurmond couldn't bring it to the top. Not on this committee. Once it's on the agenda, it has to come up in that

order. . . . It would require a vote of the committee to override the chairman's decision to do this, that, or the other thing. But in the first session of the 99th Congress, there were several discussions about just what the chairman can do, and it was pretty well established—well understood, let's put it that way—that Thurmond is not going to jiggle around the agenda once the agenda has been set. You can put things on the agenda, but they go on the bottom. He has the discretion of putting new things on the agenda in any way he wants.

The primary benefits of this precedent were reduced uncertainty and more efficient decision making. Both liberals and conservatives gained.

When we examine committee activity during the 99th Congress, however, it is apparent that Thurmond occasionally deviated from this practice. Indeed, committee staffers stressed that the queuing rule just described was not set in stone. As an aide to Charles Grassley of Iowa said, "When Thurmond introduces a bill, he has a hearing the next week, then it goes to the top of the agenda." By unanimous consent?

No, by Senator Thurmond. You have to have unanimous consent unless the chairman decides. He sets the agenda. . . . This lobbying bill [legislation to restrict the lobbying efforts of former government officials], he introduced it, held a hearing, and brought it to the top of the agenda and wanted to pass it out this past week, and everybody kind of had their mouths open, saying, "How did this happen so quickly?" Those of us having trouble with our own bills and going through all of the hoops felt this was a little unfair. But when he wants to do something, he'll do it.

As mentioned, if Thurmond regularly tore up the agenda, certain sanctions were available to committee Democrats—for example, extending debate or attempting to override the chairman with a vote of the committee. But employing such sanctions would have been costly, both in terms of member and staff time and in terms of likely retaliation by Thurmond. Thus, the chairman had a significant degree of discretion in setting the agenda. Informal guidelines existed, and they provided the modal pattern. But Thurmond brought items particularly relevant to his goals to the top of the agenda, and committee members not in his favor often had difficulties getting their legislation scheduled. Thus, Thurmond's agenda practices were characterized by a subtle mix of fairness and hardball politics.

The full force of Thurmond's agenda control was felt on antitrust policy, which was held at full committee. During the 99th Congress, the chairman wanted to consider a major antitrust initiative that had been drafted by his staff and attorneys representing various business groups.[15] Kennedy and Metzenbaum were adamant in their opposition. After the bill was introduced in June, 1985, there was considerable concern on the Democratic side that Thurmond would disregard precedent and immediately bring the legislation to the top of the agenda. In Thurmond's office, on the other hand, there was concern that Metzenbaum would use his well-honed procedural talents to block committee action. The result was an agreement between Thurmond and Metzenbaum on how to manage the legislation for 1985. An aide to the chairman described the arrangement.

> Senator Thurmond and Metzenbaum worked out an agreement to allow 1300 [the antitrust bill] to come out of the committee before the end of the first session [1985]. The deal was we wouldn't bring it up out of order . . . , which we have the right to do, [and] Metzenbaum would not filibuster and delay. He would allow the bill to be brought up, debated, and voted out.

The problem with this strategy was that the legislation did not arrive at the top of the agenda until the closing days of 1985, and there was insufficient time to report it to the floor before 1986, at which point the Thurmond-Metzenbaum agreement was no longer in force. What followed illustrates well the importance of the agenda in particular and procedural tactics in general on many Judiciary Committee bills.

The panel met to consider the bill in April, 1986, but was unable to maintain a quorum. Republican Jeremiah Denton tried to put off a dental appointment to allow a vote, but eventually had to leave. Metzenbaum then announced that he was not going to filibuster, and proceeded to speak at length against the bill, as did Kennedy. The meeting ended with Kennedy heading toward the door and Thurmond accusing the Democrats of blocking the legislation.

When the panel met the following week, Thurmond again brought up the antitrust bill, and Metzenbaum countered with an amendment that most observers believed would have brought down the entire measure if adopted. There was lengthy discussion, at which point Kennedy left the committee room. Thurmond then ended the meeting by yelling at Metzenbaum: "Walk out. Stay out as far as I am concerned."[16] The committee met and approved the legislation the following week.

So far, our discussion of agenda setting in the Judiciary Committee has emphasized the preference context, along with the location of the chairman's policy preferences. But other individual characteristics also contributed to Thurmond's leadership style. In particular, the length and nature of his experience in the Senate—both as a committee leader and as a member—increased not only his willingness to employ procedural tactics, but also his tolerance of other members using their prerogatives.

By all accounts, Thurmond provided liberal Democrats on the panel with remarkable leeway. For example, the chief obstructionist during his tenure as chairman was Howard Metzenbaum. During Thurmond's six years as chairman, however, he seldom cut off the Ohio Democrat. The following interaction during a Judiciary Committee markup in April, 1984, is indicative:[17]

> *Thurmond.* I hope there will not be obstructionist tactics used here, to give the committee a chance to vote on this matter.
> *Metzenbaum.* Mr. Chairman, I believe that S.J. Res. 5 and the proposed amendments thereto is in and of itself an obstructionist tactic.
> *Thurmond.* Then vote against it, but do not deprive this body of voting on the question, Senator.
> *Metzenbaum.* I want to say to the chairman that you are the dean, you are the dean, sir, of people in this body who have found it necessary to speak out and oftentimes at great length. It is a source of great pride to you, I know, that you held the floor for twenty-four hours, if I remember correctly, in connection with a matter in which you believed deeply. And I do not think that you would—
> *Thurmond.* That is right, but I did not obstruct any longer. They went on and voted and voted the other way.
> *Metzenbaum.* Because you could not stand there any longer.
> *Thurmond.* Well, I could have stood there longer, but I did not want to keep [the floor] any longer. We stand adjourned.

Thurmond commented about his control of the Judiciary Committee agenda, as well as other procedural practices on the committee during his chairmanship.

> I always tried to be courteous, not overbearing, and to be firm if necessary. I tried to accommodate if I could. In the eighties we were in the majority and I tried to help them with their bills. I tried to put myself in their shoes, as if I [were] in the minority.

The vast majority of senators and staffers with whom I spoke agreed with this assessment. Thurmond was fair, but his fairness had boundaries. After a certain point, he would use his procedural prerogatives to counter dilatory tactics by committee Democrats. Perhaps Edward Kennedy best captured the sentiments of most participants when he characterized Thurmond's leadership style by simply describing him as "a professional politician."

Orrin Hatch and the Labor Committee

It is with the Labor Committee during the Hatch chairmanship that we see a committee leader most regularly and effectively employing gatekeeping powers, and the primary reason was the distribution of preferences. As was the case with the other three panels, however, the structural context set the general parameters within which Hatch worked. Recall that the Labor Committee is relatively decentralized. On the health side of the jurisdiction, which is very active, the committee is as centralized as the Commerce Committee. There is no health subcommittee, and the chair has a monopoly over agenda prerogatives. But most of the jurisdiction is parceled out to subcommittees—resembling the structure of the Judiciary Committee in many ways—and Hatch shared agenda power with the subcommittee chairs on these issues.

And as was the case with the other three panels, these structural factors had consequences for agenda politics. On health issues, Hatch could block items he opposed at the very beginning of the process. Because there was no alternative forum in the committee, Hatch's agenda control was relatively unconstrained. In other policy areas, however, subcommittee chairs marked up their own legislation, with or without Hatch's support, building momentum and significantly altering the strategic environment in which the chairman exercised his scheduling prerogatives. Hatch could close the gates at the point of the full committee markup, but pressure from other senators and outside groups to allow full committee action was greater than when no preliminary action had occurred. Needless to say, committee members were sensitive to the interests of the chairman, but Hatch's discretion was much less pronounced on these issues than it was in the area of health policy.

Within these structural limits, the preference context on the Labor Committee shaped Hatch's approach to priority setting, an approach that was critical for understanding committee politics from 1981 to 1987. Recall that the chairman led a coalition of seven conservative Republicans; that ranking Democrat Edward Kennedy led an opposing coalition of seven liberal Democrats; and that there were two moderate to liberal Republican swing voters, Robert Stafford and Lowell Weicker. On most Labor Committee issues, Stafford and Weicker were closer to Kennedy than they were to their own chairman, generating Orrin Hatch's central strategic dilemma as committee leader.

Asked about his chairmanship of the committee, Hatch emphasized the importance of his agenda prerogatives.

There was constant pressure from the Democrats on the agenda, and they were very good at it, to give them credit. . . . But I controlled the agenda. As long as the Democrats wanted something, they had to be accommodating.

Democrat Howard Metzenbaum, also a committee member, agreed with Hatch on this point.

> The chairman of the committee didn't have the votes to control his own committee. . . . Senator Kennedy had the votes to win and that's what counts: whether or not you have the votes. . . . Senator Hatch's style was to use the schedule—not putting items on the calendar, not pushing things.

As Edward Kennedy recalled: "The chairman has enormous power, [such as] setting the agenda, the prerogatives of leadership. . . . We had a difficult time [under Hatch] advancing our issues."

In short, Hatch chose to restrict the size of the agenda to preclude what he feared would be an avalanche of liberal initiatives, initiatives he otherwise would have been unable to control because he lacked the votes. As a result, the committee did not meet very often, and the flow of legislation slowed markedly. Committee Democrat Paul Simon of Illinois stressed the impact of Hatch's strategy on the productivity of the Labor Committee.

> There wasn't much activity when Orrin was chairman. Orrin isn't an activist, and there were not a lot of meetings. Also, he was facing Weicker and Stafford, who more often voted with the Democrats.

An aide to Edward Kennedy remarked:

> Hatch really doesn't want to do more than the required reauthorizations. He's got a few little bills that he gets excited about, but they're more of a symbolic nature. He doesn't have the votes. If you're a chairman, you don't want to meet if you're going to keep losing votes and you can't control the bills.

Conservatives viewed pressure from committee Democrats to expand the size of the agenda as an attempt to generate publicity and embarrass the Republican party. Indeed, a "we-they" attitude permeated much of the Hatch staff, an attitude that was reinforced by a widespread belief during the first session of the 99th Congress that Edward Kennedy was a likely candidate for the Democratic presidential nomination. As one Hatch staffer put it:

> We have a numerical majority, but they have an ideological major-ity. . . . Obviously there are issues that the Democrats want to pursue.

They believe that these issues give them an opportunity to shine, to get lots of press, and to make the Republicans look cruel and hard-hearted. A Republican sitting on this committee is going to be generally unwilling to provide them with that forum. . . . We don't want to provide a campaign stage for somebody running for president. That's not the purpose [of] this committee. This committee is funded by taxpayers' dollars, and it's not the "Kennedy for President" campaign committee.

Hatch's efforts to restrict the size of the committee agenda and focus on policy areas in which he had the votes to win were particularly effective on health issues because of the absence of a subcommittee layer. An adviser to the chairman for health policy commented that

you see confrontation, particularly at the staff level. It waxes and wanes. Kennedy's agenda is broader than Hatch's. Kennedy would like to get into not only a wider range of issues, but be more activist in the role of the federal government in health care. So he is always continually pushing for more hearings, different types of hearings, trying to bring bills to markup that Hatch doesn't want to see brought to markup, amendments which we think will be ill advised. Constraining the agenda, keeping it under control, is probably the staff director's major function.

On issues falling within the jurisdiction of one of the panel's six subcommittees, Hatch's scheduling practices varied, depending on the subcommittee chair. Four of the subcommittees were chaired by fellow conservatives who shared Hatch's preferences, for the most part. In these areas, Hatch was seldom confronted by measures he opposed, and the subcommittee chairs generally shared his priorities and moved the legislation he supported.[18] But swing voters Robert Stafford and Lowell Weicker chaired two important subcommittees: the Subcommittees on Education and the Handicapped, respectively. As might be expected, there was significant full committee-subcommittee tension in these issue areas because of ideological differences between Hatch and the two subcommittee leaders.

Weicker's initiative to increase the federal role in providing protection for the mentally ill (S.974)—discussed in the opening pages of this chapter— is illustrative of the consequences for agenda politics. When Weicker reported bills opposed by the chairman, Hatch used his power over the full committee agenda to extract substantive concessions from Weicker in return for a place on the schedule. It should be emphasized, though, that Hatch had significantly less discretion in these instances than he did with health policy. Weicker's bills tended to develop a broad base of support as they moved through the subcommittee process, and Hatch faced the prospect of being circumvented if he pushed his procedural powers too far. This is one reason why he attempted to stop S.974 via Strom Thurmond during the subcommittee markup. Hatch's relationship with Stafford and the Education Subcommittee shared many of these dynamics, but they were less pronounced because the preferences of the two senators were relatively similar on many educational issues.

As was the case with Strom Thurmond and the Judiciary Committee, contextual factors, along with the location of Hatch's policy preferences relative to the committee rank and file, go a long way toward explaining agenda politics on the Labor Committee. But other individual characteristics of Orrin Hatch may have played a role, particularly his proximate career plans. One effect of restricting the Labor Committee's agenda was to significantly reduce committee activity. The expected costs of reducing activity would have been higher for Hatch had he intended to retain his chairmanship in the next congress. A committee chairmanship provides a senator with a very visible forum for influencing public policy, for building a reputation for effectiveness within the institution, and for advancing the interests of the folks back home. It is difficult to pursue these goals when the committee is inactive. But during much of 1986, Hatch expected to shift to a leadership position on the Judiciary Committee, where he would have the working majority he lacked on Labor. As a result, reducing committee activity was less damaging to Hatch's political goals. In the 99th Congress, he restricted the Labor Committee agenda, but he was the most active member of the Judiciary Committee, with the possible exception of Strom Thurmond.

Conclusion

Agenda setting clearly matters on all four panels. Scheduling decisions are the central prerogative of leadership: They determine the set of issues actively considered in committee, and they help structure relationships between the full committee chair and other committee members. At the same time, it is also apparent that there are striking differences in the nature of agenda setting across the four committees and four chairmen.

On the Commerce Committee, John Danforth faced a plethora of relatively routine reauthorizations. As a result, the emphasis often was on efficiency in managing the work load, although the chairman's scheduling prerogatives clearly had political consequences. Items of particular relevance to Danforth's policy interests or the residents of Missouri quickly went to the top of the agenda. But for the most part, the emphasis was administrative.

The agenda-setting stage played a greater role in the politics of the Environment and Public Works Committee. The combination of consensus in committee and conflict on the floor raised the importance of the order in which bills were considered. By moving certain items to the top of the agenda, Robert Stafford was able to bring them to the floor more rapidly and increase the time available for ironing out problems in the full Senate.

In contrast to Commerce and Environment and Public Works, procedure was central to Judiciary Committee politics, primarily because of the distribution and intensity of preferences on committee issues. Committee deliberations often unraveled into procedural warfare, with Strom Thurmond trying to move conservative legislation and liberal Democrats using a range of dilatory tactics to slow it down. Although informal guidelines existed for scheduling, Thurmond had the right to tear up the agenda when it promoted his goals, and he made active use of his scheduling powers to accelerate legislation he favored and derail legislation he opposed.

Orrin Hatch often lacked the votes to win on policy in the Labor Committee, and agenda control functioned as a substitute for political support within the panel. Indeed, as should become apparent in succeeding chapters, Hatch's strategy of restricting the agenda to those issues on which he had the votes set the tone for committee politics in general.

In short, the styles exhibited by the four chairmen at the agenda stage differed markedly. Structural arrangements set the boundaries for agenda decision making, but the crucial variables for explaining behavior at that stage of the committee process were the intensity and distribution of preferences on committee issues—both in committee and in the full Senate—and the location of the chairman's policy preferences within that distribution. Other individual characteristics were relevant, but the key factor for understanding agenda politics on all four panels was who had the votes, and why.

Notes

1. See Price 1972.

2. Congressional scholars have not given sufficient attention to the policy-making consequences of changing time constraints in the institution. But for an important exception, see Oppenheimer 1985.

3. Oppenheimer 1985.

4. It should be noted that some combination of these alternatives was also a feasible strategy.

5. These arguments are adapted in part from theoretical work on agenda control by Shepsle (1979), Shepsle and Weingast (1981), and Denzau and MacKay (1983). It should be clear from the discussion in this section, however, that a game-theoretic approach is most appropriate for modeling agenda politics.

6. For example, Oleszek provides an in-depth description of the dilatory tactics available to members of the Senate on the floor. See Oleszek 1976. For a more general treatment, see Oleszek 1989.

7. Senate Judiciary Committee markup of S.919 (a bill to amend the Equal Access to Justice Act), May 17, 1984. Manuscript.

8. Whether a chair has a majority on an issue depends on the content of existing law, as well as the chair's preferences and the location of the median viewpoint in committee. However, the closer a chair's preferences are to the median position, the more likely it is that he or she will have the votes to win. The importance of the median position in committee for the content of committee outcomes was first demonstrated by Black (1948).

9. There are exceptions, however. Some issues considered by the committee generate significant conflict. In the early 1980s, for example, the Federal Trade Commission Reauthorization evoked broad interest because of efforts to regulate the professions, and the Reagan administration repeatedly targeted the Consumer Product Safety Commission. In addition, during the 99th Congress, the panel considered tort reform and the sale of Conrail, both highly salient issues. Scheduling was more consequential on these matters.

10. Gettinger 1985, 754.

11. Asbell 1978, 119.

12. There also was disenchantment, particularly among committee Democrats, because of a perception that Danforth was not doing enough to protect the panel's partial jurisdiction over trade issues. Danforth was chairman of the International Trade Subcommittee on the Finance Committee, and preferred to keep these issues in that panel.

13. Additionally, I spoke with committee staff aides about a sample of ten bills marked up by the Environment and Public Works Committee in 1985—a sample that contained all of the significant legislation considered by the panel that year. None of the aides mentioned dilatory tactics on these items.

14. Senate Judiciary Committee meeting, November 14, 1985. Manuscript.

15. The bill, S.1300, pertained to the provision of joint and several liability in price-fixing cases. It was one of the more significant antitrust issues considered by the committee during the Thurmond chairmanship.

16. Senate Judiciary Committee markup of S.1300, May 1, 1986. Manuscript.

17. Senate Judiciary Committee markup of S.J. Res. 5, April 26, 1984. Manuscript.

18. But for an exception, see Richard Fenno's treatment of Dan Quayle and the Job Training Partnership Act (1989).

CHAPTER 3

Interactions with Subcommittee Leaders

We have explored how committee chairs use their agenda prerogatives, how the process of agenda setting varies, and why. A central theme has been that, even when examining a leader's formal powers, it is essential to emphasize the strategic and interactive nature of leadership behavior. In other words, it is impossible to understand the actions of congressional leaders without considering the perceptions and decisions of the led.

The purpose of the next three chapters is to analyze how committee leaders interact with other important political actors. Senate chairs and ranking minority members deal with a rich variety of individuals and groups, ranging from staff aides and lobbyists to the president of the United States, and a full accounting of these relationships is well beyond the scope of any individual study. But the academic literature on congressional policy-making, along with the observations of participants in the process, suggests that three sets of relationships should be singled out if we are to understand leadership behavior in Senate committees: interactions between full and subcommittee leaders; interactions between the full committee chair and ranking minority member; and, finally, interactions between senators off the panel and leaders in committee.

This chapter examines interactions with subcommittee leaders. Chapter 4 focuses on interactions between the two full committee leaders. And chapter 5 is about the impact of the Senate as a whole on decision making in committee.

A Brief Note on Method

In describing the interactions between full committee leaders and other political actors, I continue to rely heavily on the perceptions of senators and Senate staff aides. These interactions are usually subtle, complex, and not particularly conducive to quantification. However, an attempt has been made to balance the relatively impressionistic nature of interview data with more systematic empirical work whenever possible.

In examining how full committee chairs and ranking minority members interact with other senators, it is useful to consider who participates in committee deliberations, as well as the form of participation. As a result, I collected data about participation in committee for a sample of sixty-two bills marked up in the Commerce, Environment and Public Works, Judiciary, and Labor panels during the 99th Congress, primarily in 1985. Information was collected about which senators participated in contested roll calls, which senators successfully modified a piece of legislation during the amendment process in subcommittee or committee, and which senators had a concrete impact on the content of the draft brought into markup. For each committee member and each bill, it was then possible to construct a rough indicator of participation for the pieces of legislation considered by that panel. The participation indicator serves as a dependent variable in a statistical analysis of who participates in committee decision making. An in-depth discussion of these data and the statistical analysis is provided in appendixes A and B.

It should be emphasized, however, that these more systematic results were fully consistent with the informal perceptions of senators and staff aides. Consequently, the exposition in this chapter, as well as that in chapter 4, emphasizes the perceptions of politicians. The statistical results in appendix B are cited primarily for purposes of corroboration.

Subcommittee Power?

When we examine the internal operations of Senate committees, it is apparent that full committee chairs and ranking minority members are not alone in power.[1] Most legislation falls within the jurisdiction of one or more subcommittees, and subcommittee chairs and subcommittee ranking minority members are potential competitors for policy-making influence.

By all accounts, subcommittee leaders are important players. Max Baucus of Montana compared subcommittees on Environment and Public Works with subcommittees of the Finance Committee.

> Subcommittee chairmen are influential, although they're more influential on Environment and Public Works than they are on Finance. Finance subcommittees don't hold formal markups. [But] there is some tendency for subcommittee chairmen [on Finance] to take the lead in full committee—Mitchell on health, Moynihan on Social Security.

Paul Simon discussed the role of subcommittees on the Judiciary and Labor committees in similar terms.

> Subcommittee assignments matter on the Judiciary Committee. I'm not interested in Howell Heflin's issues about the structure of the courts, but I did become interested in the refugee problems [considered by a different subcommittee]. . . . The problem is that senators are spread so

thinly. . . . Often we can only put in an appearance. That doesn't bother me when I'm participating. It increases my clout.

And according to a staff aide to Orrin Hatch:

One thing about committees: It's very much a division of labor in the manufacturing sense. There isn't enough time for anything else. On any labor bill in this committee, Nickles [then subcommittee chair] is going to have the most influence, and Hatch the second most. Senator Metzenbaum [subcommittee ranking minority member] will have the most for the Democrats. It's a division of labor in the classic manufacturing sense.

The statistical treatment in appendix B strongly supports these comments. On the Commerce, Environment and Public Works, Judiciary, and Labor Committees, the number of offices actively involved on a bill tends to be just three or four, and subcommittee leaders, along with the full committee chair and ranking minority member, are disproportionately likely to fall within the subset of active committee members.

Why are subcommittee leaders so important in the Senate? Because of pressing time constraints, members of the Senate have to be selective in their involvement in legislative work.[2] Most senators employ one or more staff aides to monitor the committees on which they are members and search for items that may be relevant to their interests. For instance, during the 99th Congress, staffers for Charles Grassley of Iowa, a subcommittee leader on both Judiciary and Labor, met in Grassley's office on a weekly or biweekly basis to decide on legislative priorities. A senior aide to Grassley for Labor Committee issues described how they chose when to involve the office, and his description illustrates well the calculus of involvement.

You can define your priorities in many different ways. There are positive priorities and things you want to be out front on. There are sort of negative priorities—things you want to make sure you don't get hurt by. Your interest is in protecting yourself . . . , the effect on the home state. . . . Part of it is time. The number of items that go through on which you really have an opportunity to do a good job, really know there are no alligators out there, is small. I always try to consult the relevant groups in Iowa. . . . Sometimes there are things you just think are lousy ideas. . . . There's only 100 members up here and a lot of work.

Such considerations are typical. Because of the size of the work load, Senate offices weigh the expected benefits and costs of involvement in deciding how to allocate their resources. Senators choose the mix of issues and levels of involvement that maximize the difference between the benefits of participation (i.e., goal promotion) and the opportunities forgone. As a result, participation in committee deliberations tends to be selective, narrow in scope, and centered on those senators with intense preferences on the issue or access to the resources and procedural prerogatives necessary to participate effectively.[3]

The more relevant an issue is to a legislator's constituency or general policy agenda, the more intense will be the legislator's preferences among the array of feasible policy alternatives, and the greater the returns from legislative activism. The preferences of subcommittee leaders tend to be particularly intense on legislation within their jurisdictions because of the nature of the subcommittee assignment process. For the most part, senators choose their own subcommittee assignments. Committee members from each party meet separately in caucus at the beginning of a congress, and subcommittee assignments are allocated in order of committee seniority. On the majority side, subcommittee chairs are selected in the first round. The most senior member on the panel chooses a subcommittee to chair, then the next most senior, and so on until all members of the majority party have selected a subcommittee.[4] Then the process is repeated until all of the subcommittee posts allocated to the majority have been filled. A similar process occurs on the minority side, but in the first round, members choose subcommittees on which to be ranking minority member. Thus, the nature of the subcommittee assignment process ensures that those committee members with intense preferences in a policy area are most likely to be members of the subcommittee having jurisdiction over these issues. This is particularly so for subcommittee chairs and ranking minority members, since the subcommittee was their first choice.

Subcommittee leaders also are more likely to be equipped with the resources necessary to participate effectively. Those senators with access to committee staff resources are best able to gather the information necessary to shape policy, and subcommittee leaders tend to have disproportionate access to the committee staff.[5] Even on very centralized panels such as the Commerce Committee (where full committee leaders control the staff), committee aides tend to work most closely with the relevant subcommittee chair and ranking minority member. According to a staff aide to Republicans on the Commerce Committee:

> There is a lot of subcommittee member input during committee markups because the senators on the subcommittee are the ones most likely to get information from the staff. Although I work for Danforth, when I am working on an issue which concerns the Consumer Subcommittee, I work closely with Kasten [then Subcommittee Chair Robert Kasten]. Of

the 17 senators, he's one of the two or three who is likely to be able to comment intelligently on it during markup.

We provide information to other Senate staff when an interest arises, but we don't work very closely with them. Let's say Trible wants to know more about amusement parks. His staff member would contact us and we'd brief him. He'd then go back to Trible and brief him. But that's not the same as having us brief the Senator directly, reiterate the importance of things constantly, and prep him for markups. That's what we do with Kasten.

The procedural prerogatives exercised by subcommittee leaders also function as a resource for exerting legislative influence. Recall from chapter 2 that within their narrower jurisdictions, subcommittee chairs can have many of the same procedural prerogatives exercised by full committee chairs. On decentralized panels such as Judiciary and Labor, subcommittee chairs are gatekeepers: They control their own agendas and can block legislation they oppose. A subcommittee chair's gatekeeping powers generate incentives for other senators to consider his or her preferences when drafting legislation to be referred to the subcommittee. Legislation that diverges sharply from those preferences is unlikely to be scheduled. Subcommittee leaders also have certain procedural advantages at succeeding stages of the process, which serve to strengthen their strategic position during committee deliberations.[6]

In short, subcommittee chairs and ranking minority members are important in committee policy-making for a combination of reasons. They generally are among the most interested senators when it comes to legislation emanating from their jurisdictions, providing motivation for legislative activism. They have disproportionate access to staff resources, making legislative activism possible. And they also have certain procedural advantages relative to rank-and-file committee members that buttress their role in committee deliberations. As a result, how a full committee chair or ranking minority member interacts with the subcommittee leaders of his or her party is an important component of leadership behavior in committee.

Understanding Interactions Between Full and Subcommittee Leaders

Full committee leaders choose a mix of delegation and monitoring strategies in their interactions with subcommittee leaders.[7] By *delegation,* I am referring to a decision made by a full committee leader not to participate extensively—either personally or through staff—in the construction of a draft brought into markup or in the modification of the legislation in subcommittee or full committee markup. A decision by a full committee leader not to participate in the drafting and amendment stages is implicitly a decision to delegate policy-making responsibility to other members of the committee, most often the subcommittee leaders.

I am not arguing that committee decision making is driven by leadership decisions to delegate or not to delegate. Senate committees are not hierarchical in organization, and committee members make their own decisions about when to participate. Activism among subcommittee leaders arises primarily from their own interests and resources, and not from administrative decisions made by a full committee leader. Still, full committee chairs and ranking minority members have to make choices about when to become involved in legislative work and to what extent, and the decision not to take the lead on an item can be usefully conceptualized as a form of delegation, at least from the full committee leader's perspective.

By *monitoring*, I am referring to time and resources allocated by a full committee leader toward gathering information about the legislative activities of other committee members. Monitoring is essentially an alternative form of involvement. Rather than participate directly in drafting or amending legislation, a full committee leader allocates resources toward monitoring the efforts of those senators who are constructing the draft or devising language for amendments. Monitoring efforts generally take place at the staff level, and all full committee leaders employ them to some extent. For example, Strom Thurmond's staff on the Judiciary Committee was organized along functional lines, with full committee aides responsible for following legislative activity in one or more of the subcommittees. Hatch's staff on the Labor Committee was organized in a similar fashion.

Both delegation and monitoring involve costs and benefits, and the relative value of each is conditioned by a combination of contextual and individual characteristics, as well as expectations about the behavior of other committee members. Delegation can be a useful leadership tactic because it frees up resources for other initiatives. Committee leaders control a portion of the full committee staff, but allocating resources to one measure reduces the quantity available for other pieces of legislation. Thus, there often are incentives for committee leaders to share power, that is, to delegate important policy-making responsibility to other committee members. The greater the extent of delegation, the greater the quantity of leadership resources released for other activities.

But delegation also can be costly. Political leaders hold their cards closely for a reason. The more a chair or ranking minority member is involved in the substantive work on an item, the more control he or she has over the outcome. On some bills, a full committee leader may simply lack the votes to win, and no level of participation by the leader will significantly alter the final result. On most measures, however, there is room for maneuvering: A leader can affect legislation by allocating time and resources to committee deliberations. The size of the impact depends on the nature of the legislation and the larger political context, but direct involvement by a full committee leader will usually have some effect on the probability that legislation will diverge sharply from his or her interests. The more a full committee leader delegates, the greater the chance that his or her preferences will not be fully represented. Thus, delegation frees up resources and lowers the direct costs of decision making for a leader, but it generates alternative costs—the need to monitor the actions of those legislators shaping the draft and participating in the amendment process.

An additional cost to delegation also deserves mention. Senators often derive significant political benefits from being perceived as leaders on important national issues. Leadership activities generate media attention and thus provide senators with opportunities to take positions in a public forum and, perhaps, to claim credit for passing bills favored by their constituents. Delegating significant policy-making responsibility to other committee members makes these activities more difficult, and such forgone opportunities affect the relative value of delegation as a leadership tactic.

In short, committee leaders face a trade-off. The greater their direct involvement in the nitty-gritty of legislative work, the fewer resources available for other items. But allowing other senators to take the lead may require that resources be allocated to monitor their actions. As the resources necessary for direct involvement in constructing a draft and devising amendments increase, incentives to share responsibility become more pronounced. But the greater the likelihood that sharing responsibility will result in an outcome that diverges from a committee leader's preferences, the greater the incentives to monitor the activities of other senators. The efficient strategy is to select the mix of delegation and monitoring that minimizes the sum of these two costs.

Interactions between full and subcommittee leaders on the four panels are explored in succeeding sections of this chapter, but seven propositions should be emphasized from the beginning.

—When we examine the structural context, it is apparent that more centralized panels provide committee leaders with a larger share of the staff resources and agenda prerogatives necessary to influence legislation. As a result, on committees such as Commerce and Environment and Public Works, full committee leaders are better able to bear the costs of direct involvement and thus are less likely to delegate.

—Aspects of the preference context also influence a leader's choice of delegation and monitoring strategies. We need to consider the extent to which other senators share the full committee leader's policy preferences. If the preferences of a full committee and subcommittee leader are identical, delegating to the subcommittee leader probably will not have an appreciable impact on the outcome. If the views of full committee and subcommittee leaders differ, however, delegation can be costly, requiring that significant resources be allocated to monitoring efforts.

—Full committee leaders also consider preferences among the subcommittee rank and file. Delegating to a subcommittee chair or ranking minority member tends to increase the role of the subcommittee in general. For instance, delegation may make the subcommittee markup of a bill a more visible and active stage in the committee process, and if the preferences of rank-and-file subcommittee members differ markedly from those of the full committee leader, the potential costs of delegation rise.

—Individual characteristics can influence the political value of delegation and monitoring. Consider the intensity of a full committee leader's policy preferences on an item. The more important an issue is to a leader, the less inclined he or she will be to delegate extensively. On Environment and Public Works, for example, Robert Stafford's most important priority was the Superfund program, and he was much less inclined to delegate policy-making responsibility on that issue, compared to other committee bills. The less intense a leader's preferences, the lower the political cost should the outcome diverge from those preferences, and the greater the value of delegation as a political strategy.

—Similarly, leadership experience can also play a role. Relationships between full committee and subcommittee leaders tend to develop over time. The more often a full committee chair interacts with a subcommittee chair, the more information each senator has about the goals, preferences, and operating style of the other member. As a result, a full committee chair is better able to gauge when it is necessary to become active on an issue the longer he or she has been in the position.

—Proximate career plans may shape delegation strategies through their effect on a committee leader's commitment to the panel. The more a leader's attention is pulled away from the jurisdiction, the greater the benefits of delegating to the relevant subcommittee chair or ranking minority member.

—And what about the benefits and costs of legislative activism to *subcommittee leaders*? After all, their behavior helps shape the delegation and monitoring strategies adopted by full committee chairs and ranking minority members. On some issues, leaders of the subcommittee of jurisdiction do not have intense preferences, providing incentives for them to defer to leaders of the full committee and to allocate their own resources elsewhere. In more salient policy areas, the preferences of subcommittee leaders are relatively intense, their involvement is extensive, and any deference toward full committee leaders is limited. Thus, exploring how full and subcommittee leaders interact requires that we consider the strategic behavior of both actors.

Danforth, Hollings, and the Commerce Committee

Of the four panels, full committee leaders play their most pronounced role on the Commerce Committee. The analysis in appendix B reveals that, in general, subcommittee chairs and ranking minority members participate more at the drafting and amending stages than full committee leaders, but the Republican side of the Commerce Committee is an important exception. Here, the legislative impact of John Danforth (relative to the various subcommittee chairs on Commerce) exceeded the impact of Stafford, Thurmond, and Hatch (relative to the subcommittee chairs on their panels).

The structural and preference contexts explain much of Danforth's policy-making clout in the Commerce Committee. As chairman, he controlled the committee staff and thus had the resources necessary to shape a broad cross-section of the reauthorizations considered by his panel. Subcommittee chairs do not hire and fire committee staffers and therefore depend extensively on aides who work for the full committee chair. In addition, subcommittee chairs often lack intense preferences on the programs within their own jurisdictions. They want them reauthorized but usually are willing to depend on the chairman's staff for moving legislation through committee.

On the typical Commerce Committee bill, committee staffers work with the subcommittee leader of their party in constructing a draft. But throughout the process, they regularly confer with more senior aides to ensure that the legislation is consistent with the preferences of the full committee leader of their party. Thus, although staffers work most closely with the relevant subcommittee leader, the preferences of the chair and ranking minority member are incorporated into the draft.

Still, subcommittee leaders seldom lose on the Commerce Committee. Nancy Landon Kassebaum, who chaired the important Aviation Subcommittee during the 99th Congress, spoke to this point.

> We don't have formal subcommittee markups, but staff members and outside interests are meeting informally. The technical work is done there . . . developing alternatives. . . . You try to work things out in advance in an informal way. . . . There is no guarantee that a subcommittee will prevail in full committee, but in aviation, I can't think of anything the full committee didn't approve.

A veteran aide to Democrats on the panel contrasted Commerce Committee subcommittees with the subcommittees of its House counterpart, the Energy and Commerce Committee.

> Usually on the Republican side, depending on the issue, they [senators] try to follow the subcommittee chairman's lead. . . . Because we don't have subcommittee markups, it looks like it's less powerful than in the House . . . , but the bills are really sort of drafted in subcommittee, if you see what I mean. Then the whole committee acts on things, but this committee is pretty good about listening to each other. It's what a member cares the most about, expertise, years of working on that issue.

On Commerce Committee issues, the primary source of a subcommittee leader's power tends to be informational. Committee member Wendell Ford remarked that

> the chairman of the subcommittee carries the bill in committee. I don't think it [not having subcommittee markups] detracts from the subcommittees. It takes out another layer.

Do subcommittee chairs have more influence than other committee members? Ford continued:

> Yes. The subcommittee knows the details. [It is] familiar with the bill. It's a process of "I lean on you and you lean on me." You look to the leaders for advice. You have confidence in them. . . . You look toward Senator Nunn on defense because you have confidence in him.

In an environment of imperfect information, senators and their aides look to specialists on the committee (usually the subcommittee leaders) for cues about whether it is necessary to become actively involved and about how to vote. If an issue area is complex and a member's interests are being adequately represented by another senator, the optimal response is to focus on other issues and take cues from the subset of senators who specialize in the matter. These specialists may move the outcome in the direction of their preferences to a certain extent because other committee members are willing to grant them some discretion in return for the information they provide. But if the specialists shade the outcome too much, confidence in their bill will be eroded and other senators will become active.[8] Because subcommittee leaders on the Commerce Committee lack staff and agenda prerogatives, they exert power only to the extent that other committee members listen to them.

Delegation and Monitoring

Because of the Commerce Committee's immense work load, the chair's mixture of delegation and monitoring strategies is central to his or her leadership. Relative to former chairman Bob Packwood, John Danforth often held his cards close, particularly during his first year as chairman. A veteran aide to committee Democrats compared the two senators.

> [Packwood] had less of a tight rein on things, more of a let people do their own thing and then stop it when it reached something he didn't like—much more finesse. Packwood took a hands-off approach except for the things he really cared about. Danforth keeps a tighter rein on things and is more likely to step in early on relative to Packwood. . . . They're very different in their management styles and ways of dealing with other members. It has to do with letting people do what they want until they step across a line. Danforth keeps much tighter control.

These remarks were echoed by a staffer who worked for both men.

> In terms of the ____ Subcommittee, we had an informal message from Packwood that he needed to focus his energy on communications and surface transportation. He felt we could go about doing our business and not have to involve him except in a few cases, as long as he knew what we were up to. Danforth gave us a different message. He really wanted to know and be involved in all things that we were doing.

> [Danforth's] staff has been a little more hands-on about knowing what happens. If a member raises a potential objection with something, Packwood might [have] seen it as isolated and said, "Well, we'll just go ahead and roll right over it." Danforth would probably say we can wait until the next markup and talk about it and maybe work something out.

Nancy Landon Kassebaum, a member of the panel during both chairmanships, noted that

> Packwood and Danforth were both pretty independent chairmen. Pack-
> wood was good about letting you go with it. On the other hand, if it's
> something he wants to get involved in, he just goes with it.

Asked about which chairman got involved on a wider array of committee
issues, she replied:

> I would say that Packwood was more selective on issues. [But] Danforth
> is more laid back as chairman. You always had a better idea where
> Packwood stood on an issue. Danforth is less clear.

Both chairmen were more likely to dominate their subcommittee chairs
than were the chairs of the Environment and Public Works, Judiciary, and
Labor Committees. Still, Packwood and Danforth allowed subcommittee
leaders to play a significant role in committee deliberations. Because the
distribution of preferences among committee Republicans was relatively homogeneous, the probability of a subcommittee chair taking over a bill and
steering it away from the chairman's preferences was relatively low.

Still, Packwood tended to delegate more than Danforth, in part because
Danforth was a new chairman in the 99th Congress. Danforth had less information about issues and member preferences and less experience using the
committee staff to search out information. As a result, he allocated more
staff resources toward monitoring the actions of subcommittee chairs. And
because he was new to the job, there was considerable uncertainty among
other committee members about his preferences, strategies, and overall operating style.

Ernest Hollings and Subcommittee Ranking
Minority Members

Asked about the leadership style of Ernest Hollings, ranking Democrat on the
Commerce Committee during the 99th Congress, an aide to another Democrat
on the panel commented that

> Hollings can be very confrontational and an extremely forceful speaker.
> He can get very involved in Communications, Merchant Marine, and
> Consumer. On Product Liability he is adamantly opposed: "This is the
> worst piece of legislation I've seen in my twenty years in the Senate." He
> can be very confrontational when he cares a lot.

Those who observed both Hollings and Howard Cannon of Nevada—his
predecessor as ranking Democrat on the Commerce Committee—felt that

Hollings was more actively involved in legislative work. According to one staffer:

> Cannon was very deferential to subcommittee chairmen, and he let them go. Hollings wants to know about everything. There are people that he trusts to do the right thing, but he wants to know about it. He has wide interests. . . . He was not that involved with the Consumer Product Safety Commission or NHTSA. That's because Riegle, Ford, and Danforth were really involved, and he figured that dialogue was pretty exhaustive. On the Consumer Product Safety Commission, he trusts Ford.

The analysis of appendix B supports these observations: Hollings often was part of the subset of committee members active on a piece of legislation. But the analysis also reveals that Hollings did not play as significant a legislative role on the Democratic side of the panel as Danforth did among committee Republicans.

The nature of the structural context suggests why. Like Danforth, Hollings had near-monopoly control over committee staff resources for his party. But on the Commerce Committee, as on all Senate committees, the minority staff was much smaller than the majority staff. As a result, the magnitude of Hollings's informational advantage relative to Democratic subcommittee leaders was significantly smaller than the advantage Danforth enjoyed relative to the various subcommittee chairs.

When Hollings did take the lead, however, his staffers were careful to include the ranking minority member on the subcommittee of jurisdiction. As one of Hollings's aides observed:

> You always check with them [the subcommittee ranking minority members] on everything. If I set up a hearing, I check with Russell Long, who's ranking on Surface Transportation. Whenever there's an issue . . . , I always check with his office. . . . He's part of the system. Hollings will always say, "Well, where is Russell on this issue, where's my ranking?"

Staffers also noted that Hollings placed great value on his working relationship with Danforth, and on bills where Danforth was strongly committed and Hollings in opposition, Hollings tended to take a less active role. As a result, subcommittee leaders were more likely to take the lead on the minority side than they were on the majority side, but on issues relevant to Hollings's interests, he was clearly the dominant player among committee Democrats, and often on the Commerce Committee in general.

Stafford, Bentsen, and the Environment
and Public Works Committee

There was also a tendency on the Environment and Public Works Committee to concentrate policy-making responsibility at the full committee level. As was the case on Commerce, the centralization of structural arrangements within the committee was a key causal factor. Most subcommittee staffers owed primary allegiance to one of the full committee leaders, and relatively little work was done in formal subcommittee markups during the 99th Congress. But Robert Stafford was more inclined to delegate than John Danforth, and committee members emphasized the importance of subcommittee chairs and ranking minority members to an extent not found on the Commerce Committee. I asked Stafford about the division of labor on Environment and Public Works during his chairmanship, and he stressed the contributions made by subcommittee leaders: "We had good people: Chafee, Gorton, Evans. On the Democratic side, it was Mitchell, Baucus, and Lautenberg. They were the leaders and the thought framers on environmental legislation." Indeed, staffers on the committee often described the panel in terms of "the big four" or "my big four": Stafford, Bentsen, and the two leaders of the subcommittee of jurisdiction.

When we examine the analysis in appendix B, the more pronounced role played by subcommittee leaders on Environment and Public Works relative to the Commerce Committee is apparent. On the minority side, the legislative impact of Ernest Hollings and Lloyd Bentsen relative to their subcommittee ranking minority members was fairly similar. But among committee Republicans, it is clear that there existed a greater sharing of power on the Environment and Public Works Committee. Subcommittee chairs generally took the lead on substantive questions, while Stafford ran the process.

Issue Complexity, Staff Resources, and the
Distribution of Information

Senators routinely cited the extreme complexity of environmental issues when explaining the policy-making clout of full and subcommittee leaders. For instance, asked about selective participation in committee, Senate Majority Leader George Mitchell, an active member of Environment and Public Works, described it as "the natural order of things in a legislature," and went on to emphasize the importance of the distribution of information for understanding the role of subcommittee leaders on Environment and Public Works.

> There's not enough time to digest the information, to be knowledgeable, to write every bill. It's difficult to gain expertise. . . . The same relationship exists between the committee and the floor, and the subcommittee

and the committee. . . . The subcommittee members have a larger impact. They're the ones managing the legislation, leading the debate. They have more background.

Given the technical nature of the jurisdiction, senators on Environment and Public Works are particularly dependent on the committee staff for information. Recall that the staff is centralized, experienced, and highly expert, and the policy perspectives of committee aides tend to reflect the moderate environmentalism of most panel members. During the 99th Congress, the staff on Environment and Public Works revolved around a core group of senior aides, some of whom had been with the committee for two decades. Although members of the core group formally worked for Stafford or Bentsen, staff aides on Environment and Public Works tend to be bipartisan in outlook, and party differences mean very little. For instance, a staffer for committee Democrats commented on the role played by Democratic aide Philip Cummings.

> Phil is sort of the guru of the committee. He is critical for many of the members, both Democrats and Republicans. Mostly it's because he is such a resource of knowledge and the members need that: He has been working for the committee since 1966. On almost all of the bills this year, he's been a major drafter. Members go to him and say, "I want to do this." They trust him.

Similar comments were made about other senior staffers.

There were pockets of dissension on the panel, however, often led by Alan Simpson of Wyoming. Simpson argued that the staff was biased toward the environmentalist viewpoint, and, as a result, conservative westerners on the committee lacked the information necessary to influence policy outcomes. According to Simpson:

> On Environment and Public Works, there's all this talk about showers of purple mist in New Jersey that will leave you sterilized. So you either fall over passionately or you're evil. . . . The entire staff has the same mindset on Environment and Public Works. . . . About twenty people in the United States understand Superfund legislation. It takes away the yeast of legislating when all is leavened the same way. . . . I can't go to an Environment and Public Works meeting and in all confidence be sure what I hear is right, and not tilted. The staff is just too committed, too hell-bent.

Clearly, there was disagreement in the committee about whose policy agenda the staff should promote. But environmentalists and conservative westerners alike emphasized the value of staff resources as a leadership tool.

Stafford and Bentsen were influential on a wide range of committee issues through their staffing prerogatives. And as was the case on the Commerce Committee, subcommittee leaders on Environment and Public Works were influential because they worked closely with the committee staff. Other committee members had personal aides, and the committee staff certainly consulted with members outside the leadership circle. But for the most part, committee members deferred to full committee and subcommittee leaders out of necessity: They often lacked the information and expertise necessary to devise alternatives and build competing coalitions. As a result, "the big four" on a bill generally took the lead.

Delegation and Monitoring

When we examine the division of labor at the leadership level, subcommittee chairs on Environment and Public Works played a greater policy-making role than did subcommittee chairs on the Commerce Committee, but Robert Stafford shaped committee deliberations to an extent not possible for Strom Thurmond or Orrin Hatch on the Judiciary and Labor panels.

Although subcommittees on Environment and Public Works held markup sessions, Stafford controlled most of the committee staff, and the structural context was much more centralized than the distribution of resources found in Judiciary and Labor. Indeed, when we focus on staffing practices alone, Environment and Public Works does not diverge significantly from the Commerce Committee. What does distinguish Environment and Public Works from the Commerce Committee, however—and helps explain the more significant legislative impact exerted by subcommittee chairs on Environment and Public Works—is an aspect of the preference context: the intensity of member preferences on committee issues. Environmental issues tend to be much more salient than the typical Commerce Committee reauthorization. And the omnibus public works bills considered by the panel also generate more attention than most Commerce Committee initiatives. The greater preference intensity found on Environment and Public Works makes subcommittee chairs less willing to defer to full committee leaders. There are significant political rewards to taking the lead on committee issues—opportunities for position taking, influencing policy, and channeling federal money to the folks back home. As a result, subcommittee leaders on Environment and Public Works, particularly the chairs, are more active than are subcommittee leaders on the Commerce Committee.

Additionally, Stafford shared the policy preferences of the subcommittee chairs on issues within their jurisdictions, and thus had little to lose by letting them take the lead on policy. The key environmental subcommittees were the Subcommittee on Environmental Pollution, chaired by John Chafee, and the

Subcommittee on Toxic Substances and Community Development, chaired by David Durenberger. Both senators shared Robert Stafford's moderate environmentalism. Of the four westerners who often clashed with Stafford on environmental policy, three—James Abdnor, Alan Simpson, and Steve Symms—chaired subcommittees on the panel, but usually agreed with Stafford on issues within their subcommittees' jurisdictions. As a result, Stafford valued activist subcommittee leaders: They promoted his policy preferences and allowed him to allocate his time and resources to other aspects of the process.

Thus, the extreme complexity of committee issues provided an incentive for Stafford to delegate, and the fact that the subcommittee chairs generally agreed with him on policy curtailed the need for extensive monitoring of subcommittee activities. An aide to Stafford described the chairman's style in the following terms:

> In general, subcommittee people take the lead and Stafford works behind the scenes to see that a subcommittee bill is the way he wants it. He wants consensual full committee markups. Stafford is very low key about press coverage, and he lets the subcommittee chairmen take a lot of the credit. But his mark is there. . . . He's the gorilla in the closet.

A staffer to committee Democrats noted that

> he's certainly a delegator, but he's usually involved to some extent. It's an interesting mix. . . . He sets the early agenda, but as legislation moves along he becomes more reactive to other members.

The usual approach for Stafford was to dominate at the agenda-setting stage and then slowly back off as a bill took shape. Committee decision making was characterized by a functional delegation in which Stafford focused on process, while subcommittee chairs took the lead on policy.

Delegation of the sort practiced by Stafford can reduce opportunities for generating press coverage, opportunities that are often electorally valuable. But throughout his career, Stafford was less concerned than most senators about receiving media attention. And, by most accounts, his proximate career plans by the 99th Congress involved retirement at the end of his term. As a result, Stafford's behavior was seldom oriented toward position taking or publicity seeking. Instead, he systematically allowed other senators to claim credit and garner favorable press.

However, on issues such as Superfund and the Clean Air Act, where Stafford's own policy preferences were particularly intense, the chairman was much less inclined to delegate policy-making responsibility to other committee members. Stafford was largely responsible for the original passage of Superfund in 1980, and he placed great emphasis on protecting and expanding the program in the 99th Congress. As a result, he held the legislation at full committee and delegated less extensively to other senators. As one staffer said: "There's an awful lot of delegation on the committee. Stafford's nearing retirement and he's making room for the young turks, with the exception of Superfund and Clean Air, which are another matter."

Lloyd Bentsen and Subcommittee Ranking Minority Members

In many ways, Lloyd Bentsen's interactions with subcommittee ranking minority members on Environment and Public Works resembled the interactions between Ernest Hollings and subcommittee ranking minority members on the Commerce Committee. Both panels are relatively centralized, and full committee leaders have the resources necessary to influence a broad cross-section of committee legislation. But the minority staff is much smaller than the majority staff, so Bentsen's advantage in resources, relative to other Democrats on the panel, was less pronounced than the advantage enjoyed by Stafford on the Republican side.

The nature of the preference context was also conducive to extensive participation by subcommittee ranking minority members on the Environment and Public Works Committee. As was the case with committee Republicans, the breadth of interest among Democrats on the panel was wider on Environment and Public Works than it was on the Commerce Committee. Thus, relative to Hollings, Bentsen had less discretion in his choice of leadership tactics and strategies.

Individual characteristics of Lloyd Bentsen also shaped the division of labor among committee Democrats. Recall that the scope of Bentsen's issue agenda was very wide; indeed, a significant portion of his time was allocated to Finance Committee issues, the panel he was to chair in the next congress. Although Bentsen had the experience and staff resources necessary to be influential when his interests were evoked, he was extremely active on the Finance Committee during the period when he served as ranking Democrat on Environment and Public Works.

The key factor shaping Bentsen's level of involvement in the Environment and Public Works Committee was the intensity of his personal policy preferences, which, in turn, was primarily a function of the importance of an issue to his state. Many items considered by Environment and Public Works affected his constituents in Texas, activating a strong Bentsen presence. As committee Democrat Max Baucus of Montana said:

Bentsen's interest in the committee was Texas. His interest on Environment and Public Works was local and not national. It was Texas first from Clean Air to highway funds. . . . His approach is more national on the Finance Committee.

According to an aide to another committee Democrat:

[Bentsen] uses this committee to help the state of Texas. So the staff are all very well briefed on Texas government, Texas problems, and Texas phone numbers. Staff people directly under his patronage are talking about Texas and then the rest of the country. That's just a natural assumption, and it was also done with Randolph [former ranking member Jennings Randolph] and West Virginia.

Bentsen's interests and commitments in the Finance Committee jurisdiction diverted his attention from Environment and Public Works, and his leadership on the panel tended to focus on constituency matters.

An additional factor influencing Bentsen's selection of strategies was the size of his home state. All senators allocate a significant amount of attention to the folks back home, but these demands escalate dramatically the larger the constituency. Senators from populous states receive bigger staff allowances, but for a state as large as Texas, these additional staff resources do not countervail the greater demands on the office. Indeed, Bentsen has long been recognized as one of the busiest members of the Senate. As a result, when committee issues did not have a significant impact on his state, Bentsen allowed other Democrats to take the lead on policy. A staffer for committee Democrats remarked:

Bentsen is very quick, with a good memory. His staff is involved as needed. Because he is just about to become ranking on Finance, he's very busy. The size of the state is crucial. Bentsen has so many constituents and the demands on his time are extensive. Mitchell, for example, is from Maine, and has fewer constituents. Bentsen has to choose carefully among the things he does.

Bentsen's responsibilities and resources as ranking Democrat on Environment and Public Works paled in comparison to those associated with his subsequent position on the Finance Committee, but his office clearly monitored staff actions on the Democratic side of Environment and Public Works with great care. Two staffers for committee Democrats discussed staffing arrangements on the minority side.

> When Randolph was ranking, there was a lot of hiring done by the other members. When Senator Bentsen took over, he wanted to tighten up the ship, get people more coordinated and working for him.

> We have a staff director [who] oversees what other staff are doing, and we have two chief counsels, one for public works . . . and one for the environment. . . . Most of the staff works for Bentsen. The top three— Burdick, Hart, and Moynihan—each have a member on staff. The rest of us work for Bentsen. It's a centralized operation.

The environmentalist perspective of the staff was not always consistent with the interests of Texas, but after becoming ranking member, Bentsen centralized the minority staff to increase his leverage in committee decision making. Coordinating staff operations facilitated his efforts to monitor the activities of committee aides and, as a result, protect the interests of his constituents.

In short, the mix of delegation and monitoring strategies employed by Lloyd Bentsen on Environment and Public Works was conditioned by a combination of factors: the distribution of staff, the intensity of member preferences, the intensity of Bentsen's own preferences, the size of his state, and his intention to move to a leadership position on the Finance Committee at the beginning of the next congress. As was the case with Ernest Hollings on the Commerce Committee, Bentsen's involvement as ranking minority member on Environment and Public Works was selective, but often extensive. Both Hollings and Bentsen were potentially strong, if not overwhelming, presences when their interests were affected.

Thurmond, Biden, and the Judiciary Committee

Relative to the issues facing Environment and Public Works, there was much less uncertainty about the substance of issues considered by the Judiciary Committee. The death penalty, abortion, school prayer—these are not issues for which politicians need to lean heavily on staff expertise for information about the political consequences of their actions. Staff aides are useful for tracking developments and monitoring the process of coalition building, but most senators do not require extensive staff resources to participate effectively.[9]

However, even on panels that largely consider salient and easily accessible legislation, time constraints can still have an impact on committee deliberations. For example, the Judiciary Committee's jurisdiction over criminal law issues can be extremely technical, and, as a result, senators look to committee leaders for information. During committee consideration of the

"Justice Assistance Act" in 1983, ranking Democrat Joseph Biden commented on the consequences of time constraints for committee policy-making.

> Most of our colleagues on the House Judiciary Committee and the Senate Judiciary Committee do not have the time or the inclination to pay attention to the details of the provisions, and the hardest thing around here . . . is to get . . . our colleagues to pay attention to details.[10]

Time pressures and the distribution of information condition decision making on all committees.

The Judiciary Committee is the least "full committee oriented" of the four panels. As mentioned, preferences on committee issues tend to be intense, and the panel's internal structure is decentralized, with subcommittees regularly holding formal markups and subcommittee leaders controlling significant staff resources. As a result, subcommittee leaders generally have the interest and the resources necessary to participate actively in committee deliberations.

Delegation and Monitoring

The delegation and monitoring strategies employed by full committee leaders on the Judiciary Committee did not structure full committee–subcommittee relations to the extent that they did on Commerce or Environment and Public Works. Instead, subcommittee leaders used their prerogatives to compete with full committee leaders for power. Former committee Republican Paul Laxalt emphasized the importance of subcommittee leaders on the Judiciary Committee.

> Delegation is the nature of the Senate. . . . On routine matters the subcommittee is the basic unit. There are so many other matters to settle that delegation is necessary. Not on highly contentious issues: The death penalty and abortion transcend subcommittees, and they [subcommittee leaders] don't have a great effect. Hatch was an exception on the Constitution Subcommittee. He was a force.

The analysis in appendix B supports the more informal perceptions of participants in the process. On the Judiciary Committee, subcommittee chairs clearly played a more significant role relative to the full committee chairman than was the case on either Commerce or Environment and Public Works. Thurmond was an important player, but he often focused on procedure, while the various subcommittee chairs took the lead on policy.

The chairman's interactions with subcommittee chairs, however, varied significantly from member to member, depending on the subcommittee chair's policy preferences and the ideological composition of the subcommittee as a whole. An aide commented on Thurmond's differential treatment of subcommittee leaders.

> He delegates some, but if he delegates, it's only to the chosen few: Laxalt and Hatch, primarily. Grassley's not in there. He's deviated a little. He's been doing some oversight on the Justice Department, and that pushed him out of the circle of the trusted few. Sometimes Simpson, but Simpson is sometimes too busy. There aren't that many things he would be asked to take leadership on. Not Denton—not that many issues come up for him. Denton also has had an interest in juvenile justice issues with Specter [who was subcommittee chair]. Those issues have not been hot.

Also excluded from the "chosen few" were Charles McC. Mathias and Arlen Specter, both of whom were considerably to Thurmond's left. Mathias regularly voted with committee Democrats, and Specter was one of the moderate swing voters who determined committee policy when the panel was evenly divided. As a result, Thurmond was less inclined to give these senators a free hand, and he carefully monitored actions occurring in their subcommittees.

During the 99th Congress, Thurmond's strategy of selective delegation and monitoring was illustrated well by a bill aimed at protecting "whistle-blowers"—employees of executive agencies or private contractors who go public with information about waste or fraud. Working off legislation introduced by Dennis DeConcini in a previous congress, staff aides to committee Republican Charles Grassley drafted the legislation in consultation with officials from the Department of Justice. The legislation was a natural for Grassley, who had garnered considerable national publicity by investigating a variety of abuses in defense contracting, and who, as chairman of the Subcommittee on Administrative Practice and Procedure, had formal jurisdiction over the issue area.

As might be expected, the bill was not free from conflict: There was opposition from industry, and the Department of Justice had expressed concerns about portions of the draft. Grassley's office was particularly worried about the Justice Department's reaction, because overt opposition from Justice Department lawyers potentially could have generated major problems with Thurmond. An aide to Grassley described the underlying political dynamics.

The Judiciary Committee is normally very close to the Justice Department and [gives] its views . . . great weight. We knew we'd have a tough battle if we had to fight the Justice Department as well as what we expected from industry. . . . We were worried that Thurmond and several other members would be inclined to listen to the Justice Department and also would be the first [that] industry would go to.

Grassley's response was to work carefully with the executive branch. Thurmond's response was to carefully monitor Grassley. The staffer continued:

Mike Wootten was a Thurmond staffer. We knew we had to satisfy him and the Justice Department for the bill to move forward. . . . Thurmond reaches down into the subcommittees when he needs to, as on our bill. He knows that in the past we've had some oversight hearings and butted heads. Thurmond is normally very protective of [the Justice Department], and he wanted his staffer included in the subcommittee negotiations to make sure that Justice got a good deal. So they sent a chaperon down.

The subcommittees chaired by Mathias and Specter were likewise carefully monitored to protect Thurmond's interests and ensure that the chairman would not be surprised in full committee.

In addition to the views of the subcommittee chair, a subcommittee's overall ideological composition also shaped the mix of delegation and monitoring strategies adopted by Thurmond. During the 99th Congress, for instance, the Subcommittee on Criminal Law was chaired by conservative Paul Laxalt, but the subcommittee as a whole was much more liberal than the full Judiciary Committee.[11] Thurmond's strategic response was to bypass the subcommittee and hold criminal law measures at full committee. Laxalt supported the tactic not only because it cut down on dilatory tactics by liberals during subcommittee consideration, but also because it reduced demands on his time. As Ronald Reagan's closest friend in the Senate, Laxalt devoted much of his energy to troubleshooting for the president.

In contrast, Thurmond systematically delegated significant policy-making responsibility to the remaining subcommittee chairmen—Orrin Hatch, John East, Jeremiah Denton, and Alan Simpson. Hatch, in particular, had considerable autonomy as chairman of the Subcommittee on the Constitution, which considered a range of highly controversial issues. Indeed, a number of staffers referred to Hatch as "vice-chairman" of the Judiciary Commit-

tee during the 99th Congress. With the expected retirement of Barry
Goldwater in 1987, Thurmond planned to assume the chairmanship of the
Armed Services Committee, which would have enabled Hatch to become
chairman on Judiciary. An aide to Hatch described his employer's special
relationship with Thurmond as follows:

> In this committee, particularly on our issues, we fell heir to the dubious
> distinction of titular head. Thurmond is going on to Armed Services and
> is phasing himself out and phasing Orrin in. Plus, they've always kind of
> agreed on things and Thurmond has always been delighted to let Orrin
> take the lead: It makes it easier for him.

> It essentially works as kind of a one-two punch. They consult with us and
> we consult with them. We make the substantive arguments and Thur-
> mond will handle the procedural side. It allows him to stay out of the
> substantive fray and allows us to control [it], which is what we really
> want to do anyway.

Thurmond and Hatch were very similar in their ideological preferences.
As a result, there was little probability that legislation crafted by Hatch would
diverge markedly from Thurmond's views. Thurmond employed similar strategies with the other conservative subcommittee chairmen, with the exception
of Charles Grassley.

Joseph Biden and Subcommittee Ranking Minority Members

When we examine leadership relations on the minority side, Democrats on the
Judiciary Committee present an interesting anomaly. As the analysis of appendix B reveals, the impact of ranking Democrats on the subcommittees actually
overshadowed the role played by full committee ranking minority member
Joseph Biden. Structural factors were partially responsible for Biden's low
legislative profile on the panel. The extreme decentralization of the Judiciary
Committee staff, along with the smaller minority staff allowance typical on
Senate committees, combined to provide the ranking minority member with
little in the way of committee staff resources.

Biden's proximate career plans also may have contributed to his lack of
influence: Judiciary Committee issues are divisive, and there are incentives
for potential presidential candidates to avoid systematic position taking on
divisive issues. Most important, however, was the composition of the Democratic side on Judiciary, which severely constrained Biden's leadership. It

would be difficult to handpick a more heterogeneous group of senators. Democratic committee members ranged from Edward Kennedy and Howard Metzenbaum on the left to Dennis DeConcini and Howell Heflin on the right, with a core group of moderate liberals holding down the center. These ideological differences capture just one dimension of Biden's plight. As an aide to Dennis DeConcini noted:

> Everyone on our side is a very strong personality. About four of these members fall into the moderate category, and the rest are easily pigeonholed. Biden sometimes tries, but it's just super difficult to control. Simon's a rookie freshman, but he's a veteran of the Hill. Nobody tells Metzenbaum anything. Leahy's been around. Kennedy's a national figure. Heflin's a former Justice. DeConcini's involved in a number of issues. Byrd is minority leader and not really involved. Biden, with his aspirations toward the presidency, is sometimes extremely active and sometimes not. There are incentives for somebody with his ambitions to hang back because with these issues you're going to make somebody mad no matter what you do.

Strom Thurmond described Biden's strategic dilemma as ranking member.

> We had a good relationship and still do. I don't believe he feels they'll back him up. Kennedy and that crowd want to have their way. . . . [Biden] is pretty liberal, but he's a right nice fella. He's more accommodating and more reasonable and willing to work things out.

Because of a lack of staff resources, his career plans, and the distribution and intensity of preferences on the Democratic side, Biden chose to focus primarily on criminal law issues, which fell within the jurisdiction of the subcommittee on which he was ranking minority member. Indeed, it would be inaccurate to argue that Biden lacked influence across-the-board, as he usually took the lead on items considered by his own subcommittee. But on other matters, Biden regularly deferred to the relevant subcommittee ranking minority member.

Hatch, Kennedy, and the Labor Committee

Subcommittee chairs on the Labor Committee clearly took the lead on items falling within their jurisdictions (see appendix B), and they did so for essentially the same reasons that subcommittee chairs played such a prominent role on the Judiciary Committee—the structural and preference contexts were conducive to decentralized patterns of decision making. Subcommittees on Labor regularly held markups, and staff resources were decentralized. Preferences on committee issues were often intense, signaling high levels of member interest. But as was the case with Strom Thurmond on the Judiciary Committee, the way Orrin Hatch interacted with subcommittee chairs varied significantly across different portions of his panel's jurisdiction. And explaining why Hatch's tactics vis-à-vis the subcommittee chairs differed requires that we examine how contextual and individual characteristics varied from issue to issue.

Delegation and Monitoring

Four of the six subcommittee chairs—Charles Grassley, Paula Hawkins, Don Nickles, and Dan Quayle—were fellow conservatives, and although Hawkins and Quayle occasionally broke ranks with the chairman on issues within the jurisdictions of their respective subcommittees, for the most part these senators agreed with Hatch on policy. The two moderate to liberal swing voters—Stafford and Weicker—chaired the remaining subcommittees.

Because Hatch lacked an ideological majority in the Labor Committee, the conservative subcommittee chairs had to work with Stafford and Weicker to report legislation to the floor. But reaching out to Stafford, Weicker, or committee Democrats was problematic. Dan Quayle's efforts on the Job Training Partnership Act during the 97th Congress illustrate why.[12] Quayle forged a compromise with ranking Democrat Edward Kennedy in order to get a majority in committee. Hatch then responded with threats to block full committee consideration until the legislation was modified. Thus, the voting alignment in committee severely constrained the conservative subcommittee chairs, just as it constrained Orrin Hatch. They lacked the votes to move conservative measures, but reaching out to committee liberals alienated Hatch, who controlled access to the full committee agenda. As a result, the conservative subcommittee chairs focused on bipartisan, consensual initiatives, on which Hatch deferred extensively to them. Indeed, after the Job Training Partnership Act was behind them, interactions between Hatch and Quayle were relatively cooperative.

Hatch's interactions with Stafford and Weicker on their subcommittees were less cooperative, as indicated by the Weicker-Hatch collision on Weicker's initiative for the institutionalized mentally ill, described at the beginning of chapter 2. Weicker had the votes in committee to pass the bill as introduced, but Hatch's opposition kept the legislation off of the full committee agenda until a compromise was achieved. The potential for conflict of this sort was almost always present on legislation emanating from Stafford's Education Subcommittee or Weicker's Subcommittee on the Handicapped. Hatch explained.

> I deferred to the subcommittees, but I stepped in when there were log-jams. On Education, I gave Stafford a lot of leeway, but we watched them carefully. . . . There were limits and they knew it. . . . I threatened to shut things down at times, used some of the finesse available to the chairman.

Stafford and Weicker countered with some of the finesse available to all members of the U.S. Senate. As the two swing voters, they realized there were benefits to cooperating with each other, particularly on items in the jurisdictions of the subcommittees they chaired. Staffers spoke of an informal agreement between the two senators to support each other on bills considered by their panels. As an aide to Weicker said:

> Senator Weicker and Stafford are very close, and there is this understanding that whatever Weicker does, Stafford will support him, and Stafford has that understanding on the Education Subcommittee. . . . In full committee, he needs Stafford. It's significant to always know Stafford is there.

In addition, there was often considerable uncertainty about the positions of the two senators on committee issues. A staff aide to Howard Metzenbaum commented.

> What happens with Weicker and Stafford over here is it puts the onus on Hatch. . . . They don't do it as much as people think they do, [but] they know how to use that ability to get things from their subcommittees, things that they are concerned about. Stafford gets what he wants on education issues, and Weicker on handicapped issues.

The aide observed that there were incentives for Stafford and Weicker to hang back.

> In exchange for that [concessions from Hatch on their issues], they tend to still stay Republican, but it's a guessing game, and Hatch never really knows when they're going to jump ship on him. You can occasionally get flares, but sometimes you can go into markup not knowing who's going to win. You don't know where these two are going to be. They don't show their cards. Very rarely will Weicker and Stafford say what they're going to do.

Thus, because of their strategic importance, an informal cooperation existed between the two senators that maximized their bargaining leverage in committee.

Edward Kennedy and Subcommittee Ranking Minority Members

Edward Kennedy was clearly the dominant figure on the minority side of the Labor Committee. As the analysis in appendix B indicates, subcommittee ranking minority members did not participate more than the full committee ranking minority member on this committee—an important contrast with the other three panels, and strikingly different from what we found on Judiciary.

Structural factors alone cannot explain this anomaly. The decentralization of the panel's internal structure provided Democratic subcommittee members with staff assistance, so subcommittee leaders from both parties had the resources necessary to participate effectively. Instead, the key to understanding the magnitude of Edward Kennedy's role among Labor Committee Democrats lies in the preference context and its consequences for the nature of the active agenda, as well as in individual characteristics of Kennedy as a senator and a Senate leader.

As demonstrated in the previous chapter, the distribution of preferences in the panel led Hatch to severely constrain the set of active issues. As a result, interest in the jurisdiction among committee Democrats fell markedly, and demands from subcommittee ranking minority members to participate were less pronounced on the Labor Committee than was the case on Judiciary. Because of the narrow character of the active agenda, Democrats on the Labor Committee primarily focused on protecting their constituencies from conservative initiatives, while generating as much publicity as possible to build momentum and induce Hatch to schedule more hearings.

As a national figure and perennial presidential possibility, Kennedy was well positioned to take the lead in efforts to publicize Democratic initiatives and broaden the Labor Committee's agenda. Subcommittee leaders such as Claiborne Pell, Howard Metzenbaum, and Christopher Dodd were active on issues falling within their jurisdictions, but Democrats on the Labor Committee were usually willing to defer to Kennedy's lead. An aide to a Republican member commented.

> Metzenbaum is pretty active on food and drug safety and labor issues, and Simon is active on education. But from the rest of them you don't hear very much and they tend to follow Kennedy. Kennedy runs things on the minority side in a way Hatch never could with the majority.

The constituencies most interested in Labor Committee bills consider Kennedy one of their chief proponents in Congress. Indeed, when we examine the set of issues Edward Kennedy is most associated with, these items fall disproportionately within the jurisdiction of the Labor Committee. As a result, he dominated policy-making on the Democratic side of the aisle.

Subcommittee Government?

It is useful at this point to briefly discuss the implications of this chapter for the subcommittee government hypothesis, an argument that has been highly influential among political analysts in recent years. Some observers of congressional politics have suggested that subcommittees became more important as arenas for policy-making during the 1970s and 1980s. The result has been a dialogue of sorts about whether or not congressional policy-making approximates "subcommittee government."[13]

The subcommittee government hypothesis is important because a shift in the locus of decision making from the full to the subcommittee level implies greater policy-making fragmentation in an already fragmented institution. In other words, if the hypothesis is true, the major decisions on bills are now being made by fewer members. Since subcommittees are often unrepresentative of the full committee because of the self-selection that characterizes the subcommittee assignment process, the emergence of subcommittees as the dominant arenas for decision making would have important consequences for the shape of committee legislation and, eventually, the quality of representation on Capitol Hill.

Although no precise definition of subcommittee government exists, most observers appear to interpret the concept in terms of the organizational independence, or institutionalization, of subcommittees as decision-making units. For example, according to one account, subcommittee government occurs when

> the basic responsibility for the bulk of legislative activity (hearings, debates, legislative markups, that is, the basic writing of a bill) occurs, not at a meeting of an entire standing committee, but at a meeting of a smaller subcommittee of the standing committee. The decisions of the subcommittee are then viewed as the authoritative decisions—decisions that are altered by the standing committee only when the subcommittee is seriously divided or when it is viewed as highly unrepresentative of the full committee.[14]

As Steven Smith and Christopher Deering have argued, if we accept this definition of subcommittee government, then subcommittees in the House tend toward this pattern much more than subcommittees in the Senate. In an imaginative analysis based on data about committee staff organization, the proportion of hearings and markups held at the subcommittee versus full committee level, the proportion of committee legislation referred to subcommittee, and the extent to which bills are managed on the floor by the relevant subcommittee leaders, they conclude:

> Subcommittee government has not been fully institutionalized in either chamber, although House committees have moved farther in that direction since the early 1970s. Senate committees, if anything, on balance have moved away from forming independent subcommittees. . . . [S]ubcommittee autonomy, which by definition means restricted participation, is simply not consistent with the participatory individualism of the Senate.[15]

Few observers of the modern Senate would disagree with that assessment, and I certainly am not one of them. The primary avenues for policy-making in Senate committees are not formal subcommittee markups, but informal negotiations before the markup process begins and during full committee markup. However, if we are interested in the legislative role of subcommittees because of the consequences for committee policy-making, then we need to look beyond questions of institutionalization and simple indicators of subcommittee activity such as how often subcommittees meet in executive session. Indeed, the analysis in appendix B, as well as the text of this chapter, strongly suggests that subcommittee chairs and ranking minority members exert a significant and disproportionate influence over committee bills in the U.S. Senate. The influence of subcommittee leaders varies, and it is conditioned and constrained by the delegation and monitoring strategies of full committee leaders, but it is significant nonetheless.

As organizations, subcommittees in the Senate are not highly institutionalized and are not generally important as formal decision-making units. But they are usually composed of those senators with the most to gain or lose in the jurisdiction—again, particularly when we consider the two leaders—and on many committees, substantial staff resources are allocated through the subcommittee system. To comprehend the policy-making importance of Senate subcommittees, we need to think about the question more in terms of member preferences and the allocation of resources, and less in terms of organizational independence and institutionalization.[16] In short, the term "subcommittee government" is of limited value, and it would be best just to jettison it from our vocabulary altogether.

Conclusion

The pattern of interactions between full and subcommittee leaders varies in significant and interesting ways. Depending on committee structure, preferences, and characteristics of the leaders as individuals, these interactions range from the relatively full committee–oriented style of the Commerce Committee to the more active subcommittee leaders we found on Judiciary. And all committee leaders employ a blend of delegation and monitoring tactics, with the mixture depending on these same factors—structure, preferences, and individual characteristics.

When we gauge the relative importance of these explanatory factors, however, it is again apparent that contextual factors explain most of the observable variance in leadership behavior. Full committee leaders on Commerce and Environment and Public Works play a more pronounced role in policy-making than do full committee leaders on Judiciary and Labor because the former two panels have centralized structures, and subcommittee leaders lack staff resources and agenda prerogatives.

The preference context also matters. Subcommittee leaders are more influential on the Environment and Public Works Committee than they are on the Commerce Committee because public works programs and environmental policy usually evoke more intense preferences than the routine reauthorizations that make up so much of the Commerce Committee's jurisdiction. Because preferences also tend to be particularly intense on Judiciary and Labor Committee issues, subcommittee leaders on these panels are often key participants in committee politics.

Additionally, preference heterogeneity among the rank and file shapes interactions between full and subcommittee leaders. For example, divergent preferences among committee Republicans provided incentives for both Strom Thurmond and Orrin Hatch to carefully monitor the behavior of certain of their subcommittee chairs. Judiciary Committee Democrats were also a particularly heterogeneous group, making it extremely difficult for ranking minority member Joseph Biden to exert leadership. In contrast, Labor Committee Democrats were highly cohesive, and Hatch so constrained the committee's agenda that Democrats on the panel were often willing to let Edward Kennedy take the lead.

Certain individual characteristics are also significant. As we have seen, the delegation and monitoring strategies employed by the committee leaders under study varied from issue to issue, depending (in part) on the intensity of their personal policy preferences. In addition, John Danforth's behavior on the Commerce Committee again illustrates the importance of the learning curve to committee leadership. As a new chairman, he was still incurring the start-up costs of legislative leadership; this was apparent in his mix of delegation and monitoring strategies, particularly in 1985. And Lloyd Bentsen intended to give up the ranking position on Environment and Public Works for a leadership position on the Finance Committee; much of his attention during the 99th Congress was directed toward Finance Committee issues. But once again, contextual factors clearly dominate. By themselves, they explain most of the variation we observe in how the eight senators interacted with the subcommittee leaders of their party.

Notes

1. This section is based on arguments found in Hall and Evans 1990. See also Hall 1987 and Evans 1989.

2. Once again, I rely on Bruce I. Oppenheimer's insights about the impact of time constraints on congressional decision making (1985).

3. See Hall 1987.

4. Because the number of majority party members on a committee usually exceeds the number of subcommittees, the two or three most junior committee members on the majority side often will not be subcommittee chairs.

5. Staff members are the fundamental resource for processing legislative information in the Senate, but in dealing with an issue relevant to their goals over a number of years, senators often build up their own stock of personal expertise, and this expertise can significantly lower the costs of participation in the issue area. Although a senator's personal expertise can act as a substitute for staff work, in practice the two resources go hand in hand. Senators invest the time and effort to become experts on those issues most relevant to their interests, and they also tend to be in leadership positions on the subcommittees with jurisdiction.

6. For example, they often manage their own legislation on the Senate floor, and they are disproportionately represented in conference committee deliberations with the House. See Smith and Deering 1984 and Shepsle and Weingast 1987.

7. The discussion of delegation and monitoring strategies in this section is derived from theoretical work by Buchanan and Tullock (1962) on constitution making, and an application of their research to the subject of congressional oversight provided by Aranson, Gellhorn, and Robinson (1982).

8. The process is very similar to what John Kingdon (1989) has described as the "consensus mode of decision making" in his analysis of congressional voting decisions on the floor of the House.

9. Given the salience of many Judiciary Committee issues, it is interesting that the analysis of appendix B shows that patterns of participation on the Judiciary Committee resemble those found on the other three panels. The number of committee members working on a draft or influencing a piece of legislation via the amendment process in committee tends to be small: often just three or four senators on a committee of eighteen. While the start-up costs to effective participation are relatively low in issue areas such as school prayer, actively participating at the drafting level or through the amendment process does require an investment of time and other office resources.

The size of the investment may be less than we found on Environment and Public Works, but some allocation of member and staff time is necessary. And what are the countervailing benefits? Low levels of uncertainty on these issues allow senators to monitor each other without investing large quantities of staff time. As a result, there are incentives to allow the subcommittee leaders to take primary responsibility in drafting the legislation.

10. Senate Judiciary Committee markup of S.53, June 16, 1983. Manuscript.

11. Indeed, a liberal coalition consisting of Mathias, Joseph Biden, Edward Kennedy, and Howard Metzenbaum had the votes to defeat subcommittee conservatives Paul Laxalt and Strom Thurmond. The seventh member of the panel was Arlen Specter.

12. Fenno 1989.

13. For example, see Davidson 1981, Hall and Evans 1990, and Smith and Deering 1984.

14. Dodd and Oppenheimer 1985, 43. See also Haeberle 1978.

15. Smith and Deering 1984, 161.

16. This is precisely the argument made in Hall and Evans 1990.

CHAPTER 4

The Chair and Ranking Minority Member

CASE STUDY

An aide to Democrats on the Environment and Public Works Committee made the following observations about partisan tensions on the panel:

> There's no majority-minority split on this committee. . . . When we were negotiating with the Energy Committee on the low-level waste bill, there was a much more noticeable split. Not so much on policy, but it was still majority and minority. . . . We just don't operate that way. It's more like being a member of a family.[1]

Contrast her remarks with those of a former staff assistant to Edward Kennedy on the Labor Committee:

> Basically, you've got a bunch of very conservative Republicans like Hatch and Nickles—and that used to include Denton too—facing off against the likes of Kennedy and Howard Metzenbaum. Hatch doesn't have the votes to really do anything and Kennedy just sits there and blows cigar smoke in his face.

Relations between committee chairs and ranking minority members obviously vary, and a proper understanding of committee leadership requires that this variance be explored. This chapter examines the patterns of cooperation and conflict that arise between full committee chairs and ranking minority members, how these patterns differ across committees, and how they differ across issues considered by a single panel.

Political parties in the United States are weaker than their counterparts in other Western democracies. Party loyalty among voters in this country has declined in recent years; campaigns are increasingly candidate-centered; and party organizations in Congress lack the strength of political parties in parliamentary systems. Thus, it is not particularly useful to examine the Senate through the lens of party, and most congressional observers agree with David Mayhew's conclusion that "no theoretical treatment of the United States Congress that posits parties as analytical units will go very far."[2]

Still, how a committee chair and ranking minority member interact can tell us much about legislative leadership. Party-line votes are rare in committee, as well as on the floor, but key decisions are often made at the party level in Senate committees. Subcommittee assignments, for example, are allocated in party caucuses. To hold hearings, senators often have to work through the full committee leader of their party. And full committee chairs and ranking minority members are the senators most likely to have the resources necessary to influence a wide variety of committee bills. As a result, interactions at the full committee leadership level have significant consequences for policy-making in committee, even though congressional parties as organizations do not structure coalition building in the modern Senate.

Understanding Interactions Between the Chair and Ranking Minority Member

How does participation at the leadership level vary across the four panels? The findings in appendix B provide some guidance and are supported by the comments of senators and staff assistants. On the Commerce Committee, both John Danforth and Ernest Hollings participated extensively in legislative work, either directly or through staff, although the impact of the chairman was more pronounced. Results for Environment and Public Works are similar. Both Robert Stafford and Lloyd Bentsen were active at the drafting and amendment stages of the committee process, but Stafford played a more significant role.

When we turn to Judiciary and Labor, however, interesting differences become apparent. On the Judiciary Committee, Strom Thurmond was less active in drafting and amending committee bills than were Danforth and Stafford on their panels, but the more striking difference is on the minority side. As mentioned in the previous chapter, Joseph Biden was active on criminal law measures considered by the subcommittee on which he was ranking Democrat, but in other portions of the jurisdiction, he seldom took the lead. And when we turn to the Labor Committee, it is clear that Edward Kennedy was a regular participant: Indeed, his level of involvement rivaled that of the chairman, Orrin Hatch. Thus, full committee leaders tend to participate extensively in legislative work on all four panels, but their relative importance varies significantly.

In addition to looking at the extent to which chairs and ranking minority members participate in committee, it is also useful to examine *when* they participate. Is it typical for chairs and ranking minority members to focus their efforts on different bills, or are they drawn to the same items? Answering this question will take us one step closer to understanding how chairs and ranking minority members interact with one another.

The most important decisions on a bill usually occur at the drafting stage of the legislative process. Senators active in constructing the vehicle brought into markup generally set the range of politically viable alternatives, and thus determine the contours of debate at succeeding stages of the process. As a longtime staffer to Republicans on the Environment and Public Works Committee commented:

> I've always felt that there's a lot to being the one who originates the papers, who does the first draft. There's a lot of influence in that, and in setting the agenda too. Whoever gets to do the drafting—even though the other side can make changes—whoever puts it down on paper first is setting the tone, even if it gets edited.

Indeed, an important source of leadership power in Senate committees is the tendency for chairs and ranking minority members to be disproportionately active (relative to other panel members) in shaping the draft version of legislation, primarily through their staffs.[3] As a result, further light can be shed on the way full committee leaders interact by examining patterns of involvement at the drafting stage of the process.

For the sample of sixty-two bills described and analyzed in the appendixes, I asked knowledgeable staffers which senators, directly or through staff, had a concrete impact on the content of the draft brought into markup. Each piece of legislation was then placed in one of four categories: (1) both full committee leaders influenced the draft; (2) the chair influenced the draft, but the ranking minority member did not; (3) the ranking minority member influenced the draft, but the chair did not; and (4) neither full committee leader was active at the drafting stage of the legislative process. The percentage of bills falling in each category, by committee, is indicated in table 4.1. These data allow us to explore—in a tentative fashion—the extent to which a chair and ranking minority member tend to influence the same pieces of

TABLE 4.1. Committee Leadership Influence at the Drafting Stage, in Percentage

Committee	Both Chair and Ranking Minority Member	Chair	Ranking Minority Member	Neither
Commerce	12.5%	37.5%	18.8%	31.3%
Environment and Public Works	40.0	30.0	0.0	30.0
Judiciary	16.7	22.2	0.0	61.1
Labor	50.0	11.1	5.6	33.3

Source: From staff interviews.

Note: Total sample is 62 bills. For Commerce, N = 16; for Environment and Public Works, N = 10; for Judiciary, N = 18; and for Labor, N = 18.

legislation, and the results generate some interesting questions about leadership behavior in the four committees.

First consider the two relatively bipartisan committees, Commerce and Environment and Public Works. Full committee leaders were clearly active at the drafting stage on both panels—the chair or ranking Democrat influenced the draft on more than two-thirds of the bills marked up in each committee. But important differences between Commerce and Environment and Public Works emerge when we compare the number of bills on which both full committee leaders were drafters. On Environment and Public Works, Robert Stafford and Lloyd Bentsen were both active at the drafting stage on 40 percent of the bills, while the analogous figure for Danforth and Hollings on Commerce is just 12.5 percent. Why were Stafford and Bentsen more likely to focus on the same set of issues than were Danforth and Hollings? And what does this suggest about leadership interactions in the two committees?

Now consider the two more partisan committees, Judiciary and Labor. Participation at the drafting stage differed markedly between the two panels. On over 60 percent of the Judiciary Committee bills, *neither* full committee leader was a drafter. And Thurmond and Biden were both active at the drafting stage on just 16.7 percent of the bills. When we examine the Labor Committee, however, a strikingly different pattern is apparent. On 50 percent of the bills in the sample, *both* full committee leaders were drafters, while the proportion of bills on which neither had an impact on the draft was just one-third. Since Judiciary and Labor were both partisan committees, why are the results in table 4.1 so different between the two panels? In particular, given the ideological distance between Orrin Hatch and Edward Kennedy, how could both senators be influential on so many of the bills considered by the Labor Committee?

Danforth, Hollings, and the Commerce Committee

The distribution of preferences on the Commerce Committee was consensual, and the personal policy preferences of John Danforth and Ernest Hollings did not diverge significantly on most committee issues. Still, as table 4.1 demonstrates, the two leaders seldom worked together at the drafting stage. One or the other was active on most committee issues, but relative to the other three panels, they were less likely to collaborate. Why?

The answer lies in the personal policy preferences of Ernest Hollings. The typical Commerce Committee reauthorization generates little interest, and Hollings did not have intense preferences on most of the items considered by the panel. Instead, he primarily focused on three sets of issues during the 99th Congress: communications issues, for which he was also ranking Democrat on the subcommittee of jurisdiction; major administration initiatives such as the proposed sale of Conrail, on which he usually assisted Danforth in managing the committee process; and any proposals relating to product liability reform, to which he was adamantly opposed. On other items, action at the drafting level was dominated by Danforth, as well as the relevant subcommittee chair and ranking minority member.

In contrast, John Danforth, as full committee chair, was expected to manage the work load. And he did influence the draft on most bills considered in committee, primarily through his control over majority staff resources. Hollings employed fewer staff assistants and was not expected to be highly involved in all committee issues. And given the consensual nature of most of these reauthorizations, there was little return for intense involvement by the ranking minority member. Hollings and Danforth were usually in agreement, and Hollings's interests were protected by the chairman, as well as the ranking Democrat on the subcommittee of jurisdiction.

Hollings's tendency to delegate significant policy-making responsibility to other Commerce Committee Democrats also reduced the potential for personal conflict with Danforth, facilitating cooperation between the two committee leaders. Indeed, with the exception of product liability reform, observers of Commerce Committee politics noted that Hollings strategically softened his opposition to items strongly supported by the chairman.

Recall the discussion in chapter 2 of the Danforth bill aimed at Carl Icahn's move to take over TWA, an important employer in the chairman's state. Danforth had a strong constituency interest in the legislation for obvious reasons. Ernest Hollings, in contrast, viewed the Danforth bill as undue governmental interference in the marketplace, and he was in opposition on policy grounds. Howard Metzenbaum, not a member of the Commerce Committee, also opposed the measure, and threatened to lead a fight on the Senate floor. As a staffer for Hollings recalled: "Hollings [raised] substantive problems, but probably wouldn't have fought the bill. He felt it was bad legislation, but he has to work with Danforth more often than Metzenbaum."

During the committee markup, a number of senators expressed reservations about the legislation because it so obviously was aimed at a single firm rather than a general policy problem, and committee Democrat Wendell Ford had some amendments relating to labor protection. But senators quickly coalesced around Danforth in an attempt to help the chairman protect his constituents, and the legislation was reported to the floor by a margin of fifteen to one without modification. Hollings cast the single opposing vote but did not actively oppose the measure. Indeed, he was not even present, and voted no by proxy.

A similar approach was evident on a Danforth bill aimed at protecting communities from professional sports team relocations (also discussed in chap. 2). There was considerable concern in early 1985 that the Cardinals might leave St. Louis, depriving Danforth's constituents of one of their professional football franchises. Hollings opposed the sports bill, again because he viewed it as undue interference in the marketplace. A draft was provided by lawyers for the National Football League, with staff assistants to Danforth making revisions. An aide to Hollings commented.

> The NFL conferred with Danforth and Eagleton [and] basically supplied them with a draft. . . . Danforth put in a few safeguards [including] some criteria for termination [of team owners]. That was for Hollings.

Thus, Danforth's office moved the legislation quickly, but made some changes to dampen the intensity of Hollings's opposition. The bill was marked up and reported to the floor by a margin of ten to six. Hollings voted no, but did not actively oppose the measure.

In short, the interests of Danforth and Hollings seldom clashed on Commerce Committee issues. Hollings's preferences were not intense on most of the reauthorizations, and Danforth's staff was responsible for the bulk of the legislative work. But when their preferences did diverge and Danforth's preferences were intense, Hollings tended to back off. As aides to the ranking minority member often stressed, their boss placed great importance on maintaining a good working relationship with Danforth. Systematically taking the lead in opposing him on items he cared about would have alienated the chairman and made cooperation at the leadership level more difficult on other Commerce Committee issues.

Stafford, Bentsen, and the Environment and Public Works Committee

Environment and Public Works has a history of cooperation at the leadership level, dating back to partnerships between former Democratic Senator Edmund Muskie of Maine and a succession of Republicans that includes John Sherman Cooper of Kentucky, Howard Baker of Tennessee, James Buckley of New York, and Robert Stafford. Indeed, Stafford was often referred to as the milder half of the Muskie-Stafford "fire and ice team."[4] A senior aide to committee Democrats described how bipartisan patterns of decision making developed on Environment and Public Works.

> It began in the seventies and the pattern has continued. There are some differences, but they tend to be ideological rather than partisan. . . . The style of collaborative working began under John Sherman Cooper, continued with Howard Baker, and then Stafford. Muskie always dominated when he was subcommittee chairman, but that was because of his exper-

tise, his contribution, his willingness to sit in the chair and talk for days. But everything was always open when we were in the majority and the minority staff was always included. The Republicans have just continued the process.

Bipartisanship arises on Environment and Public Works because of the preference context in committee. Preferences are often intense on committee issues, but there has long been broad-based agreement among Republican and Democratic members over general questions of policy. When conflict does occur, it usually concerns how to best implement these objectives. During the 99th Congress, there existed an opposing coalition of conservative westerners, but their impact on environmental policy was not significant. Thus, while consensual decision making on the Commerce Committee was primarily due to low levels of preference intensity, on Environment and Public Works, bipartisanship resulted from shared values.

The Stafford-Bentsen relationship is best described as collaborative, with Stafford playing the more significant role on most committee issues. As demonstrated in table 4.1, both leaders influenced drafts on a wide range of committee bills, including all major legislation considered by the panel in 1985. Staffers to committee Democrats regularly commented on their inclusion at all levels of the process, often emphasizing that minority status allowed them to play a more reactive role. According to two Democratic aides:

> The great thing is that the majority has to set up the hearings and I get to free ride. . . . I get to sit in on the planning sessions, but I don't have to do any of the administrative work, which is the only way I could handle three subcommittees.

> The majority gets thirty-five slots [on the committee staff]; the minority, eighteen. The majority has [the] responsibility of taking care of administrative tasks and moving bills forward. We have a very close working team among the big four. We share the work load. But the minority has the luxury of sitting back and reacting.

Such reactive tactics are not useful on all panels. Democratic staffers on the Judiciary Committee never spoke of "the luxury of sitting back and reacting" to conservative initiatives on abortion, gun control, or prayer in public schools. One reason, of course, is that there was an underlying consensus on Environment and Public Works, and staff work often focused on interpreting and explaining the highly complex issues in the jurisdiction. But given the magnitude of Bentsen's commitments on the Finance Committee, as well as the smaller size of the minority staff, it simply was not feasible for Bentsen to systematically take the lead on Environment and Public Works. Although he influenced the draft on all major bills considered by the committee, he was often dependent on the initiatives of other senators.

An exception, however, was anything relevant to the interests of Texas. Staff assistants to Stafford were always careful to anticipate any negative effects on Bentsen's constituents. As one Stafford aide said:

> We always seem to be working around Texas, so they have a great deal of influence because they take a very hard line about not wanting any federal regulation of this or that sort. They figure prominently in any kind of negotiation because Texas state people seem to take the attitude that whatever changes being attempted in a federal statute are not going to affect them in a favorable way. They're a presence. You feel like you always have to clear things with Texas. . . . We're very sensitive to Texas.

Thus, to a greater extent than Stafford's, Bentsen's interests were targeted toward provisions that directly affected his state. The chairman was primarily concerned about the general thrust of committee policy and was more than willing to incorporate Bentsen's preferences. A common approach was for Stafford to set the early agenda. Staffers for the majority and minority, working together with executive branch officials, then shaped the vehicle to be brought into markup. Bentsen's office watched for potentially negative effects on Texas and, as they arose, expressed concern to Stafford and the committee staff. Thus, Bentsen's preferences pervaded the process, but his influence was narrower in scope than the influence exerted by the chairman. In short, their interests were complementary, fostering a cooperative working relationship between the two full committee leaders on Environment and Public Works.

Thurmond, Biden, and the Judiciary Committee

In contrast, the Senate Judiciary Committee has long been one of the most ideological committees in Congress. It has jurisdiction over issues that galvanize and deeply divide public opinion, and this conflict in the electorate is reflected in the intensity and distribution of preferences in committee. The Judiciary Committee was split during the Thurmond years, with committee conservatives enjoying a solid working majority. Because liberal Democrats on the panel lacked the votes to defeat conservative initiatives, they responded with dilatory tactics to decrease the probability that these measures would become law. Indeed, Judiciary Committee deliberations often took on a push-me–pull-you character, with Thurmond trying to facilitate committee action, and liberal Democrats employing a range of delaying tactics to slow or block items they opposed.

Preferences on the committee were polarized, and Thurmond and Biden usually confronted one another from opposite ends of the ideological spectrum. Thus, one would expect relations between the two full committee leaders to be strained and rife with conflict. The pattern of interactions between Thurmond and Biden was usually cooperative, however. Indeed, Thurmond has referred to his Democratic counterpart as "my Henry Clay," alluding to Clay's reputation as "the Great Compromiser."[5] Given that there is so little middle ground on many Judiciary Committee issues, how were Thurmond and Biden able to achieve a significant degree of cooperation at the leadership level?

Once again, the information in table 4.1 is instructive. First, on over 60 percent of the bills in the sample, neither full committee leader had a concrete impact on the content of the draft brought into markup, indicating the extent to which policy-making responsibility on the panel was decentralized. On 22.2 percent of the bills, Thurmond influenced the draft, while Biden did not. Biden affected drafts on only 16.7 percent of the bills, and in each case, Thurmond's office was also active at the drafting stage.

Biden's legislative efforts primarily dealt with issues falling within the jurisdiction of the Subcommittee on Criminal Law, on which he was also ranking minority member. Without doubt, the most important criminal law measure considered by the committee during Thurmond's chairmanship was the "Comprehensive Crime Control Act of 1984." This legislation was the culmination of over a decade of bargaining and negotiation; its policy consequences were profound; and it revealed how a degree of cooperation between Thurmond and Biden was possible in a policy area that often generated considerable conflict.

The version of the bill brought into markup in 1983 contained an array of provisions that had been before the committee in previous years, ranging from bail and sentencing reform to measures relating to drug penalties and the insanity defense. Before hearings were held, Thurmond and then subcommittee chair Paul Laxalt planned to include in the legislation highly controversial provisions relating to capital punishment, habeas corpus, and the exclusionary rule. With these items included, many Democrats intended to fight the legislation.

In response, Biden proposed that the more controversial provisions be removed and considered as separate pieces of legislation. A Republican staffer included in the negotiations described the process.

During the hearings, Biden and Kennedy said there were a lot of good parts to the bill and asked why it was burdened with controversial sections. A deal was finally worked out in Thurmond's president pro tem office. There must have been six or seven Republicans there at one time. It was a big meeting. . . .

What we got was the deal that we would take out of the package those sections that the Democrats didn't like and construct a new package, with Thurmond, Biden, Laxalt, and Kennedy as cosponsors. They would serve as a junta and act in union. If any one of those four objected to an amendment in committee, all four would line up in support. It was a veto power.

This alliance between Strom Thurmond, Joseph Biden, Paul Laxalt, and Edward Kennedy was crucial to timely Senate action on the legislation, and the primary force behind the so-called junta was Joseph Biden. A close aide to Biden described his boss's general approach to the partisanship inherent in many criminal law matters.

Biden perceives crime issues as partisan, but potentially bipartisan: that there's much that can be done. He watched through the Kennedy chairmanship, and was concerned in the initial Thurmond chairmanship, that everybody was getting bogged down on very emotional issues like the death penalty and the exclusionary rule: things that had everybody charged. . . .

Biden approached Thurmond and said, "Let's sit down and agree on what we can agree on. If we've got forty items and we can only agree on twenty, fine. Then you get a veto on the ten you don't want, and I'll get a veto on the ten I don't want. But we'll take the twenty, stick together through the process, and if somebody wants to add amendments, then no: There's no amendments unless it's agreeable to both of us."

The junta approach disturbed some committee members, but a majority of the panel saw it as a useful political strategy. After the markup, Biden spoke for most when he commented that "[w]e've learned that the only way to get action is to agree on what we agree on and move on it, and fight over what is left."[6]

Thus, a degree of cooperation between Thurmond and Biden was possible because of the distribution of preferences in committee on criminal law matters. Most crime control issues have some aspects that are controversial, and others on which there is considerable room for agreement. Thurmond and Biden were able to cooperate by avoiding those areas that generated intense conflict, while focusing on those with middle ground. The comprehensive crime control bill illustrates this general approach quite well. There was considerable support for sentencing reform, for example. But on provisions pertaining to the death penalty or the exclusionary rule, the distribution of preferences was highly polarized. Thurmond and Biden were able to coalesce by striking the more divisive provisions from the package, and uniting behind more consensual ones, such as that dealing with sentencing reform.

In short, cooperation between the two full committee leaders did not result from compromise per se: They did not simply split the difference. Rather, cooperation was achieved by carefully selecting the issues on which to legislate. Similar tactics were employed on other criminal law legislation, although the process was usually less structured than the junta approach used on the comprehensive crime control bill.

On other committee issues such as abortion or school prayer, however, dropping the divisive language would have required gutting the core provisions from committee legislation. The substantively important aspects of these bills tend to be controversial, and nothing resembling the junta approach would be politically feasible.

What was Biden's role as ranking minority member on these items? Thurmond generally had a working majority and did not need the votes of liberal Democrats such as Biden, Kennedy, and Howard Metzenbaum to win in committee. But Democrats on the panel had available a range of dilatory tactics that provided them with the leverage necessary to influence committee politics. Other Democrats may have expected Biden, as ranking minority member, to exert a leadership role in organizing obstructionist tactics— behavior that would have significantly altered his relationship with the chairman. Such a role was unnecessary, however, because of the presence on the panel of Howard Metzenbaum of Ohio, the preeminent obstructionist in the U.S. Senate.

The Metzenbaum Clearance Process

As a liberal Democrat who did not hold a full committee leadership post, Howard Metzenbaum might have had little policy-making impact during the years that Republicans organized the Senate. Instead, he was easily one of the institution's most powerful members. Metzenbaum influenced public policy during this period by systematically blocking items he opposed. Most often, these bills were special interest measures supported by particular senators for parochial reasons. But Metzenbaum was also extremely effective at blocking conservative initiatives pushed by Republicans such as Strom Thurmond and Orrin Hatch.

In the early 1980s, Metzenbaum developed a formal clearance process on the floor of the Senate in which no legislation could be passed by unanimous consent unless it was cleared by his office. Given the scarcity of floor time, party leaders are forced to consider as much legislation as possible by unanimous consent. Indeed, toward the end of a session, it is very difficult to secure floor time for bills not of major importance unless unanimity has been achieved. The leadership simply lacks the time to spend hours considering minor legislation on the floor of the Senate. As a result (particularly toward the end of a session, or as a recess approaches), Howard Metzenbaum has enormous influence. By objecting to a measure, he often can block floor consideration, effectively killing the bill. I asked Metzenbaum about his legislative style.

> It's not really a clearance process: Any member could do the same thing. If a bill is coming up and I don't know what it is, I stop it. . . . Most things pass by unanimous consent. . . . Senator Byrd once said, "If we didn't have a Metzenbaum, we would have to invent one." Senator Baker said, "Yes, but only one."

A senior staff assistant to Edward Kennedy commented on Metzenbaum's general importance to the liberal agenda.

> Metzenbaum is an absolutely essential element of the Senate. . . . You always need one or two guys like Metzenbaum because they are great foils for the other people. There's an awful lot of stuff that people get asked to do that they don't believe in. They use the process to say, "I'd love to help you, but we'll never get it by Howard."

> There's an awful lot of fights where the liberals will vote no if they really have to, but you've got to have a Metzenbaum whose willing to let Dole [then majority leader] know that if he brings it up, he's willing to tie up the place for five days, screw up the week's schedule, offer twenty-nine amendments. You've got to have him.

Indeed, by the 99th Congress, the Metzenbaum clearance process was so institutionalized that, on the form used by Senate Democrats to clear legislation for floor action, there were boxes for the floor leader, the relevant committee leader, and Howard Metzenbaum.

Metzenbaum employs a similar approach in the committees on which he is a member. As one of his aides observed, "There are very few issues that come out of any of the committees that we sit on that we do not have some impact on, or slow down, or speed up." Another staffer commented on Metzenbaum's tactics in the Judiciary Committee during the Thurmond chairmanship.

He doesn't want to let any bill out of committee that he is not comfortable and familiar with, if at all possible. I take it upon myself to become familiar with every bill on the agenda every week. I say to him every week, "These are OK and these are not."

I asked the staffer about the time investment necessary to maintain that level of activity.

It's not that hard. There are only about ten bills on the agenda and they are the same bills week after week. Look at S.37, Hatch's bill on busing. You don't have to spend ten minutes on that to realize it's probably unconstitutional, to realize you're opposed. The legislative veto: Metzenbaum's against it. All I have to say is S.1145 is the legislative veto bill and he says, "OK, I'm against it," because it's been around.

It's a lot easier to make a quick decision that you're against a bill than a quick decision that you're for a bill. Once you get a problem, you say no. Any bill I say is OK, I've spent a fair amount of time looking at it. . . . It's not that hard to have a sense of whether each bill on the agenda is bad.

During the Thurmond chairmanship, Metzenbaum's Judiciary Committee staff carefully monitored all legislation considered by the committee. Whereas other members tended to focus on those issues most relevant to their constituency and policy interests, Metzenbaum was active across the board. And on Judiciary Committee issues that were anathema to the liberal Democratic agenda, Metzenbaum was more than willing to take the lead in obstructionism, both in committee and on the floor. He did not employ dilatory tactics on all bills he opposed, but when Metzenbaum's preferences were intense, committee conservatives were sensitive to the possibility of such tactics. Indeed, Metzenbaum has been appropriately described as "the Democratic Gatekeeper."[7]

The presence of Howard Metzenbaum on the Judiciary Committee is important for understanding the relatively cooperative nature of the Thurmond-Biden relationship. On criminal law issues, the two full committee leaders were able to cooperate by strategically selecting the issues on which to legislate. A similar approach was not feasible on controversial matters falling in other areas of the panel's jurisdiction, however. On these items, Biden had three general leadership strategies from which to select. First, he could take the lead in opposing the substance of conservative initiatives by offering amendments and mobilizing public opinion. Second, Biden could take the

lead in employing a range of dilatory tactics to block committee consideration. Or, third, he simply could defer to other members of the panel on both
substance and procedure. As ranking minority member, Biden's strategic
dilemma was to select the approach or combination of approaches that would
best allow him to achieve his goals.

Taking the lead in opposing the substance of conservative initiatives on
the Judiciary Committee would have generated further publicity for Biden,
but publicity that would have associated him more closely with committee
issues. As a potential presidential candidate, there was little value to position-
taking on many of these items: They tend to divide the national Democratic
party, as well as the country as a whole. Additionally, the Democratic contingent on the Judiciary Committee was heterogeneous, ranging from liberals
such as Edward Kennedy to more conservative Democrats such as Howell
Heflin, and mobilizing a cohesive Democratic opposition on the panel was
problematic. In short, Biden's career goals and the preference context combined to provide significant disincentives for policy leadership.

The second possibility was to actively engage in obstructionist tactics,
but such behavior by Biden would have severely damaged his working relationship with Strom Thurmond. A key aim of the chairman was to move bills
to the floor, and to the extent that Biden blocked legislation, cooperation at the
leadership level on a wide range of committee bills would have been undermined. And what was the political return to Biden from taking the lead in
obstructionism? Fellow Democrat Howard Metzenbaum had developed a legislative style that emphasized the systematic use of dilatory tactics to delay
legislation he opposed. In the absence of a strong Biden presence, Metzenbaum's clearance process would fulfill the function for committee Democrats.

As a result, there were incentives for Biden to adopt the third approach—
to defer extensively to other Democrats on the panel. On items not within the
jurisdiction of the Criminal Law Subcommittee, the ranking Democrat on the
relevant subcommittee generally took the lead on substance. And when obstructionist tactics were useful to committee Democrats, Howard Metzenbaum (and Edward Kennedy, to a lesser extent) generally took the lead on
procedure.

Three Republican staffers provided comments that aptly reflect the perceptions of participants in the process.

> Biden doesn't have to take a hard line because he's got Metzenbaum and
> Kennedy: The two of them are firebrands. A lot of the time they seem to
> be leading the fight, with Biden trailing behind. A lot of that serves
> Biden's interests. Biden can come across as a reasonable, moderate
> person, but he has two other guys who are willing to fight the battle for
> him.

[Biden] carefully hides behind Senator Metzenbaum, who objects to just about everything, which is their strategy at this moment. The more they object to everything, the better off they are in terms of taking over the leadership next year. Biden allows Metzenbaum to do that, uses him in a strategic sense.

Senator Metzenbaum is really the person to go to when you're trying to move something, to ask if he has a problem with it. You don't go to Senator Biden's people. You call his people, but it's the second or third call. He doesn't decide what gets held up. If he has Kennedy and Metzenbaum opposing something, he doesn't have to do anything because they'll do it all. He doesn't even have to be there. He doesn't have to waste his good feelings with the chairman by giving Thurmond a bad time because these two will do it in spades. So he just stays in the background.

Thus, Metzenbaum's legislative style facilitated cooperation between Thurmond and Biden. On items on which the preferences of the two full committee leaders precluded joint action, Biden was relatively inactive during committee deliberations, and Metzenbaum and Kennedy took the lead. Instead, Biden focused on criminal law issues, on which a degree of cooperation with Thurmond was feasible. On other portions of the jurisdiction, however, he deferred, and this deference enabled the two full committee leaders to have a relatively smooth working relationship in one of the most polarized committees in Congress.

Hatch, Kennedy, and the Labor Committee

The Labor Committee also has jurisdiction over issues that tap ideological cleavages. Republicans and Democrats tend to have basic philosophical differences on health policy, labor law, the minimum wage, and federal aid to education. As a result, the panel has been one of the most partisan committees in the Senate for many years.[8] Asked about changes in the Labor Committee agenda, Edward Kennedy responded in a manner that captures the partisanship inherent in the jurisdiction.

There has been an important shift in the public mood. The country has really made the decisions. The question is the instrument. On issues of basic fairness, the Republicans are now caught in the crosswind.

Orrin Hatch responded in similar terms to the same question.

We accomplished a lot, but it was difficult. The Democrats had their agenda, and we had ours. We didn't do very much in the labor area. That's hard because neither side wants to give very much. . . . We kept control by listening, and we outworked them.

Partisanship in the panel was reflected in and reinforced by the distribution of preferences. During the 99th Congress, Labor was clearly the most polarized of the four committees, with seven conservative Republicans; seven liberal Democrats; and two moderate to liberal Republican swing voters, Robert Stafford and Lowell Weicker. And when we consider the preferences of the two full committee leaders, Orrin Hatch and Edward Kennedy clearly represent opposite ends of the ideological spectrum.

Given the partisan character of Labor Committee politics, the information provided in table 4.1 is illuminating. On the Judiciary Committee, the Thurmond and Biden offices did not work together at the drafting level on most committee issues. Judiciary Committee legislation is often ideologically charged, and Thurmond and Biden have divergent political philosophies. But when we examine the Hatch-Kennedy relationship, these data are strikingly different. On half of the legislation included in the sample of Labor Committee bills, *both* Hatch and Kennedy had a concrete impact on the content of the draft brought into markup. Indeed, table 4.1 suggests a degree of collaboration at the leadership level that resembles what we found on Environment and Public Works, one of the most bipartisan committees in the Senate. Why did Hatch and Kennedy tend to work together in such a partisan jurisdiction? And how was this accomplished? Once again, the key to understanding Labor Committee politics is the panel's coalitional structure: When we add moderate Republican Robert Stafford and liberal Republican Lowell Weicker to the seven liberal Democrats, Kennedy had a working majority.

Hatch worked with Kennedy because he had no other choice. As chairman, he lacked the votes necessary to build coalitions solely around committee conservatives. He had to reach out to committee liberals, or constructive legislative action would have been impossible. Kennedy also had to work with Hatch. Although Democrats had an ideological majority in the committee, Hatch controlled the agenda and could block consideration of legislation that did not incorporate his preferences. Thus, the Labor Committee was characterized by a form of split control. Hatch had the upper hand at the agenda stage, while Kennedy had the advantage when matters were brought to a vote.

One result was intense partisan conflict. Senators and staff assistants routinely described the Labor Committee during these years as one of the most partisan panels in the Senate. But the fact that each leader had a comparative advantage at different points in the decision-making process generated a bargaining environment that was conducive to uneasy cooperation, and a degree of accommodation that was not present on most Judiciary Committee issues. As one Labor Committee aide said:

> [Hatch] can't be too confrontational. It wouldn't work. If things really got out of hand, the committee could conceivably grind to a halt, and that wouldn't reflect well on anybody. . . . Hatch has to work with Kennedy.

Hatch also emphasized the accommodation that often characterized legislative work during his chairmanship: "We had a very difficult set of parameters. I certainly couldn't dictate to the committee—I wouldn't have anyway. . . . We had to accommodate. It was a classic consensus committee."

For the most part, bills that emerged from the Labor Committee during these years were either very routine measures, or more controversial items that had been reduced to the lowest common denominator to allow compromise between Hatch and Kennedy. The distribution of preferences required something approaching a coalition of the whole before legislation could be marked up. As a result, the Hatch and Kennedy offices often worked together at the drafting stage of the committee process.

This process of accommodation and compromise varied by issue, but typically it was Hatch or one of the other conservative Republicans who approached Kennedy's office in an attempt to arrive at language that satisfied senators from both ends of the ideological spectrum. An aide to one of the conservative Republicans on the panel emphasized the importance of including Kennedy's office in the early work on committee legislation.

> If you think Kennedy is going to be unfriendly, you've got to deal with him because he's going to deliver most of the Democrats. . . . Sometimes that is simply a matter of drafting a bill and going to Mr. Kennedy and negotiating, cutting a deal with Kennedy, and then laying the deal on everybody else.

Collaboration between Hatch and Kennedy was particularly frequent on health legislation, for which there was no subcommittee layer. For example, during the 99th Congress, the Labor Committee considered legislation aimed at relaxing federal restrictions on the exportation of drugs not certified as safe for U.S. consumption by the Food and Drug Administration. Under existing law at that time, exporting pharmaceuticals that had not been approved for domestic sale was illegal. Drug companies responded by simply manufacturing their products in other countries, thereby circumventing U.S. regulations. As a result, there was considerable pressure from a number of sources, including the pharmaceutical industry, to relax the ban and reduce incentives to produce abroad. Hatch had introduced legislation in 1984 that would have removed the barrier outright, but his bill died in committee because of opposition from Kennedy and other liberals, who viewed such efforts as an attempt to allow American industry to dump hazardous drugs in the third world.

After the initial draft died in the 98th Congress, Hatch's office approached Kennedy staffers in an effort to find language acceptable to both senators. They were ultimately successful, and a compromise version was introduced in late 1985. An aide to Hatch for health policy described the process—a process that was typical for health bills during the Hatch chairmanship.

> We introduced the final version in October, 1985. We had introduced an early version and then made changes along the way trying to get Kennedy on board. The version that we put out for comment in the summer was structurally different from the bill we had put out the previous year. That was largely an attempt to deal with criticisms. We worked mainly with Kennedy's office to further refine the bill and finally got a bill in October that Senator Kennedy cosponsored. . . .

> There are some members of the committee that would have liked to have avoided some of the changes we made to accommodate Kennedy, but I think they realized the political necessity of it. We were in a position of pretty much being able to count on their support, no matter what we came up with, as long as the industry would accept it. . . . Our perception was that if Kennedy signed on, all the other Democrats would fall into line as well, with the exception of Metzenbaum.

In general, on the health side of the Labor Committee's jurisdiction, the process began with efforts by Hatch staffers to devise language that reflected the chairman's preferences. Out of necessity, they then negotiated with Kennedy's office, modifying the draft in order to bring Kennedy on board as a cosponsor. The compromise was then introduced as a Hatch-Kennedy bill, and committee deliberations became relatively consensual. The underlying issue may have been controversial, but political dynamics on the panel required a broad-based consensus, or the committee was incapable of action.

Conclusion

Structure matters for understanding interactions between chairs and ranking minority members because it influences the importance of their relationship to committee policy-making. On decentralized panels such as Judiciary and Labor, subcommittee leaders usually take the lead in the crucial early stages of the committee process, and the full committee chair and ranking minority member tend to play secondary, albeit important, roles. Thus, a breakdown in relations between the two full committee leaders does not necessarily preclude all constructive action. On more centralized panels such as Commerce and Environment and Public Works, however, a cooperative working relationship between the chair and ranking minority member is essential. Most of the staff resources and agenda prerogatives are controlled by the two full committee leaders, and the locus of legislative action is similarly at the full committee level. A breakdown in relations between Danforth and Hollings or Stafford and Bentsen would have transformed decision-making practices on their panels. Conflict between Thurmond and Biden or Hatch and Kennedy, while of consequence, was more easily assimilated.

The preference context, in conjunction with each leader's individual policy preferences, is crucial for understanding relations between committee chairs and ranking minority members. Commerce and Environment and Public Works were consensual committees, and the leaders of these panels had similar preferences on committee issues. Under such conditions, cooperation is the natural order of things. Judiciary and Labor were polarized, however, and chairs and ranking minority members regularly confronted one another from opposite ends of the ideological spectrum. On Judiciary and Labor, conflict was the natural order of things.

Legislative decision making is almost always collective decision making, however, and even in the presence of significant conflict, there can be incentives for a degree of cooperation. On the Judiciary Committee, Joseph Biden employed two tactics to maintain a cooperative working relationship with Strom Thurmond. First, the distribution of preferences in the criminal law area was more conducive to compromise than were other portions of the jurisdiction, and, as a result, Biden chose to focus his legislative efforts on criminal law. Second, the Democratic contingent on Judiciary included Howard Metzenbaum and Edward Kennedy—who were more than willing to employ a range of dilatory tactics to block conservative bills—so Biden did not have to antagonize Thurmond by taking the lead in obstructionism. On the Labor Committee, a degree of cooperation between Hatch and Kennedy, although difficult to achieve, was usually a prerequisite for committee action. Hatch controlled the agenda and Kennedy had the votes. They had to work together.

The personal policy preferences of committee chairs and ranking minority members obviously are important for understanding interactions at the leadership level. A panel can have a relatively consensual distribution of preferences, but if the policy preferences of the chair and ranking minority member diverge significantly, conflict is likely. Similarly, on more polarized committees, interactions at the leadership level may tend toward cooperation if the chair and ranking minority member are in agreement on policy. For instance, if Robert Stafford had opted to chair Labor rather than Environment and Public Works, his interactions with Edward Kennedy would have been very different from the Hatch-Kennedy relationship.

Thus, the preference context is crucial for understanding how two full committee leaders interact, but it must be considered in conjunction with the individual policy preferences of the chair and ranking minority member. Other individual characteristics were relevant—for example, Lloyd Bentsen's intention to give up the ranking position on Environment and Public Works and Joseph Biden's presidential aspirations. But, for the most part, the ideological distance between two full committee leaders, conditioned by the distribution of preferences in committee, is central for understanding relations at the leadership level.

Notes

1. However, Alan Simpson and other conservative westerners on the panel often differed with the majority coalition on environmental policy.

2. Mayhew 1974, 27.

3. For a discussion of drafting behavior in Senate committees, see Evans 1989. Consult Hall 1987 for an analysis of drafting behavior in the House Education and Labor Committee.

4. For a description of the Muskie-Stafford relationship, see Asbell 1978.

5. Cohodas 1983b, 2423.

6. Cohodas 1983a, 1559.

7. Calmes 1987a.

8. For example, see Fenno 1973 and Price 1972.

CHAPTER 5

Anticipating the Floor

The emphasis so far has been on the way committee chairs and ranking minority members interact with other panel members. Congressional committees, however, are not islands of decision making. To become law, policy initiatives must be considered and approved at a succession of stages in the legislative process—the Senate floor, the House committee of jurisdiction, the House floor, conference committee, and the executive branch. Indeed, policy-making in the federal government is best analyzed as a sequence of interdependent decision-making arenas.[1] Actions taken during earlier stages set many of the boundaries for decision making at succeeding points in the sequence, and behavior at the beginning of the legislative process is often conditioned by expectations about what will happen further down the line. For instance, the alternatives considered during floor debate in the Senate are usually generated during committee deliberations, and, conversely, committee members often anticipate the mood of the full chamber during the markup stage of the process.

The purpose of this chapter is to explore the extent to which committee leaders anticipate the preferences of senators not on the panel and make concrete adjustments in legislation in committee to facilitate its passage on the Senate floor. Such strategic behavior on the part of committee chairs and ranking minority members is referred to as *anticipated reactions.*[2]

When I use the term anticipated reactions—also referred to as *prior accommodation* and *greasing the skids*—I am not referring to anticipatory behavior alone. Rather, the strategy of anticipated reactions is anticipatory behavior culminating in some concrete change in the actual content of a committee's bill. Thus, anticipated reactions is a mode through which power is exerted during the committee stage of the legislative process, but the actors exerting power are *non*–committee members. The strategic behavior of committee leaders provides the vehicle through which political actors not on the panel influence committee action.

The strategy of anticipated reactions was illustrated well by Judiciary Committee deliberations in 1985 on a joint resolution proposing a constitutional amendment to balance the federal budget. A key aide to Orrin Hatch recalled the extent to which backers of the measure took into account the mood of the full Senate during the committee stage of the process.

> I have vote counts on a quarterly basis, on a monthly basis, on how we think the floor is going on about four or five different proposals going back months. In the long run, it was the determining factor in what amendment came out of committee, and the form it was in.

The original draft of the bill was very similar to legislation passed by the Senate in 1982, and the Reagan administration was strongly in support. Although this first version certainly had the votes in committee, it stood almost no chance on the floor. Hatch's staffer continued.

> Once we got into the committee debate, it became apparent that on the floor, we were floating in the sixty-two to sixty-three area and you've got to have sixty-seven on a constitutional amendment.

The strategic reaction of committee leaders was to modify their bill to increase the probability of passage by the full Senate—that is, to employ the strategy of anticipated reactions. More concretely, they sought to bring on board one or two Judiciary Committee liberals to broaden their base of support. The aide explained:

> We saw it as very important to pick up a key liberal, someone who could bring in an extra five votes or so. The obvious target was [Paul] Simon, who, in his election campaign, endorsed the balanced budget concept. But he couldn't buy [the original measure] because of its link to GNP, so we began to tinker around.

This "tinkering" took the form of negotiations between Orrin Hatch and Paul Simon, and the result was a stripped-down version of the original bill, which was then reported to the floor with liberal support. Thurmond and Hatch opted for the stripped-down version because they believed it had better prospects on the Senate floor. Indeed, the legislation eventually garnered sixty-six votes, just one short of the number needed for passage. Although Simon was a member of the Judiciary Committee, he was not brought into the game to get the bill out of committee: Conservative senators had the votes in committee for a stronger bill. Rather, Simon was included because of political conditions in the full Senate.

Although congressional observers have long recognized that an important reason committees seldom lose on the floor is their tendency to anticipate and address the concerns of the full chamber, we know very little about the strategy of anticipated reactions and its role in legislative leadership.[3] For instance, how often do chairs and ranking minority members grease the skids? What factors influence whether or not a leader responds to potential conflict on the floor by making changes during the committee stage of the process? And, most important, how do the answers to these questions vary across different leaders, different committees, and different issues?

Why Grease the Skids?

By definition, committee leaders give something up when they employ the strategy of anticipated reactions. Legislation they send to the floor differs from what they would have recommended in the absence of expected opposition. What, then, do committee chairs and ranking minority members gain from greasing the skids? Why not report a bill that reflects their policy preferences and, if opposition arises, just fight it out on the Senate floor?

First, and most important, committee leaders try to accommodate potential opposition early on in the process because controversial measures are difficult to schedule for floor consideration. Second, concessions made in committee may enable a leader to avoid more extensive modifications at later stages in the process.

Scheduling on the Floor

Because of the work load, senators prefer to pass legislation on the floor by unanimous consent if at all possible.[4] A party leader, committee leader, or primary sponsor of a bill typically asks if there is any objection to passage. If no senator objects, the legislation is quickly passed by the Senate without debate or a formal vote. On items of low to moderate salience, the leadership will place great emphasis on achieving a consensus on substance so that the legislation can be passed quickly by unanimous consent. Floor time is scarce, particularly toward the end of a session, and party leaders are unwilling to allocate large blocks of time to anything but major legislation. Unanimous consent agreements increase the efficiency of the institution, but they also maximize the leverage of individual senators. On minor bills—and most bills considered in the Senate are relatively minor—opposition from just one senator may preclude floor action.

Individual senators can also have a great deal of leverage over whether more salient pieces of legislation are scheduled for floor debate. If unanimity on the substance of a bill is not feasible, members usually attempt to arrive at an agreement that places restrictions on the process of floor deliberations. These restrictions are called *time agreements,* and they are a form of unanimous consent agreement. But instead of consenting to pass a bill outright, senators agree to certain restrictions on how it is to be considered on the floor, such as which amendments can be offered and how much time will be allocated to debate.

Time agreements are often complex. For instance, recall from chapter 4 the Labor Committee's legislation dealing with the exportation of drugs not approved by the Food and Drug Administration for domestic consumption. Howard Metzenbaum opposed the measure, and committee leaders feared delaying tactics by the Ohio Democrat. But during deliberations in the full Senate, a time agreement was devised that was acceptable to all senators, including Metzenbaum. Assistant Republican Leader Alan Simpson of Wyoming announced the contents of the time agreement on the Senate floor.[5]

> I further ask unanimous consent that the Senate resume consideration of the pending business, S.1848 [the drug export bill] at 1 P.M. on Monday; that any roll call votes ordered with respect to amendments or motions thereto, to S.1848, on Monday be postponed until an undetermined time on Tuesday, May 13. . . . I ask unanimous consent that final passage occur on S.1848, no later than 1 P.M. on Wednesday, May 14. . . . Finally, I ask unanimous consent that the following amendments be the only amendments. . . .

Simpson then listed five senators who would be allowed to introduce amendments, and described which amendments each of them could offer. Other members of the Senate could not offer amendments, and only those amendments listed were permissible.[6] If a single senator had objected, the agreement would have had no force.

In short, if a consensus on the substance of a bill is not feasible, party leaders place great emphasis on securing a time agreement, that is, on achieving a consensus on the *process* of consideration. On some more critical pieces of legislation—the reauthorization of Superfund, for example—party leaders will schedule floor action without a time agreement, but there is almost always significant pressure to achieve prior consensus on how long debate may last. The first question aides to the majority leader ask when scheduling a bill for the floor is "How much time will it take?" As one of Hollings's staffers on the Commerce Committee said:

> If you can avoid taking up floor time, you have a much greater chance of getting a bill through. If you can bring it up by unanimous consent and not have a lot of votes, then it's much more likely to be called up than a bill where you can't get a time agreement and it's uncertain how much floor time the bill would require.

Thus, a single senator objecting to a time agreement can preclude floor consideration of even relatively important measures.

Members of the Senate often signal their objection to a measure by placing a "hold" on it.[7] The Senate hold is an informal practice by which an individual senator can delay floor action on a piece of legislation. Senators put a hold on a bill by notifying their party leader, usually at the staff level. The leadership then informs the measure's primary sponsors. Traditionally, it has not been the practice for party leaders to inform a bill's backers about the source of a hold, and while most members and staff say they can usually find out who is responsible, others comment that securing the information can be difficult.

Little has been written about the practice of the Senate hold, but participants in the process cite it as an important factor in what some congressional observers call "the new obstructionism."[8] According to Representative Edward R. Madigan of Illinois, who confronts Senate procedure during conference committee deliberations:

> I don't think there is such a thing as minority status in the U.S. Senate. . . . The ability of a senator to put a hold on a bill is power that exceeds the power of committee chairmen in the House.[9]

An aide to Republicans on the Environment and Public Works Committee described the consequences of the hold.

> Very little comes to the floor if you don't have a consensus on it ahead of time. . . . It's the age-old use of the hold. A hold on a bill was originally meant to mean: "I don't want this brought up because I'm not going to be in town." Now if a senator has a hold on a bill and it's toward the end of a congress, kaboom: It's dead—not a prayer.

The impact of a hold varies. Placing a hold on a bill may preclude further consideration. A hold may force a bill's backers to work out a compromise with the "holder." Or a hold may simply be ignored altogether. Indeed, the policy-making consequences of a hold depend on the nature of the objection, the importance of the measure, and the relevance of the bill to the goals of party leaders. However, because of the institutional need to conserve floor time, the Senate tends to back away from legislation with holds, and merely placing a hold on a bill is often sufficient to block floor action.

One reason for the potency of holds in the Senate is that they are often interpreted as filibuster threats. A senior aide to Edward Kennedy for Judiciary Committee issues explained.

> People misunderstand [holds]. They think [you just] write in and say, "I want to put a hold on a bill." You don't have any more of a hold on a bill than [the extent to which] you're willing to stand there and say, "I'm here and I'm going to start talking."

But holds are an important part of the legislative process in the Senate precisely because so many members are willing to stand there and start talking. Consider the case of Howard Metzenbaum. In the last chapter, we discussed the "Metzenbaum clearance process" and its consequences for Joseph Biden's leadership style in the Judiciary Committee, but Metzenbaum's primary impact is on the Senate floor. On a broad cross-section of legislation, if Metzenbaum is in opposition or, perhaps, is simply unfamiliar with a measure, he places a hold or objects to the request to pass it by unanimous consent. The reach of Metzenbaum's clearance process extends well beyond the occasions when he actually engages in extended debate. Over the years, he has been willing to make full and regular use of his procedural prerogatives as a member of the Senate, and his filibuster threats are viewed as credible. He does not have to filibuster much because the mere threat of a Metzenbaum filibuster is usually enough leverage to obtain substantive concessions. As Metzenbaum said, "I don't filibuster very often. I don't have to."

During the 99th Congress, Metzenbaum's clearance process influenced committee policy-making in a wide range of issue areas. At the very least, he often complicated floor deliberations. And on many bills, the prospect of a Metzenbaum hold resulted in substantive adjustments aimed at securing his support. In 1985, for example, five staffers on the Commerce Committee—of which Metzenbaum is not a member—told me that they were having what they referred to as "Metzenbaum problems": Metzenbaum had placed a hold on their legislation, or his office had voiced objections and staffers were expecting a hold. As a result, they were working closely with Metzenbaum aides to dampen the intensity of his opposition.

Howard Metzenbaum is an extreme case, but he reflects an institutional trend toward increased obstructionist tactics by individual senators on a much broader range of issues than was the case twenty, or even ten, years ago.[10] Senior members from both parties speak of the new obstructionism. Asked if he has witnessed a rise in dilatory tactics since being elected to the Senate in 1974, Jake Garn responded:

> Since I first came here, it's more common for a single senator to hold things up due to parochial issues. It used to be the great issues of the day. Now it's three bites out of the apple—filibuster the motion to proceed, the bill, and then there's the post-cloture filibuster.

Ernest Hollings voiced similar concerns.

There's been an increase in obstructionism. These bad habits about parliamentary procedure, they started with Allen [former Senator James Allen of Alabama]. A state legislature wouldn't put up with that, but this sanctified place, well, we just looked around and said, "Oh, we've got to let him do it." . . . The Senate rules are lousy. Anything can be done with Senate procedure. Anything.

This increased willingness among members of the Senate to engage in obstructionism has provided further incentives for committee leaders to both anticipate the reactions of potential opponents and make adjustments in their legislation early on in the process. When committee chairs and ranking minority members anticipate the mood of the floor and modify their bill to diminish opposition, they increase the probability that the majority leader will schedule their measure for floor consideration. Even when the number of opposing senators is small (or perhaps just Howard Metzenbaum), the alternative to greasing the skids may be no bill at all.

Forestalling Floor Amendments

Modifications made in committee may also preclude more extensive changes on the floor. Committee leaders may expect opposition on the floor if they report out the language they most prefer. Under these conditions, prior accommodation is a rational strategy for committee leaders if adjusting the legislation in committee reduces the intensity of opposition to the point where it no longer is worth the trouble for opponents to actively work against the bill on the Senate floor. The committee does not have to cave in completely: just enough so that the benefits to the opposing coalition derived from further modification do not exceed the costs of devising additional amendments, marketing them to other senators, and possibly generating ill will with sponsors of the legislation. Thus, when a committee leader makes incremental adjustments in a bill to preclude floor amendments, the changes do not necessarily indicate surrender. The alternative might be more drastic changes during the amendment process on the Senate floor.

Greasing the skids also reduces uncertainty. Particularly on complex and controversial items, few members can predict with precision how a piece of legislation will look when it emerges from a protracted floor struggle. Considering a bill on the floor by unanimous consent without debate, or subject to a time agreement restricting amendment, reduces the potential that a committee's bill will unravel in the full Senate. By incorporating the amendments of opponents during the committee process rather than waiting for floor consideration, a committee leader can better control the scope and direction of floor action.

Prior accommodation by committee leaders may also increase the speed with which a bill moves through the process. The longer an item is under active consideration, the greater the chance that preferences will change, perhaps generating demands for further modifications in a committee's legislation. Robert Stafford's efforts to reauthorize the National Endowment for the Arts (NEA) in 1985 illustrate the importance of speed and timing. The reauthorization seems relatively minor, but in recent years it has generated some controversy about where art ends and pornography begins. Before Stafford could bring his bill to the floor, some House members charged that the NEA had been funding obscene art. As an aide to Stafford recalled:

> Some congressmen claimed the Arts Endowment had funded pornographic poetry. The 700 Club was planning some kind of a presentation, and if we didn't move the bill, these offices were going to be inundated with phone calls from constituents, and there would be all sorts of obscenity amendments.

Stafford wanted to move the bill quickly, but knew he would have to spend a few hours waiting on the floor for the right opportunity. The aide described Stafford's predicament.

> Stafford is too busy to spend three hours on the floor, but as one staffer put it: "It's your choice—the thought of three months of hearings on pornographic poetry, or three hours on the floor. Do you really want to debate the issue of pornographic poetry on the Senate floor?"

Stafford decided that a few hours of his time was a small price to pay for passing the bill quickly, and, as it turned out, he did spend considerable time on the floor waiting to get the measure passed. And as the staffer recalled, "an hour after he finished, the phones started ringing off the wall."

In short, when committee leaders make adjustments to facilitate success at subsequent stages in the legislative process, there is a cost: The leader would prefer a stronger bill. Still, the strategy of anticipated reactions can generate countervailing benefits in terms of more timely consideration by the full chamber, fewer amendments on the Senate floor, and reduced uncertainty.

Understanding Anticipated Reactions

As was the case with other aspects of legislative leadership behavior, contextual factors tell us much about why some leaders grease the skids for floor action, while other leaders do not. Structural factors are relevant because legislative responsibilities in general are much more widely shared on decentralized panels like Judiciary and Labor than they are on more centralized committees like Commerce and Environment and Public Works. On centralized panels, important decisions about legislative strategy tend to be made by full committee leaders. On more decentralized panels, however, other committee members are often responsible. Thus, the anticipatory behavior of Danforth, Hollings, Stafford, and Bentsen is of particular interest for understanding leadership and policy-making in their committees. The extent to which Thurmond, Biden, Hatch, and Kennedy employed the strategy of anticipated reactions is somewhat less integral to policy-making in Judiciary and Labor, where other senators often took the lead.

But the central factor for understanding the extent to which committee chairs and ranking minority members grease the skids for floor action is the nature of the preference context on committee issues (both in committee and in the full Senate). More concretely, we need to consider (1) the presence or absence of controversy, (2) the representativeness of the committee relative to the full Senate, (3) whether or not there exists a jurisdictional overlap with another Senate committee, (4) the extent to which differences are negotiable, (5) the expenditure level, and (6) whether or not opposition on the floor has solidified at the time of committee action. Through their impact on the intensity and distribution of preferences in committee and on the floor, these variables affect the political value of anticipated reactions.

First, some degree of *conflict* is clearly a necessary condition for anticipated reactions to be a useful leadership strategy. If member preferences are very similar, then there is simply no need to make adjustments to facilitate success in the full chamber.[11]

In addition, the more *unrepresentative* on an issue a committee's membership is of the Senate as a whole, the greater the incentives to adjust the legislation in committee to mitigate floor problems. The extent to which the distribution of preferences in committee diverges from preferences in the full Senate varies from panel to panel and from issue to issue, but most committees have jurisdiction over certain items about which committee members feel differently, or care more, than do other senators.[12] Subject to certain constraints, senators select their own committee assignments. As a result, members from farming states are well represented on the Agriculture Committee, and the Energy and Natural Resources Committee has long drawn the interest of senators from oil states. On Environment and Public Works, panel members are significantly unrepresentative of the full chamber on the environmental side of the jurisdiction. In instances such as these, there may be incentives for committee leaders to strategically incorporate the views of non–committee members well before they take their bill to the floor.

The presence of a *jurisdictional overlap* also has consequences for the preference context. Senators are highly territorial when it comes to matters of jurisdiction, and even relatively noncontroversial issues can become politically charged if one committee perceives that another is moving in on its prerogatives. Additionally, members of each panel have revealed through their committee and subcommittee assignment selections that the issue is of particular relevance to their interests. The presence of a jurisdictional overlap increases the likelihood that opposition to a panel's bill will emerge from senators off the committee because of disagreements over turf and policy, generating incentives to coordinate action with the other panel before legislation is brought to the floor.

We also need to consider the extent to which *differences* on an issue are *negotiable*. If opinion is polarized and there exists no politically relevant middle ground, the only way to head off anticipated floor difficulties is to surrender. Consequentially, greasing the skids is not a viable leadership strategy if the conflict expected to arise on the floor is not amenable to compromise. There often is a lack of negotiable differences on Judiciary Committee issues, for example, decreasing the utility of anticipated reactions for Strom Thurmond and Joseph Biden.

A bill's *expenditure level* can influence the preference context and, through it, the political value of anticipated reactions as a leadership strategy. Because of the size of the budget deficit and the ensuing emphasis on holding down costs, in recent years the most significant constraints on the discretion of the various Senate standing committees have often been fiscal. One of Orrin Hatch's aides on health policy issues emphasized the consequences of the fiscal environment for committee activity.

> During the 98th Congress [1983–84], budgetary pressure was from the administration. During the 99th, it's the Congress. . . . This is the first year when the budget has been so specific. Before, the budget was very much a broad paintbrush sort of thing. . . . [N]ow if you read the report on the Budget Committee's budget . . . , it's far more specific than it's ever been before. Now we're getting down to report language, not statute. They're being very directive in their policy.

Jake Garn of Utah, chairman of the Banking Committee during the years of Republican control, echoed these comments.

> The Budget Committee has created more problems than it's solved. . . . Language in the budget resolution is more restrictive—how many housing units, how many tanks, how many airplanes—things that used to be left to the authorizing committees.

Budgetary considerations were paramount throughout the 1980s, but they were particularly pronounced during the 99th Congress. Indeed, it was in

1985 that Congress passed the Gramm-Rudman-Hollings Act, which mandated across-the-board cuts in federal spending unless the deficit was slashed by a specified amount.

In general, the higher the expenditure level on an authorization bill, the more intensely it will be scrutinized by members of the Budget and Appropriations Committees. Pressure to hold down funding levels is pervasive, but fiscal constraints are particularly binding on what are perceived to be high-ticket items. In the fiscal environment of the 1980s and 1990s, if senators not on the authorizing committee view a bill as a budget buster, it is almost a certainty that the legislation will be opened up on the floor of the Senate. As a result, on larger reauthorizations, it is standard operating procedure for committee leaders to coordinate their actions with the Budget Committee and the relevant Appropriations subcommittee. Such coordination is a form of anticipated reactions. And as funding levels rise, so does the likelihood of anticipatory behavior by the chair and ranking minority member.

In evaluating the political utility of anticipated reactions, we must also consider the *clarity of the opposition:* that is, the extent to which the preferences of potential floor opponents have coalesced around concrete alternatives to provisions in the committee bill. If floor opposition is diffuse and inchoate at the time of committee action, the chair and ranking minority member may lack the information necessary to make adjustments that will preclude opposition at later stages in the process. For instance, the political consequences of a measure may be unclear, and potential opponents may lack the information necessary to formulate concrete demands until after the committee has acted. In addition, opponents off the committee may decide to hold their cards close and strategically withhold information about their views in order to obtain a better deal from committee leaders. This tactic decreases the amount of information available to the chair and ranking minority member, thereby increasing the costs of greasing the skids for floor consideration.

Individual Characteristics

Certain individual characteristics of the eight senators also may affect the political utility of anticipated reactions as a leadership strategy. The importance of various aspects of the preference context in committee and on the floor has already been emphasized, but the personal policy preferences of the chair and ranking minority member also have an independent impact on the value of anticipatory behavior vis-a-vis the full Senate.

Consider the location of a leader's preferences relative to the preference context in committee and on the floor. By definition, engaging in anticipated reactions results in a committee bill that differs from the legislation the panel would have sent to the floor had the strategy not been employed. This adjustment will either move the bill toward or away from a committee leader's most preferred outcome. If greasing the skids moves the bill toward a committee leader's views, the leader benefits in two ways: The probability of trouble on the floor falls *and* the legislation is actually closer to the leader's policy preferences. The strategy of anticipated reactions will be particularly useful in such a situation because considering the mood of the floor actually strengthens the leader's bargaining leverage in committee.

Now consider the opposite case: Greasing the skids moves a piece of legislation further away from a committee leader's most preferred outcome. Here, the utility of anticipated reactions as a leadership strategy will depend on how rapidly the package loses value as it moves away from the leader's preferred outcome, which in turn will depend on whether the leader's legislative efforts primarily are driven by a desire to take positions or by a desire to claim credit.[13] Simply put, credit claiming resonates well with anticipated reactions, while position taking often does not.

Committee leaders like to claim credit for their legislative accomplishments. It is difficult, however, for a chair or ranking minority member to claim credit for a proposal that died on the Senate floor. As a result, legislators interested in claiming credit tend to place great emphasis on winning, and they are willing to make changes to increase the probability of passage.[14] Movement away from their most preferred outcome will lower the value they place on a package, but something is still preferred to nothing. Thus, when a chair or ranking minority member is primarily motivated by the desire to claim credit, anticipated reactions is likely to be a useful leadership tactic.

But legislative work also may be a form of position taking. A member can take a firm stand against gun control in a speech for the folks back home, but introducing and pushing legislation in committee to relax restrictions on the sale of handguns will associate the member more closely with that position. Particularly in the Senate, legislative efforts can generate press, and press generates visibility. With position taking, however, the primary goal is to associate oneself with a particular policy alternative. As a result, movement away from a position taker's most preferred position results in a dramatic decrease in the value of the package to the position taker. A committee leader primarily motivated by position taking will place greater emphasis on the purity of the policy message delivered than on the prospects for winning on the floor.[15] And under these conditions, anticipated reactions will not be a useful leadership tactic.

Danforth, Hollings, and the Commerce Committee

As we have seen, because of factors such as structural centralization and relatively low levels of preference intensity on committee issues, both John

Danforth and Ernest Hollings were major players on a wide range of Commerce Committee bills. What role did the mood of the parent chamber play in shaping their leadership strategies?

A cursory consideration of the preference context on most Commerce Committee issues suggests that anticipated reactions will not be an important leadership tactic. Most committee bills are relatively routine reauthorizations that generate little controversy, and on such items, there typically are few floor problems to anticipate and accommodate away. A closer look at the panel, however, reveals very clearly that on many committee bills Danforth and Hollings *did* anticipate floor problems during the course of committee action. Three reasons explain why.

First, although the vast majority of Commerce Committee bills are relatively consensual, on many, one or two senators off the panel may have problems with certain provisions. And because of current practices regarding the hold and other obstructionist tactics, opposition from just a few members is often sufficient to keep a bill from being scheduled for floor consideration, particularly on items that are of low to moderate salience, as are most Commerce Committee measures. Thus, the Senate hold magnifies the impact of even small degrees of dissension, and, as a result, anticipating and incorporating the preferences of senators not on the committee is often an important leadership tactic on even relatively noncontroversial items.

Second, the Commerce Committee considers a few reauthorizations with extremely high funding levels. In 1985, for example, the panel considered legislation that would have authorized almost $8 billion for the National Aeronautics and Space Administration. Because of the extreme complexity of the agency's programs, as well as its broad base of support in Congress, few members paid much attention to the substance of the measure (things changed after the Challenger disaster the following year). But the sheer size of the authorization forced staffers for Danforth and Hollings to work closely with non–committee members from the very beginning. An aide described the process.

> Knowing the mood of the Senate and what was going to occur on the floor was a constraint. We have a pragmatic view of the world because this is a big program. . . . Before we went through the sessions of cutting and realigning, before we went to the members, we sat down with the staff of the Appropriations Subcommittee on HUD and Independent Agencies and gave them an idea of what we were going to propose and got an idea of what the picture was like on that subcommittee. . . .

> We worked very closely with the Budget Committee [to] make sure Domenici didn't stand up on the floor and say it was a violation of Senate

> Budget Committee assumptions. . . . If we don't have fifty-one votes on
> the floor, we aren't going to the floor. We'll change the bill to get fifty-
> one votes.

Because of fiscal constraints, Danforth and his staff were forced to have "a
pragmatic view of the world" on most of the reauthorizations in the panel's
jurisdiction. And the larger the agency, the greater the importance that the
preferences of key actors on the Appropriations and Budget committees be
considered and incorporated into the Commerce Committee's draft.

A third reason for floor trouble on Commerce Committee bills is that the
panel does consider a few salient issues that generate significant controversy
in committee and on the floor. In 1985, for example, the panel considered
legislation to reform the nation's product liability laws—a bill that ranking
Democrat Ernest Hollings referred to as "the worst piece of legislation I've
seen in my twenty years in the Senate." Proponents of the measure expected,
and received, intense opposition from Hollings at all stages of the legislative
process.

Another item generating significant conflict during the 99th Congress
was legislation to implement the sale of Conrail to Norfolk Southern Railroad.
A majority of the Senate supported the deal, but their support was relatively
lukewarm, while opponents to the legislation were intense in their views.
Given the nature of floor procedure, Danforth and Hollings recognized that
dilatory tactics might kill the bill, or at least slow passage enough to preclude
full consideration by the House before the end of the 99th Congress. In
contrast to the reauthorization of NASA, however, committee leaders did not
modify the bill in committee in any significant way to reduce the intensity of
opposition in the full chamber. A staffer who worked on the legislation explained why.

> We tried to persuade senators to support the bill, but there were very few
> changes. It was more a question of arguing the merits. Either you're for
> the bill or you're against it, and there's not much you can do to the bill
> itself that's going to change that. Metzenbaum thinks it shouldn't be sold
> at this time, and certainly not for $1.2 billion. The only way to change
> him is to [raise the figure] so high that he can't refuse. Specter and Heinz
> fear layoffs in Pennsylvania, and nothing we can do in terms of an
> amendment will make that palatable. No matter how much labor protec-
> tion you put in there, there are going to be layoffs. That's the issue:
> Either you have the votes or you don't.

Thus, the bill was a take-it-or-leave-it item. There were few negotiable differences, so greasing the skids was not a viable leadership tactic.

The nature of Danforth's policy preferences on a measure was also relevant. Senators tend to join the Commerce Committee because it has jurisdiction over programs that affect the folks back home. Thus, it comes as no surprise that the chairman occasionally engaged in position taking. Recall that one Danforth initiative during the 99th Congress was stimulated by Carl Icahn's move to take over TWA, a major employer in Missouri, Danforth's home state. The Department of Justice and some members of the Senate viewed the measure as an undue intrusion into the marketplace, but Danforth did not attempt to adjust his bill to lower the intensity of opposition on the Senate floor. As one of his aides explained:

> In the back of our minds we knew we would have problems with pro-market types on the floor and in the Justice Department when we drafted the bill, but we sublimated those worries and said, "Let's just cross that bridge when we come to it." We had very limited options in committee. . . . We weren't really worried about the floor.

"We had very limited options in committee" is the key phrase. The legislation was an exercise in position taking. It was crucial that Danforth quickly associate himself with actions to control Icahn, and the probability of winning on the floor was a secondary consideration.

In general, Danforth made selective use of the strategy of anticipated reactions. Although preferences on most Commerce Committee bills were relatively consensual and few members were intensely interested, sticking points with one or two members often developed. Given the ease with which a single senator could derail the kinds of items considered by the committee, a small pocket of opposition was enough to provide incentives for prior accommodation. And given that so many of the panel's bills were reauthorizations, the fiscal climate of the 1980s severely limited the funds available for Commerce Committee programs. It would be inaccurate to argue, however, that the mood of the full chamber was a primary consideration on most Commerce Committee bills. On many, no floor problems were expected. On others, factors such as the goals of the chairman or the absence of negotiable differences undermined the value of anticipated reactions as a leadership tactic.

It may be that Danforth's ability to anticipate floor difficulties was hampered by his inexperience in the position of chairman. After all, greasing the skids requires information about the preferences of senators off the panel, and the quantity of information a committee leader has about member preferences on committee issues should increase with time. I found no evidence, however, that this aspect of Danforth's leadership behavior was affected by his lack of experience as chairman. Contextual factors more than countervailed.

Ernest Hollings

Of the four ranking minority members, it is most difficult to gauge the extent to which Ernest Hollings's leadership behavior was shaped by the mood of the full Senate. Danforth was primarily responsible for managing the panel's many reauthorizations, and he or his staff made most of the decisions about when to grease the skids for floor action. Hollings was involved when interested, but Danforth and the majority staff played the more significant role.

It is clear, however, that Hollings's leadership position on Appropriations influenced his approach to the Commerce Committee. In addition to being the ranking Democrat on Commerce, he was also ranking minority member on an Appropriations subcommittee with jurisdiction over many Commerce Committee programs. These dual leadership positions reinforced his clout on both panels, and his staffers on the Commerce Committee were better able to coordinate their actions with those of the appropriators. For the most part, however, Danforth was responsible for anticipating potential floor problems and making the substantive changes necessary to grease the skids and facilitate success in the full Senate.

Stafford, Bentsen, and the Environment
and Public Works Committee

On the Environment and Public Works Committee, anticipatory behavior vis-à-vis the floor was an integral component of leadership behavior. Indeed, observers of the panel often characterized its decision-making style as one of *preconsensus*. A staffer for Lloyd Bentsen explained.

> This place operates on a preconsensus basis. Everybody works very hard to develop a consensus in committee so that there aren't votes and so that we get it done and just keep the process moving. If Dole [then majority leader] hears there are going to be a lot of votes, he'll say, "Well, let's just wait, we don't have the floor time for this." . . . It's sort of what they teach us in law school: Don't ask a question for which you don't know the answer. Don't bring up legislation if you don't know people are going to agree with it.

I asked Stafford about the impact of the mood of the full Senate on policy-making in Environment and Public Works during his chairmanship.

> I wanted to have a consensus before going to the floor. By nature, on these issues you get much more done by reaching a consensus than with

confrontation. I had a policy and I made it very clear. I didn't believe in lost causes, just to make a statement.

Of the four panels under study, committee leaders on Environment and Public Works were by far the most likely to employ the strategy of anticipated reactions. On every major piece of legislation considered by the panel in the 99th Congress, expectations about the mood of the full Senate had a significant impact on the shape of the bill reported to the floor. Prior accommodation was the norm.

Like the Commerce Committee, Environment and Public Works is a relatively centralized panel, and the two full committee leaders are active on a wide range of committee bills. As a result, key decisions about when to grease the skids often were made by Stafford, Bentsen, and their aides on the committee staff. And the nature of the preference context on committee issues helps to explain why anticipatory behavior was so frequent.

Environment and Public Works regularly considers legislation that evokes the interest of a large number of senators, both in committee and on the floor, and preferences on committee bills are often intense. Decision making during the committee stage of the process tends to be consensual, but the full Senate is much less oriented toward the views of environmental groups than is the case within the panel. The unrepresentativeness of Environment and Public Works raises the prospect of significant conflict between the committee and the Senate as a whole, providing incentives for the chair and ranking minority member to grease the skids. According to committee Democrat Max Baucus: "We have agreement in committee, but because we are more environmentalist [than the Senate], our bills have problems. They don't come up until they're modified."

In addition, there are significant jurisdictional overlaps on many bills considered by Environment and Public Works. On the reauthorization of Superfund, for example, the Finance and Judiciary committees also have partial jurisdiction. Rivers and harbors legislation is sequentially referred to the Finance Committee. And the panel's jurisdiction over nuclear energy regulation is shared with the Energy and Natural Resources Committee. The presence of jurisdictional overlaps provides further incentives for the chair and ranking minority member on Environment and Public Works to consider and incorporate the preferences of non–committee members.

Conflict emerging on items considered by Environment and Public Works also tends to be amenable to compromise, which facilitates anticipated reactions. Differences are usually not over the question of "if," but "how much"—for example, how much money should be allocated for projects in a particular state, or how restrictive environmental regulation should be in a particular area. As a result, most of the disagreements that surface on Environment and Public Works Committee issues are negotiable, and greasing the skids is usually a feasible leadership strategy.

Relative to programs considered by the other three committees, the quantity of money required for the reauthorizations on Environment and Public Works is enormous. Indeed, during 1985 alone, the committee reported bills reauthorizing Superfund ($7.5 billion) and the Clean Water Act ($18 billion through 1994 for the sewage treatment program), legislation releasing to the states funds for highway construction ($12.75 billion), and a landmark omnibus water projects package (almost $12 billion).

Fiscal pressures were particularly apparent on the highways bill. Legislation authorizing funds for highway construction was the first program to affect spending considered in 1985, and there was tremendous pressure to hold costs down and keep the bill free of special interest add-ons. Authorizing money for interstate highway construction traditionally has been perfunctory, but during the 98th Congress the program became embroiled in controversy because of a plethora of proposed demonstration projects (the special interest add-ons), particularly a 2.5 billion dollar tunnel project near the district of then House Speaker Thomas P. "Tip" O'Neill, Jr.

The Environment and Public Works Committee marked up the highways bill in January, 1985. Fiscal constraints and budget politics permeated discussion during the meeting, and it was clear that major changes were made in anticipation of floor action. The markup began with an amendment offered by John Chafee of Rhode Island aimed at lowering the ceiling on spending to $500 million below the level for fiscal year 1985. After Chafee's amendment was accepted by a margin of fourteen to one, James Abdnor of South Dakota offered an amendment to strike from the bill all of the demonstration projects, and that proposal was accepted by voice vote. As a committee staffer who worked on the legislation recalled:

> The major issue was the demonstration projects. As soon as we put some in for our own members, we knew that we would hit the floor and there would be other requests. That's why they voted to take them out. That meant that no one would ask for anything because if our own members gave up their projects we were not about to entertain any from anybody else.

The very high expenditure levels involved in bills considered by Environment and Public Works tend to activate institutional pressure to hold spending down, providing incentives for committee leaders to consider the fiscal mood of the Senate and adjust for it in committee.

Thus, most aspects of the preference context are conducive to anticipated reactions on the Environment and Public Works Committee. These bills generate controversy; the panel is unrepresentative of the full Senate; there are significant jurisdictional overlaps; differences tend to be negotiable; and expenditure levels often are very high. But what about the clarity of the opposition? I have argued that it is problematic for committee leaders to grease the skids for floor action if the preferences of potential opponents have not coalesced around concrete alternatives. Environment and Public Works considers highly technical and complex issue areas, and there often is significant uncertainty about how underlying policy predispositions can best be implemented. In the presence of significant uncertainty about an issue, senators and their staff often take cues from members of the committee of jurisdiction. Indeed, participants in the process cite Environment and Public Works as one of the panels on which they lean heavily for information. Thus, preferences on committee issues often are not congealed until after the committee has acted, complicating efforts by panel leaders to anticipate and adjust for potential floor problems.

When floor problems were expected, but their form was unclear, one approach employed by Stafford and Bentsen was to leave things out: to streamline legislation in committee and move it as quickly as possible to the full Senate. This was the approach employed, for example, in the panel's reauthorization of Superfund in 1985. Superfund is highly complex, and committee leaders wanted to maximize the time available for floor debate. As a result, they moved a relatively stripped-down version through committee. An aide explained:

> When we were considering the bill in committee in 1985, we basically streamlined the bill more with an eye to getting it out of our committee with a minimum amount of discussion and debate so that we could see what kind of floor amendments would develop, and deal with them at the time of the floor.

The staffer noted that the process on Superfund was a variant of the concept of anticipated reactions.

> That's really the inverse of the process you suggest. We were not trying to shape the bill in some way to make it easier to pass, but just trying to hurry the process along because we knew the real arena would be on the floor. . . . To some extent it's anticipated reactions, but the way of doing it is not so much to shape legislation within the committee as to manage the process on the floor.

When the opposition was diffuse and lacking in clarity at the time of committee deliberations, committee leaders on Environment and Public Works still employed the strategy of anticipated reactions. They did not make concrete changes to increase the attractiveness of their legislation to the full Senate, however. Rather, they focused on streamlining legislation and reaching the floor as quickly as possible to maximize the time available for that stage of the legislative process. In short, on the Environment and Public Works Committee, the presence of significant uncertainty about potential opposition on the floor did not preclude anticipated reactions as a leadership tactic, but it occasionally influenced the way in which committee leaders greased the skids for floor action.

Lloyd Bentsen

The mood of the full Senate influenced the leadership behavior of ranking Democrat Lloyd Bentsen. As we have seen, the Stafford-Bentsen relationship is best characterized as a collaboration, although the chairman clearly took the lead in legislative strategy on most committee bills. Still, when an issue was important to Bentsen's constituents in Texas, Bentsen was the dominant player. And on these items, the ranking minority member clearly took into account the preferences of senators not on the Environment and Public Works Committee.

Efforts during the 99th Congress to reauthorize the Clean Water Act illustrate this point. Most of the controversy surrounding the bill concerned a politically popular sewage treatment grant program, which channeled $2.4 billion per year in federal money to local governments. As is often the case in the Senate, conflict arose over how to allocate the funds by state. Officials in Texas believed that their state had fared poorly under the allotment formula used in the previous authorization, and they worked through Bentsen's office to ensure that the new formula would increase their share of the pie. Because this part of the reauthorization was so important to Bentsen's state, his staff played a prominent role in devising the new formula. Also involved were aides to Robert Stafford and subcommittee chair John Chafee.

These staffers had to devise a formula that would benefit Texas, but also increase funding levels for a majority of senators in committee and in the full chamber. A Republican aide who closely observed the bill aptly summed up their dilemma.

Here's the political aspect. You had to meet the political criterion that Senator Bentsen get more money for Texas; you needed to make sure the thing would survive committee; you had to keep an eye on Kansas for Dole [then majority leader], Oregon for Hatfield and Packwood [chairs of the Appropriations and Finance Committees], and Utah for Garn [chair of an important subcommittee on Appropriations]. You needed to look out for the senior leadership, the Appropriations Committee, and the Senate. So the name of the game becomes finding formulas which will yield an increase in at least twenty-six states, and that has to include some key states.

The process began with committee staff feeding data pertaining to various allocation criteria into a computer and calculating the impact of different formulas. As one aide recalled:

> There was room to maneuver. We had Lotus set up and were playing out the states. We had Lotus set up so that suppose we multiplied this column by two and multiplied this one by three and added them together. Boom. It would give you a spread sheet: which states gain and which states lose. We tried forty or fifty formulas. You can run thousands.

Thus, committee staffers had the analytical capacity to carefully grease the skids for floor action, and the formula they devised reflected political realities in the Senate as a whole. Bentsen was a key player in this process. And on other items important to Texas, his behavior in committee was clearly conditioned by expectations about what would happen in the full Senate.

Bentsen employed the strategy of anticipated reactions because of the same factors that influenced Robert Stafford's leadership behavior: conflict in the full Senate, the presence of negotiable differences, and other aspects of the preference context on committee issues. But it also is instructive to consider the nature of Bentsen's own policy preferences on the items on which he was active. Environment and Public Works considers programs that can target significant benefits to states and localities, and these programs were of special interest to Bentsen during his service on the panel. When it comes to highway funds and sewage treatment grants, however, legislators are primarily motivated by the desire to claim credit, not the desire to take positions. On these issues, the folks back home reward results, not good intentions. Thus, Bentsen placed great emphasis on winning when he was active on Environment and Public Works, and greasing the skids for floor action was an integral component of his leadership.

Thurmond, Biden, and the Judiciary Committee

On the Commerce Committee, John Danforth made selective use of the strategy of anticipated reactions. On Environment and Public Works, the mood of the full chamber pervaded committee decision making. When we consider the

Judiciary Committee, however, it is clear that greasing the skids for floor consideration was not central to the leadership behavior of Strom Thurmond and Joseph Biden. Part of the reason lay in the extremely decentralized patterns of decision making found on the panel. Thurmond did not make adjustments in anticipation of the floor on most committee bills because other members of the committee—usually the subcommittee leaders—were responsible for key decisions about legislative strategy. But the relative absence of prior accommodation on the Judiciary Committee was primarily due to the nature of the preference context on most committee issues.

Certainly, the one crucial condition for anticipated reactions—some degree of conflict—is abundant in the Judiciary Committee. Abortion, busing, school prayer, gun control: These are some of the most divisive issues in American politics, and they typically evoke intense conflict in committee and on the floor. But two factors dampened incentives for committee leaders to grease the skids. First, during the Thurmond chairmanship, the panel was representative of the full chamber. Second, differences on Judiciary Committee issues often were not negotiable.

As chairman, Thurmond generally had sufficient support in committee to advance his agenda, although the panel's contingent of liberal Democrats tried to derail conservative initiatives with dilatory tactics. Thus, when handling controversial matters, Thurmond and his allies focused on circumventing these procedural hurdles, not on greasing the skids for floor deliberation. As a result, the Judiciary Committee was much less "floor oriented" than Environment and Public Works. In responding to my questions about anticipated reactions, a senior aide to Thurmond commented that greasing the skids is common in the Senate, but

> not so much on this committee. We have really strong dynamics in terms of the membership. We have a very broad spectrum of representation, so I think it is often a microcosm of what you would expect on the floor. We get a pretty good measure in committee. If it passes through, it usually will pass on the Senate floor. If we gain a consensus in committee, then we have a bill that's going to go all the way through. If we have a stormy time, we may get the bill out, but it's only a precursor of what's to be expected on the floor.

Because of its ideological complexion and the prevalence of delaying tactics, the Judiciary Committee was very much a "microcosm" of the full Senate during the years of Republican control. Thurmond's leadership tactics usually were driven by the internal dynamics of the committee, not the prospect of a floor fight.

An additional reason why greasing the skids is not a regular leadership tactic in the Judiciary Committee is the simple fact that committee issues often are not conducive to compromise: There is very little middle ground, and greasing the skids for floor deliberation is not a feasible leadership strategy. A staffer who worked on a death penalty measure considered during the 99th Congress explained why anticipated reactions was irrelevant to that legislation.

> That wasn't part of the thinking on this one. The first priority was [to get] it by the Democrats, and then confront the floor later. . . . [T]here isn't much that can be done to satisfy senators who oppose [it]. . . . We've debated the issue before and the main uncertainty was how far the Democrats would go to block it.

Joseph Biden

During his six years as ranking minority member of the Judiciary Committee, Joseph Biden did not play a major role on most legislation considered by the panel. Thus, even more so than Thurmond, Biden was not responsible for many of the significant decisions about legislative strategy made on his side of the aisle. There were important exceptions, however. On criminal law measures, a policy area in which Biden was actively involved, changes were made at his instigation to increase the probability of success in the full Senate. Indeed, on these bills, pressure to grease the skids for floor deliberation was more likely to originate with Biden than it was with Thurmond.

On major bills in the criminal law area, the legislative process often began with the Thurmond staff moving a draft that promised to generate considerable conflict in committee and on the floor. Then, early on in the process, usually before markup, Biden would approach Thurmond and suggest changes in the draft to broaden the base of support and improve prospects for success in the full Senate. Biden's efforts on the omnibus crime control bill, discussed in chapter 4, are illustrative. The original draft contained provisions unacceptable to liberal Democrats. Biden suggested dropping the contentious items, Thurmond agreed, and the result was a major reform of the criminal code.

Perhaps the process of prior accommodation (when it occurred at all) frequently began with Biden rather than Thurmond because the chairman was strategically hanging back and waiting for Biden to make the first move. But an additional factor was the location of Biden's policy preferences within the larger distribution of opinion on the panel. Biden was considerably to the left of the committee median, and changes in committee bills aimed at improving chances on the floor generally moved the legislation toward Biden's preferred outcome. Thus, the mood of the Senate as a whole worked to the ranking minority member's advantage in committee.

Indeed, on some bills, Biden was able to use the prospect of floor difficulties as leverage for substantive concessions from Thurmond. During the 99th Congress, for example, Thurmond introduced a bill that would have removed in price-fixing cases provisions for "joint and severable liability," an allocation scheme whereby damages awarded are deemed the responsibility of all defendants in the case. These efforts to repeal joint and several liability were opposed by the Department of Justice and many Democrats, including Biden. Thurmond had the votes to get his measure out of committee, but realized the bill faced keen opposition on the Senate floor and, in all likelihood, a quiet death in the Democratically controlled House of Representatives. As a Democratic aide who worked on the legislation recalled:

> [Thurmond] knew with Biden in opposition you [could] get it out of committee, but there would be no momentum there. It's a signal, a pattern. If you can't convince us, you can't convince them. So they worked out this deal, and Biden, Leahy, Simon, and Mathias came on board.

Thurmond made the decision to grease the skids, but Biden's preferences were the impetus for prior accommodation.

Hatch, Kennedy, and the Labor Committee

As was the case on Judiciary, greasing the skids for floor action was not central to leadership behavior on the Labor Committee during the Hatch years. Again, one reason is structural decentralization: Hatch often played a secondary role on legislation reported out of the subcommittees. But structural factors alone are insufficient to explain why committee leaders were so unlikely to grease the skids. After all, the health side of the jurisdiction was centralized and very active, and Hatch and Kennedy clearly took the lead on most health issues. Thus, a proper understanding of anticipated reactions in the Labor Committee requires that we once again consider the central feature of Labor Committee politics during the years Hatch was chairman: the distribution of preferences in committee. Edward Kennedy had the votes to win; Orrin Hatch often did not.

Hatch's leadership was felt most strongly at the agenda-setting stage of the process. Because he lacked the political support necessary to go on the offensive with controversial initiatives championed by conservatives, Hatch systematically restricted the agenda to those items for which he had the votes. These bills tended to be either routine reauthorizations or controversial measures for which an early agreement with committee liberals had been forged. As a result, even when controversial, most of the legislation that reached the markup stage was not expected to face much trouble on the floor.

Thus, because of the internal dynamics of the panel, there was usually little need to grease the skids for the full Senate. An aide to committee conservative Don Nickles underscored the link between the voting alignment and the utility of anticipated reactions as a leadership strategy.

> The way our committee is structured, we can't get a bill out unless we have agreement between the Republicans and the Democrats. We have two pivotal Republicans who will vote with the Democrats on some occasions, so everything we do is geared not only for Senate passage, but to get the thing out of committee. Once we get the thing out of committee, we usually have agreement from Orrin Hatch to Howard Metzenbaum to Ted Kennedy, and you've pretty much covered the spectrum.

The staffer emphasized that, despite all the difficulties of legislating in the Labor Committee during the Hatch years, items reported to the full Senate usually passed without trouble.

> We have, in a sense, the best of committees and the worst of committees. We have the worst in that we can't make some statements that we'd like to make on occasion. But we have the best in that if we get it worked out at the committee level, it's going to pass the Senate. On labor issues, if you have Orrin Hatch not opposed to you and Howard Metzenbaum not opposed to you, who's left?

There was some variation by issue, however. Making it through committee was usually the major hurdle, but on some measures the mood of the full chamber did influence committee action. For example, some Labor Committee programs had relatively high expenditure levels, and these reauthorizations were constrained by general pressures for fiscal austerity. The panel's reauthorization of the Higher Education Act, for instance, provided for approximately $9.7 billion for fiscal year 1987 alone. And budget constraints on the legislation were compounded when the Gramm-Rudman-Hollings budget control bill passed the Senate in the middle of Labor Committee deliberations on the Higher Education Act. I asked Edward Kennedy's staffer on this issue about the strategy of anticipated reactions.

> Yes, the Gramm-Rudman points of order. That definitely had us worried, which is why we made sure we didn't increase dramatically the graduate student loan and Pell program. We dropped the authorization levels dramatically from what current law is. We dropped it to pre–Gramm-Rudman appropriations levels plus 5 percent inflation for the majority of the programs. . . . It's a pretty conservative bill.

The sheer quantity of money involved, reinforced by the timing of the Gramm-Rudman vote, thus led to binding fiscal constraints that influenced the behavior of members in committee.

Jurisdictional overlaps also occasionally provided incentives for anticipated reactions, even in the presence of a Hatch-Kennedy compromise. The Labor Committee shared jurisdiction over health issues with the Senate Finance Committee, so on certain health items Hatch was careful to consider and incorporate the views of important members of the Finance Committee. One such example was his handling of legislation to authorize $100 million per year in block grants to states for the provision of home health care services to the elderly. The Finance Committee has primary jurisdiction over Medicare, and the home health care bill generated a turf battle that led to major changes in the Labor Committee's legislation. As an aide to Charles Grassley for Labor Committee issues recalled:

> Hatch's staff actually got quite a bit of static from the Finance Committee, but they worked with them and gradually changed the bill to satisfy some of the objections of the Finance Committee. . . . The Finance Committee forced certain changes.

Thus, on some items, very high expenditure levels or significant jurisdictional overlaps generated incentives for Hatch to grease the skids for floor action. These cases were exceptions, however. The strategy of anticipated reactions was not central to Orrin Hatch's leadership behavior on the Labor Committee because problems in moving legislation arose primarily in committee, and not in the Senate as a whole.

Edward Kennedy

Similar arguments hold for Edward Kennedy's behavior as ranking minority member on Labor: As was the case with Hatch, Kennedy's actions were almost entirely driven by the internal dynamics of the Labor Committee, and not by expectations about succeeding stages of the legislative process. Kennedy's key difficulty was getting legislation scheduled, and greasing the skids for the floor was not an integral component of his leadership. As one of Kennedy's staffers said:

> Well, we may anticipate problems if someone gets energized on some specific parochial issue, but, in general, if you work out a Hatch-Kennedy accommodation, and most things that get to the floor end up being that way, you're really kind of protected.

Although Hatch and Kennedy differ markedly as senators and as Senate leaders, their anticipatory behavior vis-a-vis the floor was very similar on Labor Committee issues during the years of Republican control.

Conclusion

On each of the four committees, the chair and ranking minority member were very similar in the extent to which they employed the strategy of anticipated reactions. Danforth and Hollings greased the skids on some bills, but not on others, demonstrating that even small pockets of opposition can provide incentives for anticipatory behavior in the modern Senate. The mood of the full chamber influenced the leadership behavior of both Robert Stafford and Lloyd Bentsen on all major issues considered by the Environment and Public Works Committee. On the Judiciary Committee, prior accommodation was not central to the leadership of either Strom Thurmond or Joseph Biden, primarily because the panel was representative of the full chamber, and differences on many Judiciary Committee issues were not readily negotiable. And Orrin Hatch and Edward Kennedy did not systematically grease the skids in the Labor Committee. Hatch controlled the agenda, and Kennedy had the votes. As a result, legislation passed by the panel had to satisfy both senators, and with a Hatch-Kennedy compromise, difficulties on the floor were unlikely.

These arguments provide the most striking evidence in this study about the importance of contextual factors—particularly the preference context—for understanding legislative leadership. When two very different committee leaders confront the same preference context, their anticipatory behavior vis-à-vis the floor is quite similar. Some differences remain, of course. On all four panels, the chair was more likely to make important decisions about legislative strategy, and the strategy of anticipated reactions was less central to the leadership behavior of the ranking minority members. In addition, aspects of a committee leader's own policy preferences affected the political value of greasing the skids. For the most part, however, on each panel the chair and ranking minority member responded in a similar fashion to the opportunities and constraints emanating from the preference context.

Notes

1. On the sequential nature of legislative behavior, see Fenno 1986.

2. The strategy of anticipated reactions is an important concept in the theoretical literature on political power. Nagel (1975, 16), for example, defines anticipated reactions as occurring "whenever one actor, *B*, shapes his behavior to conform to what he believes are the desires of another actor, *A*, without having received explicit messages about *A*'s wants or intentions from *A* or *A*'s agents." In the present study, anticipated

reactions is defined as occurring whenever members of a committee anticipate potential problems in later stages of the policy-making sequence and make changes in their bill to offset those problems. A similar definition is employed in Hall and Evans 1990.

3. The strategy of anticipated reactions has long been recognized as an integral component of legislative leadership, but empirical studies have been rare. An important exception is John Manley's exploration of Wilbur Mills's leadership style on the House Ways and Means Committee (Manley 1969, 1970). In addition, Fenno (1973) compared the importance different House committees place on winning on the floor, which is related to the strategy of anticipated reactions. See also Murphy 1974. Eulau and McCluggage (1984) discuss the links between anticipated reactions and committee power in Congress. For a study of anticipated reactions in House subcommittees, consult Hall and Evans 1990.

4. Highly useful descriptions of floor procedure in the Senate can be found in Oleszek 1989 and Smith 1989. See also Keith 1977.

5. *Congressional Record*, 99th Cong., 2d sess. May 8, 1986, S.5686.

6. In exchange for his consent to the time agreement, Howard Metzenbaum was allowed to offer an unlimited number of amendments on the substance of the bill.

7. A description of the Senate hold is provided in Oleszek 1989.

8. On the "new obstructionism," as it relates to energy policy in Congress, see Oppenheimer 1981.

9. Hook 1986, 1394.

10. See Ehrenhalt 1982 and Oppenheimer 1985.

11. Schattschneider (1960) explores the links between the level and form of conflict on an issue and political behavior. See also Price 1978.

12. Based on a systematic analysis of interest group ratings of legislators' voting records, Krehbiel (1990) argues that congressional committees are much more representative of their parent chambers than conventional wisdom has suggested. However, Hall and Grofman (1990) argue that roll call data are not sufficient to evaluate the preference outlier hypothesis, and suggest that the degree of committee bias varies by issue.

13. Mayhew 1974.

14. Mayhew 1974. For another perspective on the connections between the desire to win and legislative strategy, see Steven S. Smith 1984.

15. Mayhew 1974.

CHAPTER 6

Leadership and Power in Committee

We have explored the behavior of eight committee leaders in the U.S. Senate. A central goal has been to demonstrate that committee leadership behavior can be understood through a combination of contextual and individual factors. And a central argument has been that the behavior of committee chairs and ranking minority members is primarily shaped by the context of leadership, particularly the intensity and distribution of preferences on committee issues.

The significance of contextual factors for understanding leadership behavior raises some fundamental questions about the role played by formal leaders in the legislative process. For if the tactics and strategies of committee leaders are primarily shaped by incentives and constraints embedded in the leadership environment, then to what extent do chairs and ranking minority members make a difference in committee decision making? That is, to what extent do they exert an *independent* impact on the content and timing of committee policy? And if they do have an impact, how and why does the nature of that impact vary from leader to leader and from issue to issue?

Such questions need to be addressed if we are to understand legislative leadership and congressional policy-making. After all, the study of leadership is important because leadership behavior can influence the content of public policy. We study leadership selection because we believe *who* fills a leadership position has some effect on legislative outcomes. And we study the behavior of individual leaders to better understand how their tactics do or do not shape policy. Indeed, the study of leadership is inseparable from the study of power; otherwise, it is of limited value. In this chapter, some tentative conclusions are offered about the extent to which the eight leaders under study wielded power in committee: how much, how it varied, and why. And I close with a few brief observations about leadership and power in Congress.

Committee Leadership and the Median Voter

Social scientists disagree about the proper definition of political power, but one useful approach is to define it as "a causal relation between the preferences of an actor regarding an outcome and the outcome itself."[1] Thus, we can describe a committee leader as exerting power if his or her preferences have a disproportionate impact on legislative outcomes.

Consider the case of a committee that selects policy outcomes from a set of alternatives that can be meaningfully arrayed along some underlying dimension of evaluation—say, the traditional liberal-conservative continuum. Our theories of committee decision making demonstrate that if (1) outcomes are decided by majority rule, (2) concrete alternatives representing all points along the underlying dimension of evaluation are considered, (3) there is no uncertainty about the location of alternatives on the underlying dimension of evaluation, and (4) legislators vote for the alternative closest to their own preferences, then the final outcome of the committee process will be a policy reflecting the preferences of the median voter(s) in committee.[2]

On the Labor Committee, for example, Robert Stafford and Lowell Weicker usually shared the median position—seven conservative Republicans fell to their right, seven liberal Democrats fell to their left. As a result, the balance of power in the panel was theirs, and if information had been full and all alternatives had been on the agenda, Labor Committee decisions during the Hatch chairmanship would have tended toward the policy preferences of Stafford and Weicker.

Participants implicitly recognize the importance of the median position in committee when they discuss the role of "swing voters" or "pivotal committee members." Pivotal senators determine the outcome in close votes. Orrin Hatch described Stafford and Weicker as "pivotal" because he needed their support to report legislation to the floor. With his own vote and the support of six more conservative Republicans, he needed the two swing voters to form a majority. Thus, Stafford and Weicker were "pivotal" precisely because their policy preferences were usually located at the median position in committee. Their support was necessary for a minority coalition to become a majority.

As we have seen, however, information in Senate committees is seldom full, and the range of feasible policy alternatives is seldom unconstrained. As a result, committee outcomes often diverge from the position of the median voter, and we can expect this divergence to be in the direction of the preferences of senators, such as the chair and ranking minority member, who have disproportionate access to information and disproportionate control over which policy alternatives are considered.

Thus, leaders may exert power in committee by influencing the content of committee outcomes. But what about timing? Is a leader's impact on the pace of committee deliberations also a form of power? Consider the case of a chair who brings a bill to the top of the committee agenda and moves it quickly to the floor. As a result, the full Senate has enough time to act and the legislation passes. And assume that, in the absence of the chair's agenda tactics, insufficient time would have been available for Senate action, and the legislation would have died on the floor. Under these conditions, did the chair wield power? After all, the content of the committee's recommendation was the same in both cases. When we consider the outcome in the full Senate, however, the chair's behavior did have an impact on policy. Without the chair's agenda tactics, the final outcome in the Senate would have been the perpetuation of existing law, rather than the passage of legislation. As a result, we also need to consider how committee leaders affect legislative timing in their panels, because the timing of committee action may have an impact on the content of policy outcomes in the Senate as a whole.

The following sections are an exploration of the policy-making impact of the eight committee leaders under study. Three questions structure the discussion. First, did the leader influence the content of policy outcomes? Second, did policy outcomes diverge from the position of the median voter in committee (or on the floor) in the direction of the preferences of the chair or ranking minority member? And third, if the leader did regularly influence the content of policy outcomes, what was the source of that influence? A systematic and precise estimation of legislative power is beyond the scope of this study, but the evidence presented in previous chapters is sufficient to offer some tentative conclusions about the links between leadership behavior and political power.

Danforth, Hollings, and the Commerce Committee

Danforth and Hollings influenced the content of legislation reported to the floor by the Commerce Committee, but most committee issues were relatively consensual and policy outcomes did not diverge significantly from the position of the median voter. Rather, the two full committee leaders primarily acted to facilitate the process of coalition building—to increase their panel's ability to move legislation to the floor. Their primary contribution was to lower the transaction costs of legislative work.

Coordination and management are the central leadership tasks on the Commerce Committee. When asked about the job of chairman, John Danforth underscored the managerial side of leadership in the panel.

> I needed to bring people on board, to consult with other members and tend to their needs. There were conflicting interests and demands, sometimes reasonable and sometimes unreasonable. And there were always a lot of little things: managerial matters. Scheduling when we're to have a markup, taking into account the presence or absence of Senator *X*, working at a bill, accommodating interests.

All chairs have to deal with conflicting interests, scheduling difficulties, and colleagues with diverse viewpoints. But on the Commerce Committee, the administrative side of the job is pronounced.

Administrative duties loom large in the committee because of the nature of the preference context and the size of the work load. On most Commerce Committee issues, the preference context is relatively fluid. Three or four senators are intense in their preferences, primarily for constituency reasons, and remaining committee members tend toward indifference. Indeed, when we examine committee bills in isolation, the coalition-building process appears straightforward. The subset of interested senators negotiates with committee staffers, executive officials, and representatives of the relevant interest groups; a draft is constructed and introduced; and the panel meets and reports the product to the full Senate.

But we need to consider the size and diversity of the Commerce Committee's work load to fully understand the contributions of the chair and ranking minority member. The huge number of reauthorizations considered by the panel each year greatly complicates committee politics. And because the Commerce Committee considers issues as diverse as consumer safety and federal maritime policy, the subset of interested members differs greatly from issue to issue. Also, since committee bills tend to be low in salience, even small amounts of conflict may result in a hold, precluding action by the full body. As a result, the job of the committee is to achieve a very high degree of consensus between shifting subsets of the panel on a very large number of issues.

Within such an environment, the primary contribution that can be made by committee leaders is to minimize the transaction costs of legislative work. By transaction costs, I am referring to the time, effort, and other political resources necessary to build a successful legislative coalition. All legislative work is fundamentally transactional: It turns on bargaining and exchange. Of course, legislation is not always the product of explicit trades. Most logrolling in Congress is tacit and implicit. For example, legislators without intense preferences on an issue usually defer to more interested members, and they expect similar treatment on the items they care about. These patterns of mutual deference drive the legislative process and they are essentially transactional in nature.

Legislative transactions are costly, nonetheless. The preferences of interested members need to be gauged and evaluated; potential compromises need to be crafted; and interested members must be persuaded that one or more policy alternatives will promote their goals. These activities require time and effort.

In some jurisdictions, the potential benefits of building coalitions are large enough to induce rank-and-file committee members to invest the resources necessary to cover the transaction costs of legislative work. However, most Commerce Committee issues do not evoke much interest. Committee members want their programs reauthorized, but generally are unwilling to invest scarce personal resources in the jurisdiction. Instead, they lean on the leadership. And they have provided their leaders with the agenda prerogatives and staff resources necessary to bear the transaction costs of legislative work for them. As one Commerce Committee staffer put it, "There's a recognition that the committee runs more smoothly when the chairman is in control."

Of course, control over the staff provides full committee leaders with an important informational advantage vis-à-vis other senators, and members view the Commerce Committee staff as a source of political power. But they also emphasize the administrative burdens to an extent not evident on the other three committees. As John Danforth recalled:

> It was particularly hard to keep the staff as a whole and under one roof, rather than have the staff be balkanized into separate areas. . . . It's a very diverse and specialized jurisdiction. The subcommittee specialties are so different.

Like his colleagues, Danforth views the committee staff primarily as a tool for the entire committee to use in confronting the work load.

> We have a good staff now, and we had a good staff then. Hopefully, they're cohesive. I felt that it was important to keep the concept of the committee staff as the staff for the whole committee, rather than the personal employees of individual senators. I wanted the staff to be available to the minority and the majority, with a common purpose, rather than protecting the interests of Senator X or Senator Y. . . . I was successful for the most part, but not completely.

Danforth's impact was usually administrative. Of course, on legislation of importance to his constituents in Missouri, the chairman generally got what he wanted. And a different chair—Ernest Hollings, for example—might have been more active in the Commerce Committee's partial jurisdiction over trade. But these effects were on the margin. Danforth did not alter the direction of committee policy. Rather, he enabled other committee members to translate their own preferences into legislative outcomes. To the extent that these outcomes differed from existing law, Danforth's leadership had policy consequences.

Ernest Hollings

What was the policy-making impact of ranking Democrat Ernest Hollings? What did he contribute to committee decision making? Hollings's contribution resembled Danforth's. Committee Democrats expected Hollings to use his staff resources to minimize the transaction costs of legislative work for them.

Staffers for the minority typically worked very closely with the majority staff in gauging the preferences of important political actors, constructing policy alternatives, and providing other inputs into the coalition-building process. Thus, Hollings's primary impact on the committee was also through assisting other senators in translating their preferences into legislation, not through significantly altering the direction of committee policy.

But as ranking minority member, Hollings was less constrained in his choice of tactics and strategies than was Danforth. Danforth had to participate to a certain extent on most committee initiatives: As chairman, he was responsible for managing the committee process. Hollings had the resources to facilitate coalition building, but his administrative role was clearly secondary to the chairman's. As a result, his leadership behavior was driven almost entirely by the nature of his personal policy preferences on issues. When relatively indifferent, Hollings deferred extensively to other committee Democrats and relied on Danforth to manage the process. But when interested, Hollings was often the key player in committee, and his impact on committee outcomes was significant.

Product liability reform is a case in point. During the 99th Congress, Hollings probably cared more about this issue than any other item on the agenda. And when we consider the policy predispositions of other committee members on the issue, Hollings was clearly in the minority. Yet, in 1985 he was able to kill the initiative in committee.

Backers of the measure had walked into markup confident of a solid majority. A staffer explained.

> [T]his was a political markup. Hollings was leaning on Inouye. Gorton was gone. So they were down to nine, one more than you need. Ford was sitting out the vote because of his business connections. Kassebaum was wavering because she was getting pressure from women's groups, but ended up voting yes.

The aide then described the pivotal role played by Ernest Hollings.

> Exon was the determining factor. I don't think they were even thinking about Exon: He was an original cosponsor. Apparently, Hollings called him in the hospital [where Exon was recuperating from surgery] and convinced him to vote no by proxy.

With Exon voting no, the final vote was eight to eight to one (Wendell Ford abstained). Hollings then read into the record a statement by Exon stating that the Nebraska Democrat supported the general idea of tort reform, but believed the matter required further deliberation. The following year, John Danforth was successful in reporting another version of product liability reform to the full Senate, but when Hollings threatened a filibuster, Danforth's bill was pulled from the schedule.

Stafford, Bentsen, and the Environment and Public Works Committee

Did policy outcomes in the Environment and Public Works Committee diverge from the median position in committee toward the preferences of Robert Stafford or Lloyd Bentsen? Did Stafford or Bentsen influence the content of policy outcomes on the floor? Both senators were influential, and the foundations of leadership power on the panel were informational and procedural.

During his years as chairman, Stafford's policy preferences seldom diverged much from the median position in committee. However, he was more pro-environmentalist than the median position in the full Senate, and, consequentially, often faced opposition on the Senate floor. Thus, Stafford's strategic challenge as chairman was to manage the process so that committee recommendations would prevail in the institution as a whole.

As argued throughout this study, Environment and Public Works Committee issues are among the most technically complex considered in Congress. Executive branch officials and interest group representatives can provide valuable advice to rank-and-file members of the Senate, but by far the most useful source of information on these issues is the professional staff of the Environment and Public Works Committee. This staff provided Stafford with an important informational advantage for confronting opposition to committee legislation in the full chamber. Two aides explained how participants view the process on environmental issues.

> These bills are long and technical, and it's difficult for the senators on the committee to know what's what. If you're interested in a policy and you're not on the committee, you're up a creek. The best thing to do is go to a hold. Floor amendments are a high-risk strategy. The tendency is if it's not the way you like it, don't let it get to the floor.

> It's a sense of you know the issue much better than I do. You've rolled up your sleeves and really hashed out these things. . . . Usually they'll come in and focus on a tiny piece. In a 150-page bill, they'll be concerned about a section.

Particularly on environmental issues, information is power, and the two full committee leaders had disproportionate access to information. As a result, Stafford and other moderate environmentalists were able to shape policy outcomes.

By all accounts, however, Stafford and Bentsen did not misrepresent information. Indeed, both men were among the most trusted members of the institution, and senators and staff regularly cited their credibility. So how did their informational advantages translate into power?

To answer this question, we need to distinguish between legislative formulation and legislative interpretation.[3] On environmental policy, legislators have firm policy predispositions about the proper balance between economic growth and environmental quality. But because of the technical complexity of these issues, significant information is required to formulate concrete alternatives, and interpreting the policy consequences of these alternatives once they have been devised is usually problematic. Thus, uncertainty enters the decision-making process at two points: Information is required to create alternatives, and information is required to evaluate alternatives. Stafford and his aides on Environment and Public Works were trusted because they provided accurate information about how proposals should be interpreted. However, the force of their informational advantage was felt at the formulation stage of the process. Potential opponents often lacked the resources necessary to provide credible alternatives to committee recommendations. Indeed, Stafford seldom lost on the Senate floor.

In short, when we describe information and expertise as important leadership resources on Environment and Public Works, it is crucial to emphasize the way knowledge becomes power. Senators do not systematically mislead their colleagues about the political consequences of existing proposals. But information is the central ingredient in developing policy alternatives, and knowledge is translated into power during this stage of the legislative process.

In addition to his staff resources, Stafford influenced policy outcomes by carefully managing the process in committee. As we have seen, the chairman placed great emphasis on bringing legislation to the floor early in a session (agenda control), and on modifying legislation in committee to increase the probability of success in the full chamber (the strategy of anticipated reactions). Along with his informational advantages, these efforts made the difference between success and failure in the full Senate. During Stafford's chairmanship, all major programs in the committee's jurisdiction were reauthorized except the Clean Air Act, and environmental policy in the 1980s reflected the preferences of Stafford and other moderate environmentalists, rather than the more conservative agenda of the Reagan administration.

Lloyd Bentsen

Lloyd Bentsen is one of the most skilled legislators in the Senate: in the words of one lobbyist, "a non–back slapping Lyndon Johnson."[4] But what was Bentsen's contribution to policy-making in the Environment and Public Works Committee during his two years as ranking minority member? Did he exert power over policy? As demonstrated in previous chapters, Bentsen certainly influenced the content of major committee bills, but his impact was often narrow in scope and oriented toward issues of particular relevance to his constituents in Texas. Thus, while Bentsen was a major player on the Environment and Public Works Committee, his role in committee deliberations was less pronounced than his overall legislative record might suggest.

Why? For one, he was in the minority and controlled fewer resources than Stafford did. In addition, Bentsen was more interested in issues considered by the Finance Committee, the panel on which he intended to replace Russell Long as leader of committee Democrats. Bentsen compared the two panels.

> I enjoyed the Environment and Public Works Committee, but the jurisdiction is much smaller than the Finance Committee's. The Finance Committee is an all-consuming responsibility, particularly when we get to the floor. Everybody has an idea. . . . Environment and Public Works is bipartisan. Most of the important fights were with the House. It [becoming ranking Democrat] was not a major adjustment. [On Finance], there was an adjustment. It's one of the most important committees in Congress.

Asked about his level of activity on Environment and Public Works relative to other Democrats on the panel, Bentsen replied that "I've always believed in sharing credit."

Thus, a proper understanding of Lloyd Bentsen as a Senate leader requires that one explore his behavior on the Finance Committee, as well as his actions during his two years as ranking Democrat on Environment and Public Works. As argued throughout this study, the leadership tactics of legislators vary significantly from committee to committee and from issue to issue. But it is also clear that, when Bentsen's policy preferences were intense, he was a force to be reckoned with in the Environment and Public Works Committee. Given the technical complexity of committee issues, Bentsen's control over minority staff resources provided him with an informational advantage relative to other committee members, with the exception of Stafford. And on issues relevant to his constituents in Texas, committee policy clearly diverged from the median position toward the preferences of Lloyd Bentsen.

Thurmond, Biden, and the Judiciary Committee

As we have seen, the Judiciary Committee can be a live wire. Within such an ideologically charged environment, what role is there for leadership? And what are the foundations of leadership power?

Thurmond and Biden were more constrained in their selection of leadership tactics than were leaders on Commerce or Environment and Public Works. Because of the intensity of member preferences and the decentralization of the staff, rank-and-file members of the Judiciary Committee were less willing to defer extensively to the chair and ranking minority member. There was less uncertainty about how to interpret concrete alternatives, and members approached many committee issues with their minds made up. As a result, committee bills seldom diverged significantly from the position of the median voter on the panel. As an aide to Orrin Hatch observed about Judiciary Committee issues:

> The problem with tinkering around with something that has a life of its own is [that if] you chop a little piece off here to add it on there, well, you make somebody else mad. Somebody's mad, either side. . . . You try to pick somebody up on the left, and you lose somebody on the right. . . . Just because they're on the committee, it's automatically true that they have some influence because you're counting their votes with every amendment and figuring, "Would this fly, would it not fly?"

Relative to the other three committees under review, the independent impact of the chair and ranking minority member on the content of Judiciary Committee bills was usually very small.

Did Thurmond affect the content of policy outcomes in the Senate as a whole by greasing the skids or bringing items to the top of the agenda? He certainly tried. As chairman, Thurmond regularly lectured liberal Democrats such as Howard Metzenbaum about the evils of excessive obstructionism. He tended to place his own items near the top of the agenda. And, on occasion, Thurmond pulled legislation off the panel's schedule and brought it directly to the full Senate to avoid delaying tactics in committee. But most of these bills died on the Senate floor (or in the House) anyway. Thus, the policy consequences of Thurmond's procedural tactics were usually negligible. The Judiciary Committee simply is not conducive to a powerful leadership.

Joseph Biden

As ranking minority member of the panel from 1981 to 1987, Joseph Biden was easily the most circumscribed of the eight leaders in this study. To begin with, Biden shared all of Thurmond's constraints. Senators are unwilling to defer extensively to formal leaders on many Judiciary Committee issues, and staff resources on the minority side are even more decentralized than is the case with the majority.

But some additional factors compounded Biden's strategic dilemma. First, he usually lacked the votes to win on controversial issues, and rolling the chairman was not feasible. Second, the Democratic contingent on the Judiciary Committee was extremely heterogeneous, and often there was very little unity on the minority side of the aisle. Finally, for portions of the 99th Congress, Biden was considering a presidential run, and a close association with issues like abortion and school prayer is not necessarily the most effective strategy for securing the Democratic presidential nomination. In short, Biden had almost no room to maneuver.

There were exceptions, of course. On some important criminal law items, Biden worked closely with Thurmond, and was able to find middle ground by convincing the chairman to avoid divisive issues. Indeed, Biden was a key architect of the compromise that produced the Comprehensive Crime Control Act of 1984, a major legislative achievement. But on committee issues in general, Biden was the least influential of the eight leaders.

Hatch, Kennedy, and the Labor Committee

The cornerstone of Orrin Hatch's leadership of the Labor Committee from 1981 to 1987 was procedure. A chair's agenda prerogatives are an important part of the process on most congressional committees. But on the Labor Committee during the Hatch chairmanship, the policy-making consequences of these prerogatives were profound.[5] The magnitude of the chairman's impact on committee policy varied, however, depending on the position of existing law relative to Hatch's policy preferences and the preferences of Stafford and Weicker, the two median, or pivotal, voters.

First, consider the case in which existing law fell between the preferences of Hatch and the two pivotal voters. That is, Hatch favored moving policy to the right, while Stafford and Weicker favored shifts to the left. The distribution of preferences on many health issues resembled this configuration, with Hatch supporting greater reliance on the private sector, and Stafford and Weicker favoring a larger federal role. Under these conditions, passing conservative bills was not feasible: A majority of the committee preferred the status quo of no action. Thus, the only viable policy changes were movements away from Hatch's preferences toward the views of committee liberals, placing Hatch in a no-win situation. On these issues, the rational response (which he employed) was to close the gates and deny access to the full committee agenda.

Now, consider the case in which the preferences of Hatch and the two pivotal voters fell to the left of existing law. That is, Hatch, Stafford, and Weicker all favored greater federal intervention, but the two pivotal voters supported more liberal alternatives than did the chairman. Legislation considered by Weicker's Subcommittee on the Handicapped often fell into this category. Here, the rational response for the chairman was to threaten to close the gates if the item was not modified before full committee markup. Although Hatch wanted legislation, allowing such items to bubble up freely would have resulted in more radical departures from existing law than he favored. Since, in this case, Stafford and Weicker preferred the chairman's position to no bill at all, Hatch had the upper hand in negotiations, and the committee process usually ended with a compromise amendment resembling the chairman's views.[6]

In short, Orrin Hatch systematically pulled legislation away from the median position in committee toward his own policy preferences, but the magnitude of the impact depended on the distribution of preferences relative to existing law. When existing law fell between the positions of Hatch and the two pivotal voters, the chairman closed the gates. Since Stafford and Weicker were substantially to Hatch's left, and they had the votes to win on these items, Hatch's power over committee outcomes was substantial. When existing law fell to the right of the positions of Stafford, Weicker, *and* Orrin Hatch, the chairman was still able to pull committee outcomes from the median position toward his own views. He simply threatened to close the gates, and the result was usually a compromise that reflected his policy preferences.

Thus, there is a degree of paradox in Orrin Hatch's leadership of the Labor Committee. Compared to the other three chairmen, his political support in committee was least conducive to coalition building. But because he so often lacked the votes to win, the magnitude of his independent impact on committee outcomes (exerted via his procedural prerogatives) was clearly the largest among the eight leaders in this study.

Edward Kennedy

As ranking minority member on the Labor Committee from 1981 to 1987, Edward Kennedy was often described as "the only Democratic committee chairman in the Senate." As we have seen, Kennedy had a working majority on most committee issues. But did his ideological majority translate into political power? For the most part, the answer is no.

Kennedy's office was active on a wide range of committee bills, and in the health area, he clearly took the lead for Democrats on the panel. It would be misleading to infer from his activity level, however, that Kennedy's personal policy preferences had a significant and independent impact on the direction of committee policy. Since Hatch refused to schedule legislation unless he had the votes to win, items reaching the markup stage tended to have broad-based support. Often, these items were relatively minor reauthorizations. Kennedy took the lead for committee Democrats because of his own commitment to the jurisdiction, and because there often were few incentives for other Democrats to invest significant resources in committee bills. Thus, to a certain extent, Kennedy also filled the role played by John Danforth on the Commerce Committee—he lowered the transaction costs of legislative work for his rank and file.

In a few instances, Kennedy was able to circumvent Hatch's agenda control and move committee policy significantly to the left, over the chairman's objections. For example, one of the most significant health measures considered by the Labor Committee during the 99th Congress was a Kennedy initiative to extend the health insurance coverage of laid-off employees, widows, and divorcees. Action on this legislation illustrates the circumstances under which Kennedy could significantly influence committee policy.

Kennedy staffers, believing Hatch would not schedule the health insurance initiative for full committee markup, began searching for a vehicle to bring it directly to the Senate floor. In the fall of 1985, such a vehicle emerged in the form of the Labor Committee's reconciliation bill: a piece of legislation that had to be reported and was widely perceived as almost veto-proof.[7]

Reconciliation bills are high-priority items, and committee members usually expect a formal markup session. But Hatch viewed the legislation as a potential lightning rod for unrelated items bottled up in committee: items like Kennedy's health insurance proposal. As a result, Hatch put off holding a markup for the reconciliation bill and eventually chose to poll it out: a procedure in which a consensus package is devised informally; all committee members sign off; and no formal markup is held. An aide to Edward Kennedy described the process.

> I was supposed to do budget [reconciliation]. I kept asking Hatch's guy when they were going to hold a markup and they kept saying "next week," and next week never came. They wanted to get away without a markup.

As one of Charles Grassley's staffers later recalled:

> [T]he chairman decided to wait until the last minute on the committee's reconciliation bill, and then to poll it out. Maybe that was preferable to having a sit-down executive session, but it's sort of hard to see how because of all this stuff waiting in the wings that people wanted to move and hadn't been able to get on exec's [markups]. It just came out of the woodwork.

Members of the committee initially agreed that unrelated items such as the Kennedy health insurance bill would not be attached to the reconciliation language, but the agreement quickly dissolved. Grassley's staffer outlined the strategic context.

> So what we had was basically a highway-robbery situation in which everybody started playing the game—"We're not going to agree to this poll." One person not agreeing means it's not going to move on a poll.

As the deadline for reporting a reconciliation bill approached, it became apparent that committee members would not sign off unless additional items were tacked on. A Kennedy aide described the result:

> The bidding started. . . . In the meantime, the health guys who worked for Hatch—thinking that all things were settled and it was going to be polled out—were [out of town]. . . . At 6:00 [at night], there had been a lot of milling around. Nothing had been settled, and nobody can reach these guys. . . . So after a while, about 10:00 or 11:00, Hatch's budget guy said, "Let's just go ahead." So we put it in.

Major pieces of legislation, including Kennedy's health insurance bill and an important revision of ERISA, were incorporated into the Labor Committee's reconciliation language. Hatch later denounced the outcome, but did not fight the measure on the Senate floor.

In this case, characteristics of the budget process allowed Kennedy to do an end run around the chairman's agenda prerogatives on a significant piece of legislation. But the very byzantine nature of the process on this issue suggests the extent to which Kennedy was constrained by Hatch's agenda strategies. Circumventing the chairman on major items was extremely difficult, and such tactics seldom resulted in success. Kennedy was not "the only Democratic committee chairman in the Senate" during the years of Republican control.

Conclusion

Just as leadership behavior varies significantly from committee to committee and from issue to issue, the foundations and magnitude of leadership power also vary across committees and across issues. On the Commerce Committee, the primary contribution of the leadership was to lower the transaction costs of legislative work. Policy outcomes did not systematically diverge from the median position in committee. Rather, Danforth and Hollings facilitated bargaining and legislative exchange. On Environment and Public Works,

Stafford and Bentsen often had a significant impact on policy outcomes, which in large part was due to their informational advantage relative to other senators, as well as Stafford's control of the agenda. Thurmond and Biden influenced policy in the Judiciary Committee to a certain extent, but the magnitude of their policy impact was smaller than was the case for leaders on the other three panels. And on the Labor Committee, the source of leadership power was procedure. By systematically restricting the scope of the agenda, Hatch had a substantial impact on the direction of Labor Committee policy; and Edward Kennedy's policy-making role was sharply circumscribed by Hatch's procedural tactics.

What conditions are associated with a powerful leadership? Political scientists tend to emphasize the constraints on leadership power in Congress. Legislative leaders, they argue, lack the formal prerogatives necessary to command collective responsibility, and instead are forced to rely on bargaining, persuasion, and the provision of small favors. Indeed, if there is a unifying theme to this literature, it is that legislative leadership is mostly followership.

As we have seen, committee leaders in the Senate are highly responsive to contextual factors. And in certain policy areas, it is also apparent that committee chairs and ranking minority members exert very little influence over legislative outcomes. Judiciary Committee issues, for example, are often salient, controversial, and easy to interpret: On issues such as these, legislative leaders often lack the resources necessary to shape policy.

However, most issues considered by Congress are not like abortion, school prayer, and the death penalty. And on most matters before the institution, legislative leaders have room to maneuver. Consequentially, isolating and defining the conditions that are associated with leadership power are important tasks for congressional scholars. In this book, three sources of legislative leadership power have been emphasized: administration, information, and procedure.[8]

On issues such as those considered by the Commerce Committee, the primary contribution to be made by legislative leaders is *administrative*. These issues are of low to moderate salience, relatively noncontroversial, and constituency oriented. As a result, the preference context tends toward consensus, and few members have intense views. These items do not generate much media attention, but they constitute the bulk of the congressional agenda. And on these issues, legislative leaders can facilitate the process of coalition building by minimizing the transaction costs of legislative work. Administration and facilitation do not translate into a leadership that systematically pulls outcomes away from the position of the median voter. Rather, leaders assist other legislators in turning the median position into legislation.

But the alternative is often gridlock and existing law. Thus, the administrative side of legislative leadership has consequences for policy outcomes.

In addition, legislative leaders often have significant *informational advantages*, which can translate into political power. For example, consider issues of the sort composing the jurisdiction of the Environment and Public Works Committee: salient and potentially controversial, but also highly complex. The twin constraints of time and information have been emphasized throughout this book. Members of Congress interpret concrete policy alternatives in terms of certain underlying dimensions of evaluation: for example, the traditional liberal-conservative continuum. Legislators know where they stand along this continuum, but there often is considerable uncertainty about where concrete policy proposals are located. As a result, formulating and interpreting politically viable policy alternatives is costly. It requires information, and gathering information requires time and effort. Since formal leaders often have disproportionate access to the resources necessary to gather politically useful information, on highly complex items, they are able to move policy outcomes in the direction of their preferences. The magnitude of leadership power on these items can be expected to vary with the size of the informational asymmetry.

It should be emphasized, however, that knowledge does not become power at the point when other legislators try to interpret a leader's bill. Trust and credibility matter in congressional decision making, and formal leaders do not systematically misrepresent the political implications of their proposals. Rather, knowledge becomes power in the initial formulating of alternatives. Potential opponents of a leader's bill may lack the resources necessary to construct a viable alternative, and the result can be an outcome closer to the leader's policy preferences than would have occurred had resources (and information) been more evenly distributed.

Finally, legislative leaders often have *procedural prerogatives* that, under certain conditions, allow them to shift policy outcomes toward their preferences. But what are these conditions? After all, agenda prerogatives matter to a certain extent in all issue areas. For instance, committee chairs in the Senate can use the agenda as both a carrot and a stick. Senators who oppose a chair on an item that the chair cares about may have difficulty getting their own legislation scheduled, and, conversely, a chair can reward supporters with a place at the top of the agenda. But using agenda prerogatives as political capital in legislative exchange seldom generates an impact as large as the one exerted by Orrin Hatch on the Labor Committee during his years as chairman.

So when do a leader's agenda prerogatives permit significant alteration of legislative outcomes? Hatch's leadership suggests the answer. If we array existing law, the policy preferences of the median voter, and the policy preferences of the leader along a single underlying dimension of evaluation, then the leader's control over the agenda will significantly alter policy outcomes under two conditions: (1) If the status quo of existing law falls between the preferences of the leader and the preferences of the median voter, then the leader will deny access to the agenda and the outcome will be existing law; and (2) If the leader's preferences fall between existing law and the preferences of the median voter, then the leader will use his or her agenda prerogatives as leverage to secure a compromise that reflects the leader's preferred outcome. If we take into account imperfect information and other aspects of legislative politics, these two arguments do not necessarily hold, but they remain the general tendency.

Thus, legislative leaders influence policy outcomes because of their administrative contributions, informational advantages, and procedural prerogatives. The administrative function looms large on routine bills. When the legislative process is rife with uncertainty, a leader's informational advantages may be significant. And when political conditions are right, agenda control is important. As we have seen, the foundations of leadership power vary from issue to issue and from leader to leader. But on most matters considered in Congress, legislative leaders have the resources necessary to make a difference. Indeed, the tactics and strategies of legislative leadership are central to policy-making on Capitol Hill.

Notes

1. Nagel 1975, 29.
2. Black 1948. For an overview of this literature, consult Ordeshook 1986, chapter 6.
3. On the role of "interpretation" in legislative decision making, see Richard A. Smith 1984.
4. *Washington Post,* July 31, 1988, H2.
5. The arguments that follow are based on the work of Denzau and MacKay 1983. See also Krehbiel 1986.
6. It also is logically possible for existing law to be more liberal than the preferences of Hatch and the pivotal voters. That is, Hatch, Stafford, and Weicker all favor a more conservative policy than the status quo. On issues in the Labor Committee's jurisdiction, however, Lowell Weicker was one of the most liberal members of the Senate. As a result, the number of Labor Committee bills for which Weicker supported a shift in policy to the right was negligible during the years that I followed the committee. Placing the preferences of Hatch and both pivotal voters to the right of existing law is interesting, but such a configuration tells us little about actual Labor Committee politics.
7. Under current budgetary procedures, the authorizing committees of Congress are occasionally asked to reduce spending in the programs within their jurisdictions. The quantity of funding each panel has to cut is determined through the budget

process, but the various authorizing committees decide how these cuts will be distributed among the programs in their jurisdictions.

8. The material in this section is related to recent scholarship about the foundations of committee power in Congress. See Shepsle and Weingast 1987a, 1987b; Krehbiel 1987; Smith 1988; Gilligan and Krehbiel 1990; and Hall and Evans 1990.

Appendixes

APPENDIX A

Evidence

Although the strengths and weaknesses of the evidence in this study have been underscored in the body of the text, some questions of methodology bear further elaboration. The first section of this appendix is a discussion of the process by which the sample of sixty-two bills considered by the Commerce, Environment and Public Works, Judiciary, and Labor Committees was selected. My interviews with current and former Senate staff persons are discussed in the second section, while the third is a description of my interviews with members of the Senate.

The Sample of Legislation

Following the lead of Price (1972) and Hall (1987), I have chosen to explore congressional committee politics from the perspective of individual pieces of legislation, as well as more general perceptions of participants in the process. A sample of sixty-two bills considered by the four panels—primarily during the first session of the 99th Congress—was selected. These bills are listed in table A.1. Fifty-eight were marked up in 1985, while four were considered in early 1986. Three of the four bills marked up during the second session of the 99th Congress were Judiciary Committee bills (S.239, S.1300, and S.1923), which were included in the sample because of their subject matter interest and general salience. The final item not considered during the first session was a Labor Committee initiative (S.1965, a reauthorization of the Higher Education Act), which was included because no education legislation of comparable importance was considered in 1985.

Contained in the sample are all of the bills marked up in the four committees in 1985 for which committee consideration was more than perfunctory (i.e., there was some discussion of the provisions in the bill, or amendments were offered). A sample of more routine bills was then added to generate the total of sixty-two. For Judiciary, Labor, and Environment and Public Works, the sample includes all but a few of the items these panels marked up in 1985. Because of the very large number of reauthorizations falling within the jurisdiction of the Commerce Committee, including a lower proportion of the total number of bills considered was necessary for reasons of tractability. Thus,

TABLE A.1. Sample of Legislation, 99th Congress

Committee on Commerce, Science, and Transportation

S.100	Product Liability Act
S.259	Professional Sports Community Protection Act of 1985
S.374	U.S. Travel and Tourism Administration Appropriations Authorization
S.638	Conrail Sale Amendments of 1985
S.679	Maritime Appropriation Authorization Act for FY1986
S.721	Agricultural Trade Amendment Act of 1985
S.863	National Highway Traffic Safety Administration Authorization Act of 1985
S.990	National Ocean and Atmospheric Administration Program Support Authorization Act
S.999	Federal Communications Commission Authorization Act of 1985
S.1017	Metropolitan Washington Airports Transfer Act of 1985
S.1077	Consumer Product Safety Commission Authorization Act of 1985
S.1078	Federal Trade Commission Act Amendments of 1985
S.1084	Corporation for Public Broadcasting Authorization Act of 1985
S.1097	Methanol Vehicle Incentives Act of 1985
S.1218	International Air Transportation Protection Act of 1985
H.R.1714	National Aeronautics and Space Administration Authorization for 1986

Committee on Environment and Public Works

S.51	Reauthorization of the Comprehensive Environmental Response, Compensation, and Liability Act of 1980 (Superfund)
S.124	Safe Drinking Water Act Amendments of 1985
S.391	Interstate Highway Funding Act of 1985
S.725	Endangered Species Act Reauthorization
S.895	Nuclear Regulatory Commission Reauthorization
S.1023	Disaster Relief Act Authorization
S.1030	Public Buildings Authorization Act of 1985
S.1128	Clean Water Act Amendments of 1985
S.1567	Water Resources Development Act of 1985
S.1578	Low Level Radioactive Waste Policy Act

Committee on the Judiciary

S.40	To provide procedures for calling federal constitutional conventions
S.86	Sex Discrimination in the United States Code Reform Act of 1985
S.104	To amend chapter 44, title 18, U.S. Code, to regulate the manufacture of armor piercing bullets
S.239	To establish constitutional procedures for the imposition of the sentence of death, and for other purposes
S.274	Nuclear Power Plant Security and Anti-terrorism Act of 1985
S.300	To amend section 1951 of title 18 of the U.S. Code, and for other purposes—Hobbes Act
S.412	Malt Beverage Interbrand Competition Act
S.1200	Immigration Reform and Control Act of 1985
S.1236	To amend title 18 of the U.S. Code and other laws to make minor or technical changes as to provisions enacted by the Comprehensive Crime Control Act of 1984, and for other purposes

TABLE A.1—*Continued*

Committee on the Judiciary (*continued*)

S.1262	Refugee Assistance Extension Act of 1985
S.1300	To adjust liability in antitrust cases
S.1429	Terrorist Prosecution Act of 1985
S.1437	Controlled Substances Analogs' Enforcement Act of 1985
S.1562	False Claims Reform Act of 1985
S.1916	To preserve the authority of Supreme Court Police to provide protective services for Justices and Supreme Court personnel off court premises
S.1923	To create 34 new bankruptcy judgeships
S.J. Res. 2	Proposing an amendment to the Constitution of the United States relating to voluntary silent prayer or reflection
S.J. Res. 225	Proposing an amendment to the Constitution relating to a federal balanced budget and tax limitation

Committee on Labor and Human Resources

S.140	Children's Justice Act
S.415	Handicapped Children's Protection Act
S.484	To amend the Saccharin Study and Labeling Act
S.801	National Science Foundation Authorization Act for FY1986
S.881	To extend Title X of the Public Health Service Act
S.974	Protection and Advocacy for Mentally Ill Persons Act of 1985
S.1105	Federal Contractor Flextime Act
S.1181	Home and Community Based Services for the Elderly Act of 1985
S.1210	Public Health Service Medical Education Amendments of 1985
S.1264	National Foundation of the Arts and Humanities Amendments of 1985
S.1282	Primary Care Amendments of 1985
S.1566	To extend the Adolescent Family Life Demonstration Program for three years
S.1570	To amend the Fair Labor Standards Act of 1938 to exclude the employees of states and political subdivisions of states from the provisions of that Act relating to maximum hours, to clarify the application of that Act to volunteers, and for other purposes. (Passed as H.R. 3530, Fair Labor Standards Amendments of 1985)
S.1574	Comprehensive Smokeless Tobacco and Health Education Act of 1985
S.1730	ERISA reform (on reconciliation bill)
S.1762	Health Maintenance Organization Amendments of 1985
S.1848	Pharmaceutical Export Amendments of 1985
S.1965	Higher Education Amendments of 1985

although the sample is somewhat biased toward more salient and controversial legislation on all four committees, the magnitude of this bias is only of significance on the Commerce Committee. And across all four committees, reauthorizations are included at roughly their percentage of the total work load.

In constructing the sample, an effort was made to select legislation from all of the subcommittees of the four panels, and then to add items from those subcommittees that were particularly active. As a result, the breadth of each committee's jurisdiction is reflected in the sample, as are the relative activity levels of the various subcommittees. Unfortunately, because of low levels of activity in these areas, it was not possible to include legislation from three Judiciary subcommittees: the Subcommittees on Courts; Juvenile Justice; and Patents, Copyrights, and Trademarks. A large sample of bills from the other five Judiciary subcommittees was obtained, though, and I do not believe that these omissions have distorted our picture of leadership behavior on the four panels.

Evidence about each of the sixty-two bills was gathered from markup transcripts, staff interviews, and interviews with senators, as well as the usual media sources. The stenographic records that congressional committees keep of their markup sessions are one of the most valuable research tools available to congressional scholars, but they seldom are utilized. In part, this is because many researchers are unaware of how accessible these records actually are.[1] Indeed, it is the norm among Senate committees to keep copies of markup transcripts in committee offices, usually extending back two or three congresses.

From the markup transcripts alone, it was possible to gather information (for the bills in the sample) about which senators voted on amendments and procedural questions and how they voted, as well as information about which senators offered amendments, the views of committee members about those amendments, and whether or not attempts at amendment were successful. In addition, authorship of the draft was usually obvious from remarks in the transcripts. Typically, a markup session is opened by the chair, who announces the order of business, provides some introductory comments, and then turns the floor over to the lead sponsor of the item under consideration. The lead sponsor then describes the evolution and content of the legislation and usually cites the input of senators who participated in shaping the draft. Although the written record did not provide a comprehensive list of those senators influencing the draft brought into markup, it usually came close. Thus, the markup transcripts alone provided most of the information in the participation indicator discussed in appendix B and referred to in chapters 3 and 4.

The transcripts were also useful for developing preliminary impressions about procedural tactics and the extent to which committee members made changes in their legislation to facilitate floor action. Indeed, it was while reading transcripts of Judiciary Committee meetings early on in my research efforts that the importance of the temporal dimension of committee policy-making—namely, acceleration and delay—first became obvious. Procedural tactics are discussed openly in committee meetings, often generating heated exchanges. Markup transcripts also provided substantial information about the strategy of anticipated reactions. For instance, during the Judiciary Committee's markup of the proposed constitutional amendment to balance the federal budget, it was clear that the primary backers of the legislation had modified their draft to increase its chances of getting through the Senate. Orrin Hatch, chairman of the subcommittee of jurisdiction, repeatedly remarked that he preferred a stronger bill, but adopted a more moderate approach to maximize the probability of passage. Indeed, the negotiations leading to the stripped-down amendment aimed at bringing Democrats on board were openly discussed during committee markups, and it was clear from the transcripts that the panel was making major changes to grease the skids.

Staff Interviews

A large number of interviews with current and former Senate staff persons provided further information about the sixty-two bills, as well as more general observations about committee politics. These interviews were approximately 100 in number, and they were conducted in two waves. The first wave was conducted between October, 1985, and July, 1986; these interviews averaged approximately one hour and twenty minutes in length. In addition, a few supplementary interviews were conducted during the summer and fall of 1988. All of my conversations with staffers were held on a "not-for-attribution basis." A number of these individuals requested complete anonymity and thus cannot be directly thanked for their assistance. But I am able to note my appreciation to the following current and former Senate staff persons, who gave freely of their time and expertise.[2]

Amy Bondurant, Harold Brayman, Jim Brudney, Chris Button, Doug Campbell, Chuck Carroll, Geryld Christianson, Guy Clough, Tom Cohen, Eddie Correia, Sandy Crary, Phil Cummings, Deborah Curtis, Jim Curtiss, Dick Dargan, Paul Donovan, Jim Drewry, Loretta Dunn, David Evans, Charlie Faust, Bob Feidler, Mike Forscey, Peter Friedman, Win Froelich, Ann Garrabrant, Pamela Garvie, Polly Gault, Sam Gerdano, Scott Green, Carl Hampe, Paulette Hansen, John Hardy, Chuck Harwood, Rick Holcomb, Lisa Hovelson, Bob Hurley, Kris Iverson, Steve Johnson, Helen Kalbaugh, Kate Kimball, Marty Kress, Jean Lauver, Rick Lawson, Mary McGrane, Ken McLean, Susanne Martinez, Bill Miller, Linda Morgan, David Nexon, Ron Outen, Deborah Owen, Steve Palmer, Peter Perkins, Dan Phythyon, John Podesta, Martha Pope, Randy Rader, Marilyn Richmond, Tim Rieser, Robin Rushton, Mona Sarfaty, Steven Shimberg, Christopher Simpson, Tom Skirbunt, David St. John, Ken Starling, David Starr, David Sundwall, Steve Swain,

Nancy Taylor, Jerry Tinker, Ted Totman, James Wagoner, Cheryl Wallace, Diana Waterman, Jane West, Heather Wicke, and David Zorensky.

This study could not have been conducted without the assistance of these individuals. Of course, I alone am responsible for matters of interpretation.

For each of the bills in the sample, I spoke with staffers who had responsibility for the legislation; discussion focused on specific legislative items rather than more general questions about committee politics and legislative leadership. On average, just over three individuals were interviewed per bill. As Richard Hall has argued, structuring interviews with congressional staffers around specific pieces of legislation increases the reliability of the responses for two reasons.[3] First, the staffers are primarily asked about those matters on which they have considerable expertise and first-hand knowledge. Second, focusing on individual bills reduces the stakes of the interview for the staff person because rating a senator as inconsequential on one or two bills does not imply general ineffectiveness. Staffers may show a natural reluctance to judge the overall effectiveness of a senator, but I found few to be reluctant to make concrete comments about a senator's actions on just one or two bills.

Considerable effort was made to discuss each of the sixty-two pieces of legislation with staffers from both parties, and on all but four of the items, at least one staff person from each party was interviewed (the four bills subject to only one interview were all minor reauthorizations). The reasons for such an approach are relatively clear. First, there is the potential that the partisan loyalties of the individuals interviewed might distort their responses to questions: Talking to both Republican and Democratic staffers about legislation mitigates this problem. But the more significant pitfall to relying on the responses of staffers from just one party is that they may not be privy to information about decision making on the other side of the aisle.

The vast majority of the staff interviews were tape-recorded. In general, taping provides a much more accurate and comprehensive record of an interview, which was crucial in the staff interviews because of the focus on particular pieces of legislation. Of course, there is always the danger that the person being taped will be less than candid. Although it is not possible to judge with certainty, my general impression was that taping the staff interviews had little impact on their content. Very few of the staff persons revealed significant hesitancy about being taped, and most seemed to think the request was natural. After speaking for ten to fifteen minutes, staffers usually appeared to have forgotten the presence of the tape recorder altogether.

These interviews are best described as semistructured. A core set of questions was used in almost all of the interviews, allowing construction of the participation indicator described in appendix B. Given the constraints of elite interviewing, as well as the exploratory nature of this project, efforts also were made to keep the conversations as free-flowing as possible. Indeed, I generally found that the staffers were more than willing to speak at length, and I tried to restrict my own participation to guiding the conversation and avoiding unfruitful digressions. Questions were not always worded in the same manner, and the order in which questions were asked was not always identical across interviews. A primary goal was to establish and maintain rapport. In addition, if a staffer presented sufficient information to answer a question before it was actually asked, I avoided asking the question.

The typical staff interview was constructed around the following questions:

1. Who shaped the draft brought into markup? Which senators, directly or through staff, had a concrete impact on the substance of the draft?
2. How salient is [the relevant policy area] to members of the Senate? How much conflict does the issue usually generate? Is the committee representative of opinion in the Senate on this issue?
3. At any time during the committee process, was the bill changed, or were certain provisions not attempted, because of potential problems with other committee members?
4. Did any senators on the committee, directly or through staff, influence the process by slowing things down, or by putting things on a fast track and speeding things up?
5. During the time when the committee was working on the bill, did you anticipate potential problems on the floor (with the administration? with the House?) and change the bill for that reason? Were the changes major or minor?

At varying points during the interviews, I asked staffers to characterize the roles played (on a particular bill) by the full committee chair and ranking minority member. These questions usually were followed up with a question asking the staff person to generalize, if possible, about the overall leadership style of both leaders. Questions also were asked about the role of subcommittees in committee decision making; the role of the minority; the extent of party leaders' involvement during the committee stage; the levels of communication and cooperation with members and staff of the House committee of jurisdiction; and the way in which Senate offices decide when to become involved on a bill. Additional questions were asked about events that occurred between committee and floor consideration—for example, the presence and source of any holds or the nature of the negotiations leading up to a time agreement. Because many of the bills had been considered on the floor by the time my interviews with the relevant staff persons took place, a discussion of action in the full Senate often was possible.[4]

Member Interviews

In addition to interviewing staff persons, interviews with twenty-one individuals who were members of the Senate in the 99th Congress were conducted during the summers of 1988 and 1989. Most of the senators interviewed were members of the four committees under study, and the sample is skewed toward the leadership level. Indeed, thirteen of the twenty-one senators had experience as a committee chair and/or ranking minority member. I was also able to interview seven of the eight full committee leaders examined in this study—all but Joseph Biden.

In contrast to the staff interviews, interviews with senators were held "on the record." Through informal chats with people experienced in interviewing members of the Senate, it quickly became clear to me that the potential political costs to a senator from damaging quotations are usually high enough that most members implicitly treat all discussions as on the record unless they know the interviewer well. The time of a U.S. senator is one of the most valuable commodities in Washington, and appointments are generally scheduled in fifteen-minute bites. As a result, I did not expect to have the time necessary to develop anything approaching significant rapport and thus opted to do the interviews on the record.

Unlike my interviews with staffers, I did not tape-record the interviews with senators. I wanted to keep the discussions as casual and informal as possible, given the time constraints, and did not see that as feasible with a tape recorder sitting on the coffee table. The member interviews were relatively unstructured. In part, I wanted to corroborate other sources, but my primary goal was to get some feel for the senator's perspective on the process. For this reason, I took notes during the course of the interviews and jotted down all phrasings that I found evocative. These discussions were then reproduced as completely as possible immediately after the interview. In general, my views on elite interviewing have been heavily influenced by the appendix on participant observation found in Fenno 1978.

A list of the senators interviewed follows. The conversations ranged in length from ten minutes to forty-five minutes, for an average of about twenty-five minutes.

Max Baucus (D–Mont.)	July 8, 1988
Lloyd Bentsen (D–Tex.)	August 2, 1989
John C. Danforth (R–Mo.)	July, 1989
Pete V. Domenici (R–N. Mex)	July 29, 1988
Wendell H. Ford (D–Ky.)	July 26, 1988
Jake Garn (R–Utah)	July 12, 1988

Orrin G. Hatch (R–Utah)	July 28, 1988
Ernest F. Hollings (D–S.C.)	July 28, 1988
Paul Laxalt (R–Nev.)	September 22, 1988
Nancy Landon Kassebaum (R–Kans.)	July 29, 1988
Edward M. Kennedy (D–Mass.)	August 4, 1988
Howard M. Metzenbaum (D–Ohio)	July 12, 1988
George J. Mitchell (D–Maine)	July 7, 1988
Claiborne Pell (D–R.I.)	July 26, 1988
William Proxmire (D–Wis.)	July 14, 1988
Paul Simon (D–Ill.)	July 13, 1988
Alan K. Simpson (R–Wyo.)	August 4, 1988
Robert T. Stafford (R–Vt.)	July 27, 1988
Steven D. Symms (R–Idaho)	July 27, 1988
Strom Thurmond (R–S.C.)	September 22, 1988
John W. Warner (R–Va.)	July 14, 1988

I generally began these interviews with a specific question or set of questions about the senator's activities on a bill on which he or she made a significant contribution during 1985 or 1986. This approach emphasized my interest in concrete information, revealed that I had done some homework, and also served as an informal test of the member's personal knowledge and involvement in a matter that had been prominent on his or her agenda. Further topics varied considerably from member to member, but throughout I was extremely careful to avoid asking questions that could be answered by staff. Instead, I focused on questions that only the individual senator could answer effectively. For the most part, my interviews with senators corroborated and reinforced evidence gleaned from other sources. But they also generated some useful new information about how senators view committee politics and legislative leadership.

Notes

1. Richard Hall was the first person to tell me about the general availability of committee markup transcripts in the Senate. As further evidence of the value of markup records for analyzing committee decision making, I need only point to his ongoing study of participation and representation in congressional committees.

2. The process for selecting the individuals to be interviewed was straightforward. For the Commerce Committee, the names of the lead staffers on committee legislation are listed in the various committee calendars. On Environment and Public Works, staff participation during markup sessions is extensive enough that the names of the relevant staffers on a bill can be gathered simply by reading through the transcripts. For legislation in the jurisdictions of Judiciary and Labor, I began by

calling committee offices and requesting the names of the primary staffers. And during the course of each interview, I typically asked for the names of additional individuals who were active on the legislation, and these people were then interviewed.

3. Hall 1990.

4. Usually toward the end of an interview, a staff member also was given a form with an alphabetical list of committee members and asked to rate each as to whether "directly, or through staff, the senator had a major, moderate, minor, or no influence on the substance of the bill." The form was exactly the same as the one developed by Hall (1990) to analyze influence in House committees, and it has been employed to analyze subcommittee anticipation of full committee preferences in three House committees (Hall and Evans 1990). To incorporate legislators' influence over the process, after a staff member had completed the form, I asked the following question: "How would these ratings change if the form had been worded to include influence over the committee process on this bill—for example, dilatory tactics or speeding things up—rather than just influence on the substance of the bill?" These data were not useful for comparing leadership behavior across different issue areas, however, and therefore are not used in this book. But see Evans 1986.

APPENDIX B

Participation in Committee

A major reason why our understanding of legislative leadership behavior is underdeveloped is the difficulty of gathering useful data across a range of leaders and leadership contexts. As a result, the methodology of this study is two-pronged. First, relatively impressionistic evidence has been gleaned from interviews and committee documents; this evidence figures prominently in the text. But it is useful to combine interview data with more systematic empirical work when feasible. As a check on the perceptions of senators and staff persons, as well as material derived from committee documents, I also have conducted a statistical analysis of participation during the 99th Congress in the four committees under study. Data were drawn from the sample of sixty-two pieces of legislation considered by the panels in 1985 and 1986 (see appendix A for a description of the sample).

This book, however, does not thoroughly examine who participates in congressional committees and why.[1] The object of study is leadership behavior, and evidence about the division of labor among legislators in committee is employed only to shed further light on issues directly related to leadership in Senate committees. Thus, I do not explore in a systematic fashion the motivations and goals that lead rank-and-file committee members to participate in legislative work. Instead, I seek a general picture of the division of labor in each of the four committees during the 99th Congress. How involved are full committee leaders in legislative work? How does the extent of their involvement vary across different leaders and different committees? Answers to these questions provide a useful point of departure for the analysis of leadership strategies in chapters 3 and 4. In short, my treatment of participation in this appendix is primarily descriptive, not analytical.

Members of the Senate participate in committee work in many ways, from introducing legislation to providing language for committee reports. But three modes of participation are given special emphasis here: participation in roll call votes at some point during the markup stage of the process; participation in committee deliberations through offering substantive (nontechnical) amendments that are then included in the panel's bill; and participation in shaping the original draft brought into markup. These particular forms of participation can have a direct impact on the content of committee policy, and they have been emphasized in the existing scholarly literature on congressional committees.

Measurement

Participation has been recognized as an integral component of policy-making in congressional committees for years, but until the recent work of Richard Hall, students of committee politics have lacked the methodology necessary to examine participation in committee with much precision.[2] The major roadblock in previous studies was a lack of systematic data. Hall used a combination of verbatim transcripts and focused interviews with knowledgeable staff persons to devise an individual level, bill-by-bill measure of participation for members of the House Education and Labor Committee during the 97th Congress. The participation indicator used in this appendix is adapted from that research.

Hall's focus, however, was on participation in committee, whereas my interest centers primarily on questions about leadership and power. As a result, some of the forms of participation included in his indicator are not used here. In particular, Hall analyzed attendance and speaking during formal markup sessions. Although these activities can have a concrete impact on legislation, my observations of decision making in Senate committees, as well as the remarks of senators and staff assistants, suggest that they are much less consequential for committee policy than is the case with participating in roll call votes, offering nontechnical amendments that are eventually accepted, and participating during the drafting stage of the process. Thus, the participation indicator used here consists of these last three activities alone.

Data pertaining to voting and amendment behavior were drawn from verbatim transcripts of full and subcommittee markup sessions for the sample of sixty-two bills considered in the four panels during the 99th Congress (see app. A). From careful study of the markup transcripts, it was straightforward to code for each of the sixty-two bills (a) whether or not there was a non-unanimous roll call vote during committee consideration of a piece of legislation; (b) which senators voted in person on at least one of those roll calls; and (c) the names of senators offering nontechnical amendments subsequently accepted by the committee. Both subcommittee and full committee markup sessions were examined in gathering the data.

Participation in roll call votes (and not voice votes) was considered because roll calls tend to occur on proposals for which the result is in question or the issue is important. Occasionally, however, senators will call the roll for purposes of position taking, and the result will be unanimous. For that reason, I have excluded all unanimous votes. And if a senator's vote was cast by proxy, I did not credit him or her with having voted. This was a tough call: On some measures, proxies determined the result. But it was clear from the markup transcripts, from the interviews, and from an examination of a large number of written proxy letters that, contrary to the rules of most Senate committees, proxies tend to be relatively general. That is, any influence over the outcome resulting from the vote tends to be exercised by the senator with the proxy, rather than the member on whose behalf the proxy is being cast. These observations are fully consistent with those of Hall, and he also excluded proxy votes from his scale of participation.

The markup transcripts also provided detailed information about which committee members offered amendments, the content of the amendments, and their resolution. Using Hall's criteria, I distinguished between amendments that were obviously technical in nature, and those that were substantive. An amendment was considered technical if and only if it was explicitly referred to as technical by the amendment's sponsor, there was no disagreement from other committee members, and the question was resolved by voice vote or unanimous consent. Because technical amendments tend to be inconsequential and involve little legislative influence, they were excluded from my analysis.

In order to gather information about which senators influenced the shape of the vehicle brought into markup, I began my interviews with staffers knowledgeable about each bill by asking the following questions: "Who shaped the draft brought into markup? Which senators, directly or through staff, had a concrete impact on the substance of the draft?"[3] These questions often drew mention of a wide range of actors in addition to the relevant Senate offices, including interest groups, executive agencies, and even an occasional academic. Indeed, on some of the bills, no member of the Senate had an effect on the substance of the draft (most bills in this category were administration initiatives introduced by request). In this study, no attempt is made to distinguish between differing levels of impact on the draft, although on most drafts some senators were obviously more consequential than others. And because my focus is more on power than on participation per se, unlike Hall I only consider those senators who exerted a concrete impact on the actual substance of the draft.

Combining information gleaned from the markup transcripts and staff interviews, it is possible to construct a simple four-point indicator of participation in committee by a Senator i on some bill j:

0—did not participate;
1—a nonunanimous roll call vote occurred in either subcommittee or full committee markup, and the senator voted in person;

2—the senator offered a nontechnical amendment during subcommittee or full committee markup that was accepted and incorporated into the bill;

3—the senator was attributed with having some concrete impact on the shape of the markup vehicle.

On occasion, a senator successfully amending a bill clearly had a greater impact on the substance than did senators influencing the draft, and on a few pieces of legislation, the fate of the entire bill turned on the votes of just one or two committee members. But, in general, my interviews and the markup transcripts suggested that this simple four-point scale taps into the intensity of legislative influence on a bill rather well. It has the additional advantage of being reproducible, and it builds on Hall's previous research on the House, allowing the possibility of systematic bicameral comparisons.[4]

In the analysis that follows, I treat the participation indicator as an interval-level measure, even though it is clearly ordinal. That is, I implicitly assume that the difference in participatory impact between the various intervals is the same. For example, the difference between voting and not voting is assumed to be identical, in terms of legislative involvement, to the difference between passing an amendment and shaping the draft. These assumptions are obviously strong, but the key methodological question is whether or not they have substantive implications for the statistical results in this appendix. A series of tests was employed to gauge the extent to which the results were dependent on the particular scale employed, and it was clear that changes in scale did not significantly change the conclusions. As is the case with most ordinal-level measures, treating the participation indicator as an interval-level measure did not appear to distort the substantive interpretations drawn from the data. In short, the results in this appendix are sufficiently robust to support the tentative generalizations offered in chapters 3 and 4.

Analysis

A range of factors influences whether a senator participates in committee on a given piece of legislation, but five are of particular relevance to the study of committee leadership: whether or not a senator is (1) chair of the full committee; (2) ranking minority member of the full committee; (3) chair of the subcommittee of jurisdiction; (4) ranking minority member of the subcommittee of jurisdiction; or (5) a member of the subcommittee of jurisdiction. In addition, in the following analysis, I also controlled for the effects of three more explanatory factors: a senator's party, seniority, and whether or not he or she was preparing for a reelection campaign.[5] The literature on congressional committees and my own research suggested that these variables would shape the identities and relative involvement of senators active on a bill in committee.[6]

The relative importance of the factors affecting participation in committee was explored through four simple regression equations (each panel was examined separately). Bills falling within the jurisdiction of a subcommittee were pooled with items that were clearly full committee issues.[7] However, because legislation held at full committee may exhibit patterns of participation that differ from those characterizing subcommittee bills, a dummy variable (FCBILL) was added to the regressions, which took on a value of one if a bill was a full committee issue, and was zero otherwise. To explore the roles of the full committee chairs and ranking minority members on full committee bills, interactions were added between FCBILL and the indicators of full committee chairmanship and ranking minority member status. A summary of the variables is provided in table B.1, and results of the regression equations are presented in table B.2.[8]

As expected, the parameter estimates in table B.2 provide evidence that

TABLE B.1. Variables

PARTICIPATION	Takes on a value of three if a senator affected the draft, a value of two if he or she offered an amendment that passed, a value of one if a nonunanimous roll call occurred and the senator voted in person, and is zero otherwise.
INT	The intercept.
FCBILL	Takes on a value of one if a bill is a full committee issue, and is zero for all subcommittee issues.
FCCH	Takes on a value of one if a senator is the full committee chair, and is zero otherwise.
FCCHF	FCCH*FCBILL: An interaction between full committee chair and whether or not a bill is a full committee issue.
FCRK	Takes on a value of one if a senator is the full committee ranking minority member, and is zero otherwise.
FCRKF	FCRK*FCBILL: An interaction between full committee ranking minority membership and whether or not a bill is a full committee issue.
SCCH	Takes on a value of one if a senator is subcommittee chair for the bill, and is zero otherwise.
SCRK	Takes on a value of one if a senator is subcommittee ranking minority member for the bill, and is zero otherwise.
SCMEM	Takes on a value of one if a senator is on the subcommittee of jurisdiction, and is zero otherwise.
PARTY	Takes on a value of one if the senator is a Republican, and is zero if the senator is a Democrat.
APPREN	Takes on a value of one if a senator is serving in his or her first two years in office, and is zero otherwise.
RUN	Takes on a value of one if a senator ran for reelection in 1986, and is zero otherwise.

formal leadership status does lead to disproportionate participation. Across all four panels, the coefficients on full committee chairmanship (FCCH), subcommittee chairmanship (SCCH), and subcommittee ranking minority membership (SCRK) are positive and statistically significant and, of greater importance, large enough to be of substantive significance as well. Of the full committee ranking minority members (denoted by FCRK), only Joseph Biden on the Judiciary Committee fails to show a positive coefficient, a result that is discussed at length in chapters 3 and 4. The coefficients on subcommittee membership (SCMEM) are also positive on all four committees and statistically significant on three. Thus, for the most part, a senator's institutional

TABLE B.2.   Participation in Committee

Independent Variables	Committee			
	Commerce	Environment and Public Works	Judiciary	Labor
INT	.19[c]	.49[a]	.39[a]	.31[b]
	(.11)	(.17)	(.09)	(.14)
FCBILL	.52[b]	.43[c]	− .11	.27[b]
	(.21)	(.25)	(.13)	(.13)
FCCH	1.39[a]	1.61[a]	.80[a]	1.09[a]
	(.22)	(.41)	(.23)	(.32)
FCCHF	.87	.74	.004	1.11[b]
	(.83)	(.87)	(.52)	(.43)
FCRK	.62[a]	.58	− .12	1.06[a]
	(.23)	(.41)	(.23)	(.33)
FCRKF	− .55	− .01	.51	.47
	(.84)	(.87)	(.52)	(.44)
SCCH	1.31[a]	1.97[a]	1.87[a]	2.36[a]
	(.23)	(.42)	(.24)	(.33)
SCRK	.98[a]	.99[b]	1.49[a]	.87[a]
	(.24)	(.43)	(.25)	(.33)
SCMEM	.19[c]	.39[c]	.48[a]	.28
	(.11)	(.22)	(.13)	(.17)
PARTY	.03	− .28	− .08	− .11
	(.12)	(.21)	(.10)	(.14)
APPREN	.03	—	.24	− .07
	(.17)	—	(.15)	(.18)
RUN	.23[b]	.20	.04	.08
	(.11)	(.28)	(.11)	(.13)
R^2	.36	.30	.41	.37
N	272	150	324	288

Note: Standard errors are in parentheses.
[a] Significant at the .01 level
[b] Significant at the .05 level
[c] Significant at the .10 level

role on a bill is closely associated with the degree to which he or she participates in committee. In general, the subset of committee members participating is disproportionately composed of members holding formal leadership status on a bill, as well as members of the subcommittee of jurisdiction.[9]

Beyond these continuities, however, there are some interesting differences in the size of the parameter estimates for the various leadership positions, both within and across committees. In particular, four questions emerge: (1) Why is there little difference between the coefficients for full committee and subcommittee chairmanship on the Commerce Committee, but not on the other three panels? (2) Why is the coefficient for ranking minority member status on the Judiciary Committee negative, while coefficients for all the other full committee leaders are positive and, with one exception, statistically significant? (3) Why is there little difference between the parameter estimates for full committee chairmanship and ranking minority member status on the Labor Committee, but not on the other three panels? (4) Why does the parameter estimate for the full committee ranking minority member on Labor exceed the coefficient for subcommittee ranking minority member, a finding that also differs from the other committees? A detailed analysis of these questions is provided in chapters 3 and 4.

Notes

1. See Hall 1987 for an analysis of participation during markup sessions. Payne 1980 provides a study of participation at the hearing stage of the process. And studies of participation on the floor can be found in Sinclair 1989 and Smith 1989.

2. Hall 1987. An expanded treatment that includes data from three House committees can be found in Hall 1990. For earlier discussions of participation in House and Senate committees, see Huitt 1954, Clapp 1963, Manley 1970, Price 1972, and Fenno 1973.

3. Hall employed a similar procedure in gathering data for his scale of informal participation in the House Education and Labor Committee. However, my questions about drafting activity were more general, and my intention was to evoke an extended discussion of the source of the markup vehicle. Indeed, these discussions usually went back two or three congresses.

4. Hall used a Guttman scale technique to produce a seven-point scale of formal participation that included attendance, two levels of participation in the discussion, the offering of technical and nontechnical amendments, participation as an agenda setter, and roll-call voting. Influence over the draft was incorporated via a five-point scale of informal participation, derived from interviews with knowledgeable staff. As mentioned, these other forms of participation, while relevant for a general study of participation in committee, are less crucial when the focus is on questions of legislative leadership and power. In addition, no Guttman analysis or other scaling techniques were employed here. Crediting a senator with influence over the draft does not imply that he or she also amended the bill, or even that the senator attended the markup.

Given the time pressures facing the typical senator, some of the bills in my sample were brought up in markup when the primary authors were not in attendance. Similarly, on many pieces of legislation, there are no incentives for a bill's authors to attempt modification in committee through the amendment process. The particular hierarchy of the four-point scale in this appendix was chosen because it made good intuitive sense, because it was consistent with the perceptions of the people I interviewed, and because the activities followed a similar ordering in Hall's seven-point scale.

5. It is also conceivable that preference outliers may participate less than committee members closer to the center of the distribution of opinion in committee on a particular piece of legislation. Indicators of extremism were constructed for each committee, but they had a trivial impact on participation as measured in this appendix. Since their impact was substantively trivial, these variables were dropped from the equations. Remaining parameter estimates were not affected.

6. For a more comprehensive analysis of participation in the four committees, see Evans (forthcoming).

7. A number of pieces of legislation not marked up in subcommittee were treated as subcommittee bills. If the bill clearly fell within the jurisdiction of one subcommittee and the issue area traditionally was assigned to that subcommittee, but the legislation was held at the full committee level with the consent of the subcommittee chair, the bill was treated as originating from that subcommittee. Thus, assignment to a subcommittee does not imply that a subcommittee markup actually took place.

8. Notice that none of the explanatory variables included in the models of table B.2 varies both by senator and by bill, which is the relevant unit of analysis. Are these regression equations badly misspecified as a result? The answer depends on the substantive questions being asked. In his analysis of the House Education and Labor Committee, Hall included explanatory variables that tapped into the degree to which a piece of legislation evoked the interest of committee members. These variables varied by bill and by legislator. As expected, the degree to which a legislator's goals are evoked by a bill has an independent impact on participation in committee. Similar variables are not included in this analysis because gathering the necessary data would have required many months of additional staff interviews. But, more important, my interest is in determining the extent to which committee leaders participate relative to other senators, and not in distinguishing between the effects of member interest and institutional position on participation in committee. Thus, given my focus in this study, as well as the difficulty of collecting the data necessary for a more comprehensive approach, the specification in table B.2 is a useful and informative, albeit second-best, solution.

9. Significant effort was allocated to gauging the stability of the results under alternative specifications. Obviously, the bills in the sample differ markedly in salience and controversy, and, as a result, participation in committee is more extensive on some items than it is on others. It is conceivable that correlations between the explanatory variables and bill-specific factors not included in the models (such as salience and controversy) might distort the results in table B.2. To explore whether or not such distortions occurred, I dropped the intercept and included dummy variables for each of

the bills. There were no significant changes in the parameter estimates. I also dropped observations from each of the four committee-specific samples and repeated the regressions to examine whether or not the results were dependent on one or two bills. Again, no significant changes in the parameter estimates occurred.

References

Aranson, Peter, Ernest Gellhorn, and Glen Robinson. 1982. "A Theory of Legislative Delegation." *Cornell Law Review* 68:1–67.

Asbell, Bernard. 1978. *The Senate Nobody Knows.* Baltimore: Johns Hopkins University Press.

Austen-Smith, David, and William Riker. 1987. "Asymmetric Information and the Coherence of Legislation." *American Political Science Review* 81:897–918.

Baker, Ross K. 1980. *Friend and Foe in the U.S. Senate.* New York: Free Press.

Barber, James David. 1965. *The Lawmakers: Recruitment and Adaptation to Legislative Life.* New Haven: Yale University Press.

Barber, James David. 1966a. *Power in Committees: An Experiment in the Governmental Process.* Chicago: Rand McNally.

Barber, James David. 1966b. "Leadership Strategies for Legislative Party Cohesion." *Journal of Politics* 28:347–66.

Barber, James David. 1972. *The Presidential Character.* Englewood Cliffs, N.J.: Prentice-Hall.

Bass, Bernard M. 1981. *Stogdill's Handbook of Leadership.* New York: Free Press.

Bianco, William T., and Robert H. Bates. 1990. "Cooperation by Design: Leadership, Structure, and Collective Dilemmas." *American Political Science Review* 84:133–48.

Black, Duncan. 1948. "On the Rationale of Group Decision-Making." *Journal of Political Economy* 56:23–34.

Black, Duncan. 1958. *The Theory of Committees and Elections.* Cambridge: Cambridge University Press.

Buchanan, James M., and Gordon Tullock. 1962. *The Calculus of Consent.* Ann Arbor: University of Michigan Press.

Bullock, Charles S. 1985. "U.S. Senate Committee Assignments: Preferences, Motivations, and Successes." *American Journal of Political Science* 29:787–808.

Calmes, Jacqueline. 1987a. "Profiles in Power: Leaders Without Portfolio." *Congressional Quarterly Weekly Report,* January 3, 16–17.

Calmes, Jacqueline. 1987b. "Trivialized Filibuster Is Still a Potent Tool." *Congressional Quarterly Weekly Report,* September 5, 2115–20.

Clapp, Charles. 1963. *The Congressman: His Work as He Sees It.* Washington, D.C.: Brookings Institution.

Clausen, Aage R. 1973. *How Congressmen Decide.* New York: St. Martin's Press.

Cohodas, Nadine. 1981. "Orrin Hatch: The Mace and the Olive Branch." *Congressional Quarterly Weekly Report,* October 10, 1954.

Cohodas, Nadine. 1983a. "Senate Panel Again Approves Package of Anti-Crime Bills." *Congressional Quarterly Weekly Report,* July 30, 1559.

Cohodas, Nadine. 1983b. "Biden and Specter Play Pivotal Rights Role." *Congressional Quarterly Weekly Report,* November 19, 2423.

Cohodas, Nadine. 1987. "Metzenbaum Takes on New Role: Pragmatist." *Congressional Quarterly Weekly Report,* July 18, 1582.

Cooper, Joseph, and David W. Brady. 1981. "Institutional Context and Leadership Style: The House from Cannon to Rayburn." *American Political Science Review* 75:411–25.

Davidson, Roger. 1981. "Subcommittee Government: New Channels for Policy Making." In *The New Congress,* ed. Thomas Mann and Norman J. Ornstein. Washington, D.C.: American Enterprise Institute.

Davidson, Roger. 1985. "Senate Leaders: Janitors for an Untidy Chamber?" In *Congress Reconsidered,* 3d ed., ed. Lawrence C. Dodd and Bruce I. Oppenheimer. Washington, D.C.: Congressional Quarterly.

Denzau, Arthur, and Robert J. MacKay. 1983. "Gatekeeping and Monopoly Power of Committees: An Analysis of Sincere and Sophisticated Behavior." *American Journal of Political Science* 27:740–61.

Denzau, Arthur, William H. Riker, and Kenneth A. Shepsle. 1985. "Farquharson and Fenno: Sophisticated Voting and Homestyle." *American Political Science Review* 79:1117–34.

Dodd, Lawrence C., and Bruce I. Oppenheimer. 1985. "The House in Transition: Partisanship and Opposition." In *Congress Reconsidered,* 3d ed., ed. Lawrence C. Dodd and Bruce I. Oppenheimer. Washington, D.C.: Congressional Quarterly.

Dodd, Lawrence C., and Bruce I. Oppenheimer, eds. 1981, 1985, 1989. *Congress Reconsidered,* 2d, 3d, 4th eds. Washington, D.C.: Congressional Quarterly.

Ehrenhalt, Alan. 1982. "In the Senate of the '80s, Team Spirit Has Given Way to the Rule of Individuals." *Congressional Quarterly Weekly Report,* September 4, 2175–82.

Ehrenhalt, Alan, ed. 1987. *Politics in America: The 100th Congress.* Washington, D.C.: Congressional Quarterly.

Eulau, Heinz, and Vera McCluggage. 1984. "Standing Committees in Legislatures: Three Decades of Research." *Legislative Studies Quarterly* 9:195–270.

Evans, C. Lawrence. 1986. "Influence in Senate Committees: The Role of Formal Leadership." Presented at the annual meeting of the American Political Science Association, Washington, D.C.

Evans, C. Lawrence. 1989. "Influence in Congressional Committees: Participation, Manipulation, and Anticipation." In *Congressional Politics,* ed. Christopher J. Deering. Chicago: Dorsey Press.

Evans, C. Lawrence. N.d. "Participation and Policy Making in U.S. Senate Committees." *Political Science Quarterly.* Forthcoming.

Fenno, Richard F., Jr. 1973. *Congressmen in Committees.* Boston: Little, Brown.

Fenno, Richard F., Jr. 1978. *Home Style.* Boston: Little, Brown.

Fenno, Richard F., Jr. 1982. *The United States Senate: A Bicameral Perspective.* Washington, D.C.: American Enterprise Institute.

Fenno, Richard F., Jr. 1986. "Observation, Context, and Sequence in the Study of Politics." *American Political Science Review* 80:3–15.

Fenno, Richard F., Jr. 1989. *The Making of a Senator: Dan Quayle*. Washington, D.C.: Congressional Quarterly.

Ferejohn, John A. 1974. *Pork Barrel Politics*. Stanford: Stanford University Press.

Fiorina, Morris P. 1974. *Representatives, Roll Calls, and Constituencies*. Lexington: Heath.

Fiorina, Morris P. 1989. *Congress: Keystone of the Washington Establishment*, 2d ed. New Haven: Yale University Press.

Fiorina, Morris P. and Kenneth A. Shepsle. 1989. "Formal Theories of Leadership: Agents, Agenda Setters, and Entrepreneurs." In *Leadership and Politics*, ed. Bryan D. Jones. Lawrence: University of Kansas Press.

Foley, Michael. 1980. *The New Senate*. New Haven: Yale University Press.

Fowler, Linda. 1982. "How Interest Groups Select Issues for Rating Voting Records of Members of the U.S. Congress." *Legislative Studies Quarterly* 7:401–14.

Fox, Harrison W., and Susan Webb Hammond. 1977. *Congressional Staffs: The Invisible Force in American Lawmaking*. New York: Free Press.

Gettinger, Stephen. 1985. "New Questions Delay Action on Conrail Sale Legislation." *Congressional Quarterly Weekly Report*, April 20, 754.

Gilligan, Thomas W., and Keith Krehbiel. 1987. "Collective Decision-Making and Standing Committees: An Informational Rationale for Restrictive Amendment Procedures." *Journal of Law, Economics, and Organization* 3:287–335.

Gilligan, Thomas W., and Keith Krehbiel. 1989. "Asymmetric Information and Legislative Rules with a Heterogeneous Committee." *American Journal of Political Science* 33:459–90.

Gilligan, Thomas W., and Keith Krehbiel. 1990. "Organization of Informative Committees by a Rational Legislature." *American Journal of Political Science* 34:531–64.

Goodwin, George. 1970. *The Little Legislatures: Committees of Congress*. Amherst: University of Massachusetts Press.

Haeberle, Steven H. 1978. "The Institutionalization of the Subcommittee in the United States House of Representatives." *Journal of Politics* 40:1054–65.

Hall, Richard L. 1987. "Participation and Purpose in Committee Decision Making." *American Political Science Review* 81:105–28.

Hall, Richard L. 1990. "Participation in Congress." University of Michigan, Ann Arbor. Typescript.

Hall, Richard L., and C. Lawrence Evans. 1990. "The Power of Subcommittees." *Journal of Politics* 52:335–55.

Hall, Richard L., and Bernard Grofman. 1990. "The Committee Assignment Process and the Conditional Nature of Committee Bias." *American Political Science Review* 84:1149–66.

Hess, Stephen. 1986. *The Ultimate Insiders: U.S. Senators in the National Media*. Washington, D.C.: Brookings Institution.

Hook, Janet. 1986. "House GOP: Plight of a Permanent Minority." *Congressional Quarterly Weekly Report*, June 21, 1393–96.

Huitt, Ralph K. 1954. "The Congressional Committee: A Case Study." *American Political Science Review* 48:340–65.

Huitt, Ralph K. 1961. "Democratic Party Leadership in the Senate." *American Political Science Review* 55:333–44.

Jones, Charles O. 1968. "Joseph G. Cannon and Howard W. Smith: An Essay on the Limits of Leadership in the House of Representatives." *Journal of Politics* 30:617–46.

Keith, Robert. 1977. "The Use of Unanimous Consent in the Senate." *Committees and Senate Procedures*. 95th Cong., 2d sess.

Kingdon, John W. 1984. *Agendas, Alternatives, and Public Policies*. Boston: Little, Brown.

Kingdon, John W. 1989. *Congressmen's Voting Decisions*. 3d ed. Ann Arbor: University of Michigan Press.

Koch, Kathy. 1981. "Senate Environment Panel Becomes a Western Preserve." *Congressional Quarterly Weekly Report*, February 21, 343.

Kornacki, John J., ed. 1990. *Leading Congress*. Washington, D.C.: Congressional Quarterly.

Krehbiel, Keith. 1986. "Sophisticated and Myopic Behavior in Legislative Committees: An Experimental Study." *American Journal of Political Science* 30:542–61.

Krehbiel, Keith. 1987. "Why Are Congressional Committees Powerful?" *American Political Science Review* 81:929–35.

Krehbiel, Keith. 1990. "Are Congressional Committees Composed of Preference Outliers?" *American Political Science Review* 84:149–64.

Loomis, Burdett A. 1988. *The New American Politician*. New York: Basic Books.

Mackaman, Frank H. 1981. *Understanding Congressional Leadership*. Washington, D.C.: Congressional Quarterly.

Manley, John F. 1969. "Wilbur Mills: A Study of Congressional Leadership." *American Political Science Review* 63:442–64.

Manley, John F. 1970. *The Politics of Finance: The House Committee on Ways and Means*. Boston: Little, Brown.

Mann, Thomas E., and Norman J. Ornstein, eds. 1981. *The New Congress*. Washington, D.C.: American Enterprise Institute.

Matthews, Donald R. 1960. *U.S. Senators and Their World*. New York: Vintage Books.

Mayhew, David. 1974. *Congress: The Electoral Connection*. New Haven: Yale University Press.

Murphy, James T. 1974. "Political Parties and the Porkbarrel: Party Conflict and Cooperation in House Public Works Committee Decision Making." *American Political Science Review* 68:169–85.

Nagel, Jack H. 1975. *The Descriptive Analysis of Power*. New Haven: Yale University Press.

Neustadt, Richard E. 1980. *Presidential Power*. New York: Wiley.

Oleszek, Walter J. 1976. "Dissent on the Senate Floor: Practices, Procedures, and Customs." U.S. Library of Congress: Congressional Research Service.

Oleszek, Walter J. 1989. *Congressional Procedures and the Policy Process.* 3d ed. Washington, D.C.: Congressional Quarterly.

Oppenheimer, Bruce I. 1981. "Congress and the New Obstructionism: Developing an Energy Program." In *Congress Reconsidered,* 2d ed., ed. Lawrence C. Dodd and Bruce I. Oppenheimer. Washington, D.C.: Congressional Quarterly.

Oppenheimer, Bruce I. 1985. "Changing Time Constraints in Congress: Historical Perspectives on the Use of Cloture." In *Congress Reconsidered,* 3d ed., ed. Lawrence C. Dodd and Bruce I. Oppenheimer. Washington, D.C.: Congressional Quarterly.

Ordeshook, Peter C. 1986. *Game Theory and Political Theory.* Cambridge: Cambridge University Press.

Ornstein, Norman J., and David W. Rohde. 1977. "Resource Usage, Information and Policymaking in the Senate." In *Senators: Offices, Ethics, and Pressures.* U.S. Senate Commission on the Operation of the Senate. 94th Cong., 2d sess.

Ornstein, Norman J., Robert L. Peabody, and David W. Rohde. 1986. "Party Leadership and the Institutional Context: The Senate from Baker to Dole." Presented at the annual meeting of the American Political Science Association, Washington, D.C.

Ornstein, Norman J., Robert L. Peabody, and David W. Rohde. 1989. "Change in the Senate: Toward the 1990s." In *Congress Reconsidered,* 4th ed., ed. Lawrence C. Dodd and Bruce I. Oppenheimer. Washington, D.C.: Congressional Quarterly.

Parker, Glenn R., and Suzanne L. Parker. 1985. *Factions in House Committees.* Knoxville: University of Tennessee Press.

Patterson, Samuel C. 1990. "Party Leadership in the U.S. Senate." In *Leading Congress,* ed. John J. Kornacki. Washington, D.C.: Congressional Quarterly.

Payne, James L. 1980. "Show Horses and Work Horses in the U.S. House of Representatives." *Polity* 12:428–56.

Peabody, Robert L. 1976. *Leadership in Congress: Stability, Succession and Change.* Boston: Little, Brown.

Peabody, Robert L. 1981. "Senate Party Leadership: From the 1950s to the 1980s." In *Understanding Congressional Leadership,* ed. Frank H. Mackaman. Washington, D.C.: Congressional Quarterly.

Peabody, Robert L. 1985. "Leadership in Legislatures: Evolution, Selection, Functions." In *Handbook of Legislative Research,* ed. Gerhard Loewenberg, Samuel C. Patterson, and Malcolm E. Jewell. Cambridge, Mass.: Harvard University Press.

Peabody, Robert L., Norman J. Ornstein, and David W. Rohde. 1976. "The United States Senate as a Presidential Incubator: Many Are Called But Few Are Chosen." *Political Science Quarterly* 91:237–58.

Phillips, Cabell. 1964. "Two Senators Resort to Wrestling over Collins Post." *New York Times,* July 10, L1, 10.

Plattner, Andy. 1985. "The Lure of the Senate: Influence and Prestige." *Congressional Quarterly Weekly Report,* May 25, 991–98.

Price, David E. 1972. *Who Makes the Laws? Creativity and Power in Senate Committees.* Cambridge, Mass.: Schenkman.

Price, David E. 1975. *The Commerce Committees: A Study of the House and Senate Commerce Committees.* New York: Grossman.

Price, David E. 1978. "Policy Making in Congressional Committees: The Impact of Environmental Factors." *American Political Science Review* 72:548–74.

Price, David E. 1985. "Congressional Committees in the Policy Process." In *Congress Reconsidered,* 3d ed., ed. Lawrence C. Dodd and Bruce I. Oppenheimer. Washington, D.C.: Congressional Quarterly.

Riker, William H. 1964. "Some Ambiguities in the Notion of Power." *American Political Science Review* 58:341–49.

Ripley, Randall B. 1969a. "Power in the Post–World War II Senate." *Journal of Politics* 31:465–92.

Ripley, Randall B. 1969b. *Power in the Senate.* New York: St. Martin's Press.

Rohde, David W., Norman J. Ornstein, and Robert L. Peabody. 1985. "Political Change and Legislative Norms in the United States Senate." In *Studies of Congress,* ed. Glenn Parker. Washington, D.C.: Congressional Quarterly.

Rohde, David W., and Kenneth A. Shepsle. 1987. "Leaders and Followers in the House of Representatives: Reflections on Woodrow Wilson's 'Congressional Government.'" *Congress and the Presidency* 14: 111–33.

Salisbury, Robert, and Kenneth A. Shepsle. 1981. "Congressmen as Enterprise." *Legislative Studies Quarterly* 6:559–76.

Schattshneider, E. E. 1960. *The Semi-Sovereign People.* Hinsdale, Ill.: Dryden Press.

Schick, Allen. 1977. "Complex Policy Making in the United States Senate." In *Policy Analysis on Major Issues.* U.S. Senate Commission on the Operation of the Senate. 94th Cong., 2d sess.

Sharp, J. Michael. 1988. *The Directory of Congressional Voting Scores and Interest Group Ratings.* New York: Facts on File Publications.

Shepsle, Kenneth A. 1979. "Institutional Arrangements and Equilibrium in Multidimensional Voting Models." *American Journal of Political Science* 23:27–60.

Shepsle, Kenneth A. 1986. "Institutional Equilibrium and Equilibrium Institutions." In *Political Science: The Science of Politics,* ed. Herbert F. Weisberg. New York: Agathon.

Shepsle, Kenneth A., and Barry R. Weingast. 1981. "Structure-Induced Equilibrium and Legislative Choice." *Public Choice* 37:503–19.

Shepsle, Kenneth A., and Barry R. Weingast. 1987a. "The Institutional Foundations of Committee Power." *American Political Science Review* 81:85–105.

Shepsle, Kenneth A., and Barry R. Weingast. 1987b. "Why are Congressional Committees Powerful?" *American Political Science Review* 81: 935–45.

Sinclair, Barbara. 1983a. *Majority Leadership in the U.S. House.* Baltimore: Johns Hopkins University Press.

Sinclair, Barbara. 1983b. "Purposive Behavior in the U.S. Congress: A Review Essay." *Legislative Studies Quarterly* 8:117–31.

Sinclair, Barbara. 1986a. "Senate Styles and Senate Decision Making, 1955–1980." *Journal of Politics* 48:877–908.

Sinclair, Barbara. 1986b. "Senate Norms, Senate Styles and Senate Influence." Presented at the annual meeting of the American Political Science Association, Washington, D.C.

Sinclair, Barbara. 1989. *The Transformation of the U.S. Senate.* Baltimore: Johns Hopkins University Press.

Sinclair, Barbara. 1990. "Congressional Leadership: A Review Essay." In *Leading Congress,* ed. John J. Kornacki. Washington, D.C.: Congressional Quarterly.

Smith, Richard A. 1984. "Advocacy, Interpretation, and Influence in the U.S. Congress." *American Political Science Review* 78:44–63.

Smith, Steven S. 1984. "Coalition Leadership in Congress: A Theoretical Perspective." Presented at the annual meeting of the American Political Science Association, Washington D.C.

Smith, Steven S. 1988. "An Essay on Sequence, Position, Goals, and Committee Power." *Legislative Studies Quarterly* 13:151–76.

Smith, Steven S. 1989. *Call to Order: Floor Politics in the House and Senate.* Washington, D.C.: Brookings Institution.

Smith, Steven S., and Christopher J. Deering. 1984. *Committees in Congress.* Washington, D.C.: Congressional Quarterly.

Smith, Steven S., and Christopher J. Deering. 1990. *Committees in Congress.* 2d ed. Washington, D.C.: Congressional Quarterly.

Tolchin, Martin. 1984. "Senate Deplores Disarray in New Chamber of Equals." *New York Times,* November 25, 40.

Unekis, Joseph K., and Leroy N. Rieselbach. 1984. *Congressional Committee Politics: Continuity and Change.* New York: Praeger.

VanDoren, Peter M. 1990. "Can We Learn the Causes of Congressional Decisions from Roll Call Data?" *Legislative Studies Quarterly* 15:311–40.

Wilson, Woodrow. 1885. *Congressional Government.* New York: Meridan Books.

Index